W9-CMK-013

# STANLEY KUBRICK HAS TAKEN HIS FANS ON MANY FAR-OUT TRIPS:

—to a fighter's dressing room in *Killer's Kiss*

—to a racetrack about to be robbed in *The Killing*

—to a World War I battlefield in *Paths of Glory*

—to ancient Rome in *Spartacus*

—to the spell of an irresistible nymphet in *Lolita*

—to the edge of doom in *Dr. Strangelove*

—to the distant stars in *2001*

—to the nightmare near future in *A Clockwork Orange*

—to the lusty, brawling 18th century in *Barry Lyndon*

Now you can relive those unforgettable experiences, and learn the very personal truth about the man who engineered them, in a truly fascinating study written with superb, intimate knowledge and eloquent appreciation.

*Oversized Books in the Big Apple Film Series Available from Popular Library:*

HOLLYWOOD CORRAL
ROBERT REDFORD
ABBOTT AND COSTELLO
TEX AVERY: KING OF CARTOONS
SUPERMAN


*And soon to appear in rack-size:*

ABBOTT AND COSTELLO
SUPERMAN

# STANLEY KUBRICK A FILM ODYSSEY

**GENE D. PHILLIPS**

**Popular Library Film Series**
**Leonard Maltin, General Editor**

POPULAR LIBRARY ● NEW YORK

All POPULAR LIBRARY books are carefully selected by the POPULAR LIBRARY Editorial Board and represent titles by the world's greatest authors.

POPULAR LIBRARY EDITION

October, 1977

Copyright © 1975 by FILM FAN MONTHLY

Additional material copyright © 1977 by FILM FAN MONTHLY

ISBN: 0-445-04101-3

Photograph credits and acknowledgments: United Artists, Metro-Goldwyn-Mayer, Universal Pictures, Columbia Pictures, Warner Brothers, Joseph Burstyn

### To Alexander Walker

We welcome your thoughts and comments on the Popular Library Film Series. Address all correspondence to Leonard Maltin, 200 West 79 Street, 5-L, New York, New York 10024.

PRINTED IN THE UNITED STATES OF AMERICA
All Rights Reserved

# CONTENTS

First of all, I am most grateful to Stanley Kubrick, who not only discussed his films with me personally but has corresponded with me and encouraged me throughout the time I was preparing this book.

Of the many others who helped me I would like to mention: William K. Everson, film historian of New York University; Patrick Sheehan of the Motion Picture Section of the Library of Congress; Ted Schmitt of Universal 16, the distributors of *Spartacus;* and Donald Krim of United Artists 16, the distributors of *Killer's Kiss, The Killing,* and *Paths of Glory,* all of whom provided me with valuable research materials; also Richard A. Blake, communications editor of *America* magazine, for his careful reading of the typescript and his valuable suggestions.

Portions of this book appeared in a different form in the following publications:

"Kubrick," *Film Comment,* VII (Winter, 1971), copyright © 1971 by Film Comment Publishing Corporation, and reprinted with the permission of *Film Comment,* all rights reserved; "Stanley Kubrick" in *The Movie Makers: Artists in an Industry,* copyright © 1973 by Gene D. Phillips, and used with permission of the publisher, Nelson-Hall Company, Chicago.

# PART ONE: GETTING STARTED

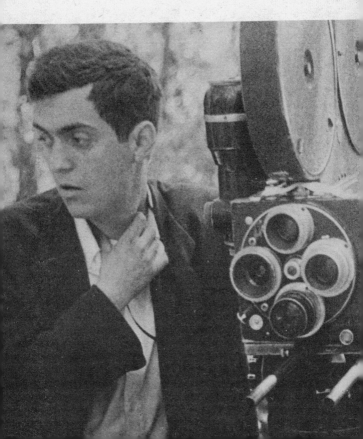

Toba Kubrick, Steven Hahn and Stanley Kubrick making FEAR AND DESIRE.

# Chapter One
# Darkness at Noon:

# Fear and Desire (1953) and Killer's Kiss (1955)

I had talked with Stanley Kubrick before, but this was the first time that I was making the trip out to his home, about half an hour's drive from London. As I drove in the gate I caught my first glimpse of the huge, rambling old house where Kubrick lives with his wife and three daughters and where he does much of the pre- and post-production work on his films. The mansion has the unmistakable air of an English manor house about it, but its owner is just as unmistakably American as the Bronx section of New York where he grew up.

Kubrick's manner of dress has become legendary, so I was not surprised when he appeared in a dark jacket and trousers, white shirt and black shoes. This ensemble, which never varies in tone, indicates that he is a man who is too preoccupied with his work to be concerned with the latest fashions. He is a soft-spoken man, whose friendly manner has a way of putting you immediately at ease. In conversation he listens intently to the person with whom he is talking, as if he stood to gain a great deal more from the interchange than his guest. Nothing about Kubrick's engaging and unassuming manner would imply to a visitor that he is in the presence of a filmmaker whose work has won him critical and popular success throughout the world.

Kubrick moved to England to shoot *Lolita* (1962) because financing was easier to come by there. He found living and working near London so congenial that he decided to settle there permanently. Since his home-office is not far from London, he is still able to keep in touch with his business, artistic, and social contacts while avoiding the hustle of big-city life and the factory atmosphere of a film studio. As one visitor to his home has put it, the Kubrick residence is a casual collection of offices and living rooms in which family life and filmmaking overlap as though the one were unthinkable without the other. For a man like Kubrick, for whom filmmaking is a whole way of life, this is probably true.

In the course of my visit I met his wife Christiane, the former Susanne Christiane Harlan, whose professional name was Susanne Christian when she was an actress in the fifties. Now, as Christiane Kubrick, she is a painter whose canvases have been exhibited at the Royal Academy in London. I also met the Kubricks' three daughters, Katherine, Anya, and Vivian, who by now are used to the stream of visitors that come to the house. But the bulk of my time with Kubrick was devoted to his recollections about his moviemaking. He is a fascinating storyteller and the many anecdotes he told me about the making of his films are spread throughout this book.

As a director Kubrick is almost unique in that he taught himself the techniques of filmmaking, and became a director without serving the usual apprenticeship in a movie studio where he would have had to work his way up to the status of director by way of lesser jobs. By the time he began directing films for the major studios he was able to command a degree of independence rare in motion-picture history. Asked why he thought that the major film companies had decided to extend wide artistic freedom to directors like himself, Kubrick replied, "The invulnerability of the majors was based on their consistent success with almost anything that they made. When they stopped making money they began to appreciate the importance of people who could make good films." Kubrick was one of the independents they turned to, and when they did, he had learned the filmmaking business from the ground up and was ready to answer the call. By the time he made his first studio-backed film, he had done two documentaries and two features almost single-handedly. Since then he has continued to supervise every aspect of production when he makes a film from scriptwriting and casting through shooting (often operating the camera himself), editing, and choosing the musical score, as well as overseeing the finished film's publicity campaign. He is, therefore, the total filmmaker; his movies are the product of his own creative imagination in a way that few other directors can claim.

Although he was probably not aware of it at the time, Kubrick began building toward his life's work as a filmmaker while still a high school student in the Bronx, where he was born on July 26, 1928. His father, a professional physician and amateur photographer, gave Stanley a Graflex camera when he was thirteen, and young Kubrick became photographer for the Taft High School newspaper. While still a student there during World War II, Ku-

**Above, two enemy officers, FEAR AND DESIRE.**

brick sold a photograph to *Look* magazine showing a string of motorists lined up as they waited for their share of rationed gasoline.

Kubrick went on to sell a picture story to *Look* which was inspired by one of his English teachers at Taft, the only person who ever managed to interest Kubrick in studies while he was in school. Although Kubrick's overall performance in high school was poor, an IQ test proved that he was brighter than most of his classmates. He was simply bored by most of his classes. "I think the big mistake in schools is trying to teach children anything," is Kubrick's comment on his education. "Fear of getting failing grades, fear of not staying with your class, etc. Interest can produce learning on a scale compared to fear as a nuclear explosion to a firecracker. I never learned anything at all in school and I didn't read a book for pleasure until I was nineteen years old."

He continued selling pictures to *Look* until graduation, when Helen O'Brien, the picture editor of the magazine, hired him full time as an apprentice photographer. Kubrick stayed with the publication for four years, until he was twenty-one. "From the start I loved cameras," he remembers. "There is something almost sensuous about a beautiful piece of equipment." At *Look,* he says, he had four years of seeing how things worked in the real world. He now feels that had he spent those four years going to college instead of gaining experience with his camera, he would never have become a film director, but would probably have become a doctor like his father.

While he was working for *Look*, Kubrick and his friend from high school days, Alex Singer, who at the time worked for *The March of Time*, used to discuss filmmaking as a career. Kubrick learned from Singer that the *March of Time* documentary shorts were budgeted at $40,000 apiece, and he speculated that he could produce a documentary for a fraction of that cost. Drawing on a picture story that he had done for *Look* on middleweight boxer Walter Cartier, Kubrick made a sixteen-minute short called *Day of the Fight* (1950). One of the employees at the camera store where Kubrick rented his equipment taught him each step of the technical side of the filmmaking business as he went along.

Kubrick did everything himself, from writing and shooting the film to dubbing in the punches and the slam of car doors on the sound track. Based on this experience he has since said, "Perhaps it sounds ridiculous, but the best thing that young filmmakers can do is get hold of a camera and some film and make a movie of any kind at all."

*Day of the Fight* opens with a neon sign proclaiming "Boxing Tonight!" and cuts to a middle-aged man scrambling for a ticket at the box office and being ushered to his seat. "What do fight fans—or rather fanatics—seek?" asks narrator Douglas Edwards. "They seek action, the triumph of force over force." Kubrick illustrates this remark with a quick succession of shots of knockout punches from several different fights. "But why do *they*—the fighters—do it?" Edwards continues. "There is the prestige of the winners; but also it is a living."

The movie then zeroes in on Cartier, "one fighter out of the record book. This, then, is the story of a fighter and of a fight." On the bleak dawning of the day of the fight the camera cuts from a poster announcing Cartier's bout, to be held at 10 P.M. that same night, to the apartment house where Cartier lives. "At 6 A.M.," says the narrator, "begins the waiting." Walter Cartier and his twin brother Vince, who is also his manager, rise to go to make their way through the deserted streets of New York for early morning Mass at a nearby church because "Cartier doesn't place all of his faith in his hands."

Kubrick quickly takes Cartier through his day, showing the various preparations such as the weigh-in, that lead up to the impending bout. Yet the director still manages to communicate that restless sense of endless waiting that the fighter experiences all day

12

long. This feeling is best sensed in the shot in which Cartier stands in his dusky living room in late afternoon staring down at the street below, and in the one in which the boxer contemplates his face in his mirror just before leaving for the arena, wondering what kind of image the glass will reflect the following morning.

Then the tempo of the film picks up as Cartier reaches the arena and begins the final stages of getting ready for the fight in his stuffy dressing room—a scene which Kubrick would draw on in making his second feature, *Killer's Kiss*.

It is time at last to go into the ring. The crowd cheers as the fighters are introduced and this noise carries over into the next shot, that of a young man standing on a street in downtown New York City, intently listening to the fight on his portable radio—someone who looks very much like young Stanley Kubrick.

While the two fighters sit in their corners waiting for the bell to sound, Cartier is photographed at the opposite end of the ring through the legs of his opponent—a shot that would be repeated in *Killer's Kiss*. Kubrick shoots the fight from a variety of angles and edits them together in rapid succession, thereby imparting to the viewer the intensity of the battle, which culminates in Cartier's kayoing the other boxer. As his manager leads the winner through the ropes and down into the smoke-filled auditorium toward his dressing room, the narrator concludes, "A day in the life of a man who fights for his existence, the end of another working day."

Kubrick spent the $3,900 which he had saved while working for *Look* on making this short film and sold the distribution rights for $4,000 to RKO for its *This Is America* series. By the age of twenty-two Kubrick had made a film on his own (for one tenth of the cost of a *March of Time* documentary) and it had shown a profit, however modest. From that time onward Stanley Kubrick was hooked for life on moviemaking. By this time he felt that he had outgrown his interest in still photography and so he quit his job at *Look*.

RKO advanced him $1,500 for a second short, *Flying Padre* (1951), for its RKO Pathé Screenliner series. "It was about Father Fred Stadtmueller, a priest in New Mexico who flew to his isolated parishes in a Piper Cub," Kubrick explains. The opening shot is a pan over the vast plateaus and canyons of New Mexico, after which the camera tilts upward to encompass the little plane coming in for a landing on a prairie. Two lone cowboys on horseback await the priest to escort him to a funeral service which he is to conduct.

Even at this early stage of his career Kubrick was interested in bringing the viewer into the action as much as possible. So here, he photographs Fr. Stadtmueller inside the cockpit of his plane from

**FEAR AND DESIRE.**

various angles, even shooting upward at one point from the floor through the controls. He was also aware of the importance of catching significant details that will bring a scene to life. Hence the burial scene is punctuated with close-ups of an aged man and woman watching the ceremony as the little group of mourners huddles together around the grave. Later, when the priest has to fly a mother and her child to a hospital, Kubrick again puts us in the cockpit of the plane with the priest, showing the land below rushing by and finally disappearing as the Piper Cub gains speed and takes flight, once more lending the audience a feeling of participating in the action.

Around this time Kubrick made a third short which I ran across quite by accident just before this book went to press. In 1953 the Atlantic and Gulf Coast district of the Seafarers International Union commissioned him to make a half-hour documentary called *The Seafarers* about the life of the men who sail American cargo ships. One might be tempted to dismiss the movie as a mere industrial documentary except for the fact that it contains several instances of a young filmmaker reaching to photograph in an inventive and creative way what could otherwise have been a perfunctory film done as a routine assignment. It is also Kubrick's first film in color.

In the early hiring hall sequence Kubrick moves among the men with his camera, photographing their intense expressions as they vie for good berths on their favorite ships. In fact Kubrick, who as usual served as his own cameraman, constantly moves his camera about in each scene, whether on ship or off, in order to keep visually alive what could so easily have been a static documentary. He is forever looking for—and finding—interesting images to punctuate the film. The scene in the seamen's bar starts with a close-up of a mermaid carved out of wood to look like an ornament on the prow of a ship, and then the camera pulls back to show the men grouped round it at the circular bar. The sequence at the Marine Hospital begins with a shot of the flower garden on the grounds filling the screen in stunning color before moving on to show the convalescents enjoying the view and the sunshine.

Only rarely does the film fall into looking like a conventional documentary, as when a group of seamen are pictured spending some of their shore time in reading and in writing letters in the union library. There is a somewhat stagey quality about the way that they are rather self-consciously "arranged" at the tables from foreground to background. On the other hand one shot in particular hints at the promising things to come for the young director. Several seamen are grouped round a table discussing grievances with a union representative with a single lamp above their heads shedding light on their conference. This lighting and composition would be repeated to great dramatic effect in *The Killing* in the scene in which the thieves plan their strategy for the race track robbery.

All in all, *The Seafarers* is a worthy piece of work for a filmmaker still finding his way and gaining experience, and is all the more significant for being the only movie which Kubrick shot in color until *Spartacus,* almost a decade later. The young director then decided to make his first feature film. He borrowed $10,000 from his father and his uncle, a Bronx druggist, and added $3,000 of his own. Then he went on location to the San Gabriel Mountains near Los Angeles to shoot *Fear and Desire* (1953), which is about a futile military patrol trapped behind enemy lines in an unnamed war.

The script for *Fear and Desire* was written by Howard Sackler, another old friend of Kubrick's from high school days, who later wrote the award-winning play and film *The Great White Hope.* Other friends helped out during the location shooting in the mountains, assisting Kubrick in setting up and putting away the equipment each day; and three Mexican laborers were engaged to transport the boxes of materials to and from the location site. Ku-

brick's first wife Toba served as dialogue director. But it was Kubrick himself who filled all of the jobs associated with shooting a film: he was director, cinematographer, prop man, and general factotum.

Since he had saved money by shooting his short subjects without sound and adding the sound track to the film afterward, Kubrick tried the same method with *Fear and Desire.* However, because post-synchronizing a sound track for a feature film is more complex than dubbing sound for a short, Kubrick ran into problems that added $20,000 to the $9,000 which had already been spent on shooting the picture. As a result, *Fear and Desire* never earned back its initial investment, even though independent distributor Joseph Burstyn was able to book the film on the art house circuit, where it garnered some good reviews.

Mark Van Doren, for example, singled out some scenes, such as the one in which an enemy general is shot, as visually compelling. It was the respected critic James Agee whom Kubrick recalls as making the kindest remark about *Fear and Desire.* After seeing the movie, Kubrick and Agee had a drink in a Sixth Avenue bar in Greenwich Village in New York. "There are too many good things in the film," said Agee, "to call it arty." Nonetheless Kubrick still thinks of the film as inept and pretentious, although it was still important in helping the young director at twenty-five to gain invaluable experience in his craft.

In a letter to the distributor of the film, Joseph Burstyn, which is quoted in Norman Kagan's *The Cinema of Stanley Kubrick,* the director described *Fear and Desire* as a poetic allegory, "a drama of man lost in a hostile world—deprived of material and spiritual foundations—seeking his way to an understanding of himself, and life around him." There is, furthermore, "an unseen but deadly enemy" lurking around him, an enemy who is shaped from the same mold that he is.

The allegorical intent of the picture is made clear from the beginning, as a narrator sets the mood of the film: "There is war in this forest; not a war that has been fought, nor one that will be, but any war. And the enemies that struggle here do not exist unless we call them into being. . . . Only the unchanging shapes of fear and doubt and death are from our world. These soldiers that you see keep our language and our time, but have no other country but the mind."

The four men who make up the military patrol on which the film focuses are Lieutenant Corby (Kenneth Harp), Mac (Frank Silvera), Fletcher (Steven Colt), and Sidney (Paul Mazursky, later to become a film director himself). Their plane has crashed behind enemy lines and Lieutenant Corby suggests that they build a raft and float down the river out of enemy territory. While they are moving through the woods, the quartet comes upon some enemy soldiers, whom they summarily ambush and kill. Next they happen upon a girl, whom they tie to a tree and gag, fearing that she would otherwise turn them over to the enemy. Sidney, who has been on the verge of hysteria ever since the plane crash, becomes more and more upset as his craving for the girl grows inside of him. Finally he unties the struggling girl and, as she tries to run from him, shoots her. In a panic he disappears into the forest.

When the others return, Mac persuades them to kill an enemy general whose headquarters they have come across nearby. Mac insists that this one courageous act will finally give meaning to their otherwise aimless lives, and they agree. Corby and Fletcher are to move in on the general and his aide and kill them while Mac employs diversionary tactics to preoccupy the general's guards. When Corby focuses the general and his aide through his binoculars, he discovers that the general is a double for him and the general's aide is a double for Fletcher (the general and his aide are played by the same actors who enact the roles of Corby and Fletcher). Fletcher shoots both of the men, but the general does not die immediately. He crawls toward the edge of the porch and Corby fires, finishing him off. As Corby looks into the general's dead face, he sees his own countenance staring back at him. These images thus round off the film's theme that the basic brotherhood of mankind cannot be destroyed even by war, for the enemy is but a reflection of one's self.

At the end of the film, Mac, severely wounded, is seen lying on the raft which he and his comrades had built earlier, floating toward the shore. With him is Sidney, still traumatized by what he has done, whom Mac has picked up along the way. Standing on the shore waiting for them are Corby and Fletcher, who show no signs of satisfaction over having successfully completed their mission.

Kubrick is perhaps too hasty in writing off *Fear and Desire* as a "student film." *Film Quarterly* points out that the movie's 'mateurish quality makes its virtues all the more obvious. Chief among those virtues is Kubrick's handling of the camera with which he creates limpid visual images, particularly in the shadowy forest scenes. As the spoken prologue suggests, the forest becomes a metaphor for the jungle of man's own psyche, the heart of darkness of which Joseph Conrad wrote.

All four central characters are prey to the fear of death and to the desire for the girl they discovered in the woods. Sidney succumbs to both by attacking the girl, then killing her because he is afraid that she will report him, and finally by withdrawing into a state of shock because of what he has done. His plight underscores more than anything else in the film the thought that perhaps one's most deadly enemy is the man within and that therefore, as the prologue would have it, it is in the country of the mind that man's real battles are fought.

"The ideas which we wanted to put across were good," Kubrick has commented to Alexander Walker in *Stanley Kubrick Directs*; "but we didn't have the experience to embody them dramatically." Nevertheless, a great deal of the thought-provoking content of the movie does come across, especially in Mac's insistence on lending some meaning to his empty life by doing something courageous while he still has the chance. Kubrick's own description of the film—as a drama of man deprived of material and spiritual foundations, lost in a hostile world in which he seeks to understand himself and the life around him—could well serve as the keynote for all of the director's films. In each of them Kubrick presents someone who is trying to cope with the tough world in which he finds himself.

Thus in his next film, *Killer's Kiss* (1955), Kubrick shows us the struggles of a second-rate prizefighter to rise above the tawdry existence to which he is tied. Both *Fear and Desire* and *Killer's Kiss* belong to a trend in American cinema that was just nearing its end when Kubrick began making films, as does *The Killing*, which I will discuss in the next chapter. French film critics labeled this cycle of postwar American films *film noir* ("dark film"), indicating that a somber, cynical vision of life was reflected in these films which were made during the decade following World War II.

The new pessimistic tinge which several American movies exhibited in this period grew out of the disillusionment which had resulted from the war and its aftermath. As Paul Schrader has written in his brilliant essay on *film noir* in *Film Comment*, this disillusionment was often mirrored in melodramas in which a serviceman returns home from the war to find a corrupt society which was not worth fighting for. *Film noir* was also exemplified in war pictures that showed the ugly side of war, which had been absent from the glamorous "bond-selling" war films of the early forties. It is easy to identify *Killer's Kiss* as an example of the kind of *film noir* that exhibited the corrupt postwar world, and *Fear and Desire* as the type that showed war in all of its ugliness.

The sober look at life presented in these films was in keeping with the movement toward greater realism in the cinema that followed the Second World War. Audiences had grown accustomed to the

realism employed in wartime documentaries and fiction films about the war, and continued to expect this same brand of realism in postwar films as well, not only in pictures that dealt directly with the war, but in other kinds of movies too, such as crime melodramas. These films were frequently shot on location and called forth more naturalistic performances from the actors in order to match the authentic settings.

Schrader enumerates several elements that were usually evident in *film noir*, of which the following are noticeable in *Killer's Kiss*. The film takes place almost entirely at night, often in murkily lit rooms, alleys, and side streets. The actors move about in this dark, brooding atmosphere, which gives the movie a hopeless mood. "There is nothing the protagonist can do," writes Schrader. "The city will outlast and negate even his best efforts," and this is why the hero and heroine of *Killer's Kiss* flee the city at the film's end.

*Killer's Kiss*, originally titled *Kiss Me, Kill Me*, was co-scripted by Kubrick and Sackler. They built their story around some exciting action sequences which would carry the weight of the film and not be costly to shoot, including two key fight scenes and a chase through some lower Manhattan warehouses. Kubrick shot *Killer's Kiss* in the shabbier sections of New York, which gave the film a visual realism unmatched by the post-synchronized sound track (although Kubrick had become more expert in post-dubbing than he had been when he made *Fear and Desire*).

The hero of the story is a young fighter named Davy Gordon (Jamie Smith) who is already a has-been. We discover him pacing in the waiting room of Grand Central Station, awaiting the departure of his train. Over the sound track we hear his voice as he begins to recount the events of the past few days in an effort to sort them out for himself. "It all began just before my fight with Rodriguez," he muses, and we cut to a poster advertising Davy's fight, then to Davy examining his face in the mirror of his cheap furnished room. There are photos stuck all round the edges of the mirror which show his Uncle George and Aunt Grace on their farm near Seattle. The pictures represent the cleaner life which Davey has left behind but not forgotten.

His only companion seems to be his pet goldfish, which he dutifully feeds, indicating a softer side to his nature. Davy is the type of *film noir* hero who is hard-boiled on the surface in order to hide from the brutal world around him the more human, emotional side of his personality. There is one shot of Davy seen through the fishbowl as he peers into it, symbolizing that he is imprisoned in the narrow life which he leads as is the fish in its bowl.

In his loneliness he has taken to staring at Gloria Price (Irene

22

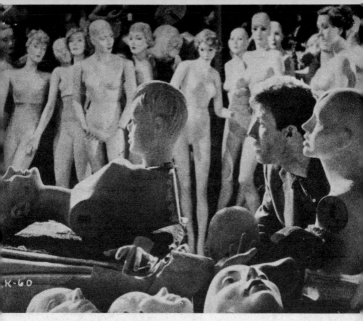

**Jamie Smith, KILLER'S KISS.**

Kane), the girl who lives across the way, whose window is just opposite his. That she is equally lonely is reflected in the fact that at other times she snatches looks at him from her vantage point. They are two isolated individuals whose ability to watch each other from a distance only further emphasizes their separateness. Later they leave their building at the same time, their paths crossing in the lobby as Davy makes for the subway on his way to his fight and Gloria meets her boss Vince Rapallo (Frank Silvera), who is waiting at the curb to drive her to Pleasureland, the dance hall where she works as a hostess. Vince's possessiveness is immediately apparent when he inquires how long she has known Davy. "He just lives in the building," Gloria replies in a bored tone of voice.

While riding the subway Davy reads a letter from his Uncle George, whose voice is heard over the sound track reminding Davy that "we still miss you a lot." There follows a series of shots of Davy in his dressing room getting ready for the fight, intercut with shots of Gloria dancing with a succession of anonymous partners in Pleasureland to canned music from an old phonograph.

In his office Vince turns on his television set to watch Davy's bout and invites Gloria in on the pretext of seeing the fight. By the device of Gloria and Vince looking at Davy's match on television,

Kubrick neatly joins the two parallel lines of action for a moment. The TV announcer describes Davy's career as one long promise without fulfillment.

The scene shifts to the arena for what Peter Cowie calls in *Seventy Years of Cinema* "one of the most vicious boxing matches ever seen on the screen." Kubrick's experience in making *Day of the Fight* undoubtedly helped him to give to the arena scenes in *Killer's Kiss* a ring of authenticity. He photographs much of the fight through the ropes to make the viewer feel that he is witnessing the bout from ringside. At crucial moments the director moves his hand-held camera into the ring, first showing Davy's opponent Kid Rodriguez lunging at the camera as if at Davy's jaw, and then showing Davy slumping to the floor in a daze. At this point Kubrick turns the camera upward to catch the overhead lights glaring mercilessly down on the felled fighter.

As Davy lies on the mat and the announcer gives an obituary for Davy's career in the ring, the scene returns to Vince's office, where he is busy seducing Gloria. It almost seems as if the neurotically jealous Vince feels that he has won Gloria from Davy by having had her watch the boxer lose the prizefight. Afterward Gloria wanders along the grubbiest part of Forty-second Street toward the subway while Davy broods in the darkness of his room about his final failure to make it as a fighter.

When he sees her enter her room across the way and begin to undress for bed, Davy watches with undisguised interest until his phone rings. It is Uncle George, offering his condolences over the bout and inviting Davy to come back to Seattle to live and work on the farm. The camera is on Davy as he talks; behind him is a dresser, in the mirror of which we can see Gloria's reflection as she gets into bed. In a single shot, perfectly composed, Kubrick shows us Davy's erotic interest in the girl registering on his face as he talks distractedly to Uncle George, while at the same time we see the dreamlike image of Gloria in the mirror, which is the true object of his attention at the moment.

When Davy himself turns in, he has a dream in which the camera speeds down a narrow slum street, photographed in a negative image, rendering the scene darkly grotesque. The dream sequence (which has an affinity to the astronaut's ride through the space corridor in *2001*) seems to be a nightmarish premonition of the life-and-death chase through the streets and across the rooftops of lower Manhattan which will climax the film.

Davy is awakened by a scream and sees through the window that Gloria is being assaulted by Vince. Her assailant flees when he hears Davy coming, leaving him to comfort Gloria. She ex-

24

plains that Vince had come to ask her to become his mistress and when she sneered at the idea he became violent. Davy assures her that Vince will not come back; Gloria falls into a childlike sleep as the camera cuts to a close-up of the doll which hangs atop her bedstead, suggesting that, despite her present life, Gloria is still an innocent at heart who has been tarnished by the corrupt atmosphere of big-city low life.

Davy wanders around her room, affectionately examining the personal articles on her dresser: a bottle of perfume, a music box, some family photographs. When she awakens the next morning and they breakfast together, he asks her about the people in the photographs. One is her father; the other is her sister Iris, who is wearing a ballet costume (played by the late Ruth Sobotka, a member of the New York City Ballet, and Kubrick's wife at the time). As Gloria begins her long monologue about the tragedy that enveloped her family, we see Iris dancing alone on a dark stage, illuminated by a spotlight.

Gloria's mother died when she was born and her older sister Iris grew up to be the image of their dead mother. As a result their father, Mr. Price, favored Iris over Gloria. When Iris was twenty she gave up her promising dancing career to marry an older man who agreed to support his bride's ailing father and younger sister in the bargain. Mr. Price died after a prolonged illness and Gloria hysterically berated Iris for making them all miserable. Iris went up to her room, turned on a recording of one of her favorite ballets, left Gloria a note asking forgiveness for meddling in other people's lives, and slashed her wrists.

As the vision of Iris pirouetting on the lonely stage fades slowly away, Gloria concludes her monologue by saying that she took her job at Pleasureland partially as a penance for her ingratitude to her dead sister. "I told myself," she concludes, "that at least Iris never had to dance in a place like that, a human zoo. And then I felt less unhappy."

Norman Kagan in his book on Kubrick comments that Gloria's story, "besides being cookbook Freud, has little to do with the rest of the film," and speculates that the long ballet sequence was added to bring the film up to the slim feature running time of sixty-four minutes. Granted that this flashback-within-a-flashback complicates the narration of the story, it also sheds light on Gloria's character as surely as the stage spotlight illumines Iris. Through Gloria's memories we learn how a basically decent girl like her became implicated with Vince and Pleasureland, and why she allows the situation to go on: out of a vague sense of expiation to her dead sister. Kubrick agrees that the sequence, besides being a tribute to his wife's skill as a dancer, adds interest to Gloria's character.

In Grand Central Station once more, we see Davy still nervously awaiting his train for Seattle, recalling now how he told Gloria of his plans to return to the family farm: "Looking back, I wonder why I believed her when she said that she would come with me," he says to himself. "She was so scared that she would have grabbed at anything." Thus the viewer at last learns the source of Davy's anxiety while he paces the station floor: he desperately hopes that Gloria will arrive in time to go with him as she had promised. This is a nifty suspense hook on which to hold the film-goer's interest as Davy goes on with his story.

Davy recalls how he asked Albert, his manager, to pay him for his last fight immediately so that he could make the trip to Seattle with Gloria. Albert agrees to meet him at 8:15 P.M. in front of Pleasureland, where Gloria must go to tell Vince that she has quit her job and to pick up her last paycheck. This situation sets up the intricate and ironic plot twists that lead to the climax of the picture. While Davy awaits Albert in front of the dance hall, two drunken Shriners snatch his scarf and he pursues them down the street. In Vince's office Gloria once more turns down his offer to stay on as his mistress. Angered when Gloria sneers at his pathetic efforts to keep her, Vince throws her out without paying her salary.

For the next scene Kubrick adroitly places his camera at the top of the stairs that lead up to Pleasureland from the street. Below, Albert can be seen through the double glass doors as he stands next to Gloria. Both of them, unknown to each other, are waiting for Davy, who has not yet returned with his scarf. One of Vince's henchmen goes down the stairs and through the door and motions to Gloria to come with him, while his partner waits on the landing above. As the first man accompanies Gloria back up the stairs toward the camera (and past a sign that ominously warns "Watch Your step"), the other hood proceeds down the staircase away from the camera and takes up a position outside the building next to Albert.

When Davy returns with his scarf, there is no one in the doorway in front of Pleasureland. Vince's boys, thinking that Albert is Davy, have backed him into an alley where they begin to rough him up as a warning to stay away from Gloria. Kubrick has lit this scene expressionistically, making it all the more menacing; the two thugs are seen as dark silhouettes; while Albert pleads for his life, slatted shadows, cast by a grating in the alley, fall across his cringing form. There is a scuffle in which the two hoodlums bash the hapless fight manager's head in. The camera, peering into the alley from the street, holds on the two men as they move away from the scene of the crime and one of them goes back nonchalantly to retrieve his hat. This last little detail, implying as it does the killers' calloused lack of concern for what they have done, brings the scene to a striking close. It represents the kind of neat touches that distinguish even the earliest Kubrick films.

Gloria and Davy finally meet in the doorway at Pleasureland and then go back to the tenement to pack. But when Davy goes to Gloria's room to meet her after he has moved out of his room, he finds that she and all her belongings are already gone. This shock is followed by another, as he overhears the building superintendent being informed by the police that Davy is wanted for the murder of his manager.

Davy tracks down Vince with a gun and forces Vince to take him to the warehouse loft where Gloria is being held. At the warehouse Vince's men overpower Davy, but he escapes by jumping through a window to the street below. (In the chase scene that follows Davy's white socks change unaccountably to black—the only lapse in continuity I have detected in a Kubrick film.)

Davy runs down streets and through alleys, up a fire escape and across rooftops in his efforts to elude Vince and his hoods. At one point Kubrick stations his camera on a flat rooftop and watches Davy jog from the farthest edge of the roof toward the camera, thereby giving the viewer the feel of Davy's exhausting run without ever moving the camera. Finally Davy takes refuge in a warehouse storeroom filled with department store mannequins. Vince finds him, nonetheless, and the two men face each other for what both of them know is going to be a struggle to the death.

The partially dismantled dummies grotesquely prefigure the violence that the two protagonists are likely to inflict on each other. Vince hurls a torso at Davy, then grabs a fire ax from the wall. Davy fends off his assailant with the broken bodies of the mannequins until he is able to seize a pike-tipped window pole. The opponents viciously batter among the debris like two gladiators (almost anticipating Kubrick's later film *Spartacus*), flailing at the camera with their deadly weapons.

Finally Davy delivers the death blow off camera. There is a close-up of the smashed head of a dummy as the sound of Vince's scream of pain elides into the screech of a train whistle in Grand Central Station, recalling a similar shot in Hitchcock's *The Thirty-nine Steps* in which the scream of a woman discovering a corpse melds with the whistle of the train which is carrying the hero away from the scene of the murder of which he is accused.

Davy brings the story up to date by recounting that he was cleared of Vince's death because he acted in self-defense, but that he has now lost Gloria, probably for good. Up to this point in the film the exterior scenes have taken place mainly at dusk, at night, or at dawn, in true *film noir* fashion. This dark, brooding atmosphere is quickly dispelled as the camera cuts to a bright, sunshiny day outside the station, where a cab is just drawing up to the curb. Gloria gets out and rushes inside to join Davy in his flight from the city to the fresher life on the farm. They embrace and kiss as the camera pulls away, losing sight of them in the congested crowd of passersby hurrying through the station.

In their departure from the brutal big city, which has proved a harsh and unpleasant place for both of them, one can see early indications of Kubrick's dark vision of contemporary society. In his films Kubrick shows us modern man gradually being dehumanized by living in a materialistic, mechanized world in which one man exploits another in the mass effort for survival. In his later films which probe into the future, Kubrick further suggests that man's failure to master the world of the present can only lead to man's being mastered by the world of the future.

Like *Fear and Desire, Killer's Kiss* was financed by Kubrick with the help of his friends and relatives, this time for $75,000. Money began to run out during the post-production work and Kubrick was unable to afford an editing assistant. He therefore had to spend four months just laying in the sound effects "footstep by footstep," as he puts it. In any case Kubrick created his sound track with skill. For example, his use of recordings of prizefight crowds, coupled with the fact that he keeps his camera close to the ring throughout the arena sequence, creates the illusion that the darkened area beyond the ring is crowded with fight fans. In reality the auditorium was virtually empty beyond the first couple of rows during the shooting.

Kubrick holds *Killer's Kiss* in only slightly more esteem than he does *Fear and Desire.* When I told him at our first meeting that I had not yet been able to see his first two features, he smiled and said, "You're lucky," since he regards both films as amateur efforts. It is significant, however, that Kubrick was able to sell *Killer's Kiss,* a film made completely outside the Hollywood studio system, to United Artists, a major company, for worldwide distribution. "It made a profit for United Artists," he says, "though it was mostly released as a second feature."

Accordingly United Artists invited him to make a series of low-budget program pictures for the neighborhood circuits, but he turned down the offer, not wishing to commit himself to making second features indefinitely. This was a wise decision on Kubrick's part, as is borne out by the experience of other directors. When Fred Zinnemann (*High Noon, A Man for All Seasons*) turned out some fast low-budgeters at M-G-M in the early forties, the studio offered him nothing else for years. "I had a strong feeling of going backward," he once told me. "It was frustrating to do donkey work when I felt that I had already done more than enough of an apprenticeship."

Kubrick was saved from this situation when an old friend from high school days, Alexander Singer, introduced him to James Harris, a wealthy young man who wanted to try his hand at producing motion pictures. Kubrick and Harris, both of whom were only twenty-six years old at the time, formed a three-picture partnership which enabled Kubrick to rise from the rank of promising newcomer to that of major director.

Above, Marie Windsor and Elisha Cook, Jr.

# Chapter Two
# The Last Holdup:
## The Killing (1956)

Kubrick's first important film, *The Killing,* was a tough and tightly knit crime thriller about a racetrack robbery carried out by a group of down-at-the-heels small-time crooks who hope to pull off one last big job to solve all of their individual financial crises. Like Kubrick's first two features, *The Killing* comes at the end of the *film noir* cycle in American cinema mentioned in the previous chapter.

"After ten years of steadily shedding romantic conventions," Paul Schrader writes in his *Film Comment* article on the cycle, "the later *noir* films finally got down to the root causes" of the disillusionment of the period: the loss of heroic conventions, personal integrity, and finally psychic stability. The last films of the trend seemed to be painfully aware that "they stood at the end of a long tradition based on despair and disintegration and did not shy away from the fact." Certainly *The Killing* does not.

Furthermore, *The Killing* also reflects another element of *film noir* that Schrader points out as endemic to that type of movie: it utilizes a complex chronological order to reinforce a sense of hopelessness and lost time in a disoriented world. Based on Lionel White's novel *Clean Break,* Kubrick's tightly constructed script follows the preparations of the makeshift gang bent on making a big pile of money by holding up a racetrack. They have planned the robbery to coincide with the actual running of the seventh race, and Kubrick photographs the heist in great detail with all of its split-second timing. He builds suspense with great intensity by quickly cutting from one member of the gang to another in a series of flashbacks that show how each has simultaneously carried out his part of the plan. All of these parallel lines of action lead inexorably to the climactic moment when the ringleader gets away with the loot.

Pauline Kael, who agrees with Kubrick that *The Killing* marks the real beginning of his career, says in *Going Steady* that robbery pictures tend to be terribly derivative of earlier robbery movies, but that it is still possible for a director to bring a fresh approach to the project: "to present the occupational details of crime accurately (or convincingly), to assemble the gang so that we get a sense of the kinds of people engaged in crime and what their professional and non-professional lives are like. A good crime movie generally has a sordid, semi-documentary authenticity about criminal activities," she concludes, "plus the nervous excitement of what it might be like to rob and tangle with the law."

All of these elements are evident in *The Killing*. In giving us a glimpse into the seedy lives of each member of the gang involved in the robbery, Kubrick has given the film a touch of sleazy authenticity that raises it well above the level of the ordinary crime movie.

"The budget was larger than the earlier films, $320,000," he notes. "This time we were able to afford good actors." The director elicited a high order of ensemble acting from a group of capable Hollywood supporting players who rarely got a chance to give performances of such substance. Sterling Hayden plays Johnny Clay, the tough organizer of the caper. Jay C. Flippen is Marvin Unger, the cynical older member of the group; Elisha Cook, Jr., is George Peatty, the timid track cashier who hopes to impress his voluptuous wife Sherry (Marie Windsor) with stolen money, since he cannot otherwise give her satisfaction; and Ted De Corsia is Randy Kennan, a crooked cop. They and other cast members help Kubrick create the brutal atmosphere of the film.

Sterling Hayden remembers Kubrick during shooting as always confident about what he was doing: "I have worked with few directors that good. He's like the Russian documentarians who could put the same footage together five different ways, so it really didn't matter what the actors did—Stanley would know what to do with it."

Kubrick was also confident that his method of telling the story by means of fragmented flashbacks would work as well on the screen as it did in the novel. "It was the handling of time that may have made this more than just a good crime film," he says. Another thing that attracted him to White's book, Alexander Walker points out very perceptively in *Stanley Kubrick Directs*, is that the novel touches on a theme that is a frequent preoccupation of Kubrick's films: the presumably perfect plan of action that goes wrong through human fallibility and/or chance: "It is characteristic of Kubrick what while one part of him pays intellectual tribute to the rationally constructed master plan, another part reserves the skeptic's right to anticipate human imperfections or the laws of chance that militate against its success."

We shall see reverberations of this theme most notably in films like *Dr. Strangelove,* in which a mad general (again played by Sterling Hayden) upsets the carefully planned U.S. nuclear fail-safe system, and in *2001,* in which Hal the "infallible" computer goes lethally awry. But this theme asserts itself in other Kubrick films as well, including movies as different as *Spartacus* and *Lolita.*

It is clear from the outset in *The Killing* that the tawdry individuals whom Johnny Clay has brought together to execute the racetrack robbery comprise a series of weak links in a chain of command that could snap at any point. Add to this the possibility of unexpected mishaps that could dog even the best of plans, and the viewer senses that the entire project is doomed from the start. Nevertheless, one is still fascinated to see how things will go wrong, and when.

Surprisingly, most of the film was shot on studio sets, except the exteriors at the track and at the airport. Even with the biggest budget of his career to date, Kubrick had to work quickly and economically to bring the film in within that figure. Harris contributed $130,000 to the budget, and United Artists furnished the rest. "During shooting," Harris once told *Newsweek,* "there was an air of resentment all around us," since there were not very many producers and directors in their twenties working in Hollywood at the time. "Stanley had his own ideas how things were to go and people resented his encroaching on their contributions."

Because of union regulations Kubrick could no longer act as his own cameraman, and so veteran cinematographer Lucien Ballard was engaged to shoot the film. Occasionally friction developed between director and cameraman when they disagreed on how a shot should be lit. Eventually, however, a mutual respect developed between the two men. Kubrick, after all, is one of the few movie directors who has belonged to the cinematographers' union and who still operates his own camera from time to time when making a film. In fact, Jeremy Bernstein noticed while *2001* was in production a decade later that Kubrick often took Polaroid shots of a camera setup in order to check lighting effects with his cinematographer, Geoffrey Unsworth. "I asked Kubrick if it was customary for movie directors to participate so actively in photographing a film," Bernstein records in *The New Yorker,* "and he said succinctly that he never watched any other directors work."

During the credits of *The Killing* there are several shots of the preparations before a race: the starting gate is brought into place, the horses line up in their positions, etc. It is a tribute to Kubrick's naturalistic direction that when the film cuts from these documentary shots of the track to the betting area, few filmgoers suspect that the action has shifted to a studio set. The voice of the narrator further contributes to the documentary air of the picture. He introduces each of the characters, describing why each is implicated in the plot.

First there is Marvin Unger. "At exactly three forty-five on a Saturday afternoon in September," the narrator begins, "Marvin Unger walked toward the cashiers' windows at the racetrack. Despite his lifelong antipathy for gambling, he had bet on all of the horses in the same race. He realized that his method would cause him to lose in the long run, but he was shooting for higher stakes." Marvin is helping to set up a well-planned robbery so that he can obtain enough money to retire with financial security. He stands at the window of cashier George Peatty. When the winner of the race is confirmed, Marvin writes an address and meeting time on the back of his winning ticket and pushes it through the window to Peatty. He gives a similar note to track bartender Mike O'Reilly (Joe Sawyer).

"About an hour later," the narrator continues, "Patrolman Randy Kennan had some business to attend to." Kennan keeps a rendezvous in a cheap bar with a gambler to whom he is heavily in debt. He stalls his creditor with the promise that he is shortly to come into a large sum of money.

At 7 P.M. that same evening Johnny Clay is opening a bottle of beer in the dingy kitchen of a flat while he describes his accomplices to his girlfriend Fay (Colleen Gray). "None of these guys are criminals in the ordinary sense of the word," he explains. "They all have little problems they have to take care of. Take Marvin Unger, who is nice enough to let me stay here in his apartment. He is no criminal." To quell Fay's misgivings about Johnny's getting involved in a major crime after recently getting out of prison, her lover says, "Anytime you take a chance you had better be sure that the stakes are worth it because they can put you away just as fast for taking ten dollars as for taking a million." Johnny arranges to meet Fay at the airport after the robbery so that they can go away together, and sends her away.

"Half an hour earlier, at approximately six-thirty, Mike O'Reilly came home." The bartender greets his bedridden wife, whom he cannot afford to send to a specialist. Mike daubs her forehead with his handkerchief and consoles her with the promise of better days ahead as he fingers the scrap of paper which Unger has given him.

Some of the strongest dramatic scenes in the film are those between mousy George Peatty and his sluttish wife Sherry. George is hopelessly in love with Sherry and is constantly afraid that she will two-time him with another man, something she has already done repeatedly. Kubrick gives us a thumbnail sketch of their ugly, unhappy relationship in just a few lines of dialogue. Trying to lure his wife's attention away from the pulp magazine she is reading, George opens with, "I saw something sweet on the way home tonight." "Was it a candy bar, George?" she asks without looking up.

Undaunted, George goes on, "It was a couple sitting in front of me on the train. They called each other papa and mama." "Is that what you want us to do, George?" "Forget it, Sherry. What's for dinner?" "Steak. If you can't smell it cooking it's because it's still down at the supermarket."

Maddened by her constant condescension, George blurts out that he is involved in a big operation that will make them rich. Sherry shrewdly tries to pry more of the details from him, but George, aware that he has already said too much, becomes evasive. "My own husband doesn't trust me," she pouts. Sherry later tells her lover Val (Vince Edwards) what she has been able to

**Elisha Cook, Jr., Sterling Hayden and Jay C. Flippen, THE KILLING.**

wheedle out of her husband. Ironically, she is as submissive to this cheap crook as George is to her.

At the meeting which Johnny has called with his fellow conspirators, he goes over the intricate plans which he has laid. A single overhead lamp illumines their worn, defeated faces as they talk, leaving them surrounded by a darkness that is almost tangible. It is this darkness that seems to hover around Kubrick's characters in many of his films and which they desperately seek to keep from engulfing them—usually without success.

Sherry unexpectedly interrupts these deliberations when she is heard snooping around in the corridor outside Marvin's apartment. George weakly whimpers that she must have found the address while going through his pockets, since she is a very jealous wife. This incident shakes the whole group's sense of security about the venture, but Johnny is able to reconfirm their confidence that the plan has not been damaged by Sherry's interference. The group disperses and Marvin goes out onto the street to smoke a cigarette. As he leaves the building he passes a parked car, and the camera moves in to show Val and one of his henchmen casing the place.

Back home George presses Sherry to find out if Johnny tried anything with her, and she denies it. Given Johnny's scorn for her, she is probably telling the truth for once. George nonetheless is thinking of pulling out of the whole deal because of the harsh way in which Clay treated them both. But Sherry, getting into bed and pulling George toward her in a fatuous embrace, gets him to agree to stick with the gang.

"Three days later," the narrator says, "Johnny Clay began the final preparations." He hires a wrestler named Maurice to start a fight with the track bartender to distract the police from the robbery. Clay meets the wrestler in a most unlikely place, a chess and checkers parlor. (In point of fact, however, the wrestler who played the role was in real life a chess addict like Kubrick with whom the director had played many times in Washington Square.)

Clay next visits sharpshooter Nikki Arane (Timothy Carey) at his farm. Johnny hires Arane to shoot down Red Lightning, the favored horse, during the course of the seventh race. This will delay the official decision on the winner of the race and enable Johnny to make a bigger haul before the betters arrive at the cashiers' windows for their payoffs. Nikki fondles a puppy all the time that he and Johnny discuss the proposition, which explains his hesitation to shoot an animal. "You're not being asked to commit first-degree murder," Johnny chides; "it isn't even murder. The worst

36

they could get you for is shooting horses out of season." The last item on Johnny's agenda is to rent a motel room where he can temporarily store his rifle and hide the loot immediately after the robbery.

Tension begins to mount as the day of the holdup dawns. "Four days later, at 7 A.M., Sherry Peatty was wide awake," says the narrator. Badgering her nervous spouse at the breakfast table, she gets him to admit that today is the day. The only possible weakness in the film is the implausibility of George's being quite as naive and ineffectual in dealing with his wife as he is portrayed to be. But the two performers breathe a great deal of credibility into their handling of these scenes, particularly Elisha Cook, Jr., whom Penelope Houston describes in *Contemporary Cinema* as "the prototype of all sad little men."

"At the track the favorite, Red Lightning, was given only half a portion of feed, and Johnny Clay began what might be the last day of his life." Ironically, it will be the last day of life for just about everyone involved in the project *but* Johnny. The mastermind of the holdup stops at his motel room, where he transfers his rifle from a violin case to a flower box. Now things move swiftly. At 8:45 A.M. Clay deposits the box in a locker at the bus station and puts the key to the locker in Mike O'Reilly's mailbox.

Having snatched the key from the mailbox, Mike heads for the bus station, which he reaches by 11:29 A.M. He just has time to pick up the flower box and board the racetrack special, which almost leaves without him. The film is filled with suspenseful moments like this one, where a single slip could upset the whole plan that Johnny has worked out with such careful timing. Similarly, in the employees' locker room at the track, a friend of Mike's insists on storing the flower box in a refrigerator instead of allowing the contents to wilt in Mike's locker. Mike irritably stuffs the box into his locker with a hasty explanation that offends his buddy but does not make him suspicious. Nearby George Peatty, who has overheard what has just transpired, takes a pistol out of his lunch box and pockets it.

From this point onward Kubrick begins to follow each separate strand of the robbery plot through to its completion, doubling back each time to show how each of the elements of the elaborate plan is implemented simultaneously with all of the others. Kubrick repeats the shots from the credit sequence of the horses getting into starting position for the seventh race each time he turns back the clock to develop a different step in the complex robbery plan, thereby situating the viewer temporally.

"At three thirty-two Officer Kennan set in motion his phase of

the operation." Kennan phones in to headquarters that his radio keeps going dead, hoping by this ruse to avert suspicion from himself later in the afternoon when he stops taking police calls while he is otherwise occupied.

"Earlier that afternoon Maurice the wrestler started for the track. He was to be there by 4 P.M." Maurice goes immediately to the bar and observes Johnny standing by the employees' entrance nearby. Then the wrestler starts a fight with Mike the bartender and takes on the entire track police force. One by one they leap into the frame and grab for Maurice, who picks them up, twirls them around, and sends them sailing across the floor. At 4:23 P.M. Maurice is finally overwhelmed by superior numbers and taken into custody while Johnny, unobserved, slips through the track staff's door, which has been unlocked for him by Peatty. So far so good.

The narrator takes us back to 11:43 A.M., when Nikki Arane left his farm in his sports car. He arrives at the track parking lot at twelve-thirty, and bribes the black parking attendant to let him have the position he requires in order to draw a bead on Red Lightning. The attendant mistakes Nikki's patronizing manner as genuine kindness and comes over from time to time to chat with Arane. At one point the attendant offers Nikki a lucky horseshoe. We see once more the shots of the horses approaching the gate for the seventh race, then cut back to Nikki, who is getting more nervous by the second at the thought of the attendant's standing by and witnessing what he is about to do. Finally he explodes at the black, who walks away in anger.

Nikki tensely watches the race through his gunsight. At precisely 4:23 P.M., he pulls the trigger and brings Red Lightning down. Thirty seconds later Arane is dead. His sports car blows a tire as he tries to drive out of the parking lot, leaving him within the range of a track guard's pistol shot. Lying next to Nikki on the cement is the lucky horseshoe that he had been given a few minutes before.

Now the clock rolls back to 2:15 P.M. as we see the robbery from the point of view of its key figure, Johnny Clay. In directing *The Criminal* (1960, alternate title: *The Concrete Jungle*), Joseph Losey decided not to film in detail the racetrack robbery that climaxed the picture. "It seemed to me the important thing was to see the exterior aspect," he explains in Tom Milne's *Losey on Losey*, "to see how they got in, and then see them come out and escape. The fact that inside somebody points a gun at somebody else, and someone puts lots of money into satchels, is not to me interesting." In *The Killing*, however, Kubrick has built his film from the beginning toward the peak where all of Johnny's meticulous planning suddenly converges on the moment when he enters the cashiers' office and scoops up $2 million. Hence it was artistically right for him to depict this moment for the audience in detail, and he does so.

Johnny passes George Peatty's window as George gives him a frightened, furtive look. Johnny cues Maurice to start his fight at the bar and stands by the employees' entrance to the track. George opens the door, Johnny moves by him and enters the locker room, where he retrieves his rifle from Mike's locker and puts on the rubber mask and gloves which were also in the flower box. With typical Kubrick irony, the face on the mask is frozen into a perpetual grin.

Thus disguised, Johnny bursts into the cashiers' room and orders them to fill his large laundry sack with all the money it will hold. As they do so the track announcer can be heard in the background: "We don't have any exact information on Red Lightning's spill but we do know that the jockey was not seriously injured." Then Johnny makes his getaway, heaving the bulky bag, which now contains his mask, gloves, and gun as well as the cash, out of an open window. Later we learn that Officer Kennan was stationed below the window to catch the loot as it hit the ground and transfer it to the motel room where Johnny would pick it up later.

Kubrick begins to draw the last threads of the plot together as Johnny's companions in crime assemble in Marvin's shabby living room to await Clay's appearance with the money. The men sit around drinking nervously and listening to radio reports of the "daring holdup" at the track. George's hand, anxiously nursing a glass, is in the foreground, suggesting the tension that permeates the room.

"Where is Johnny?" George whines. "Why does his timetable have to break down *now*?" There is a knock at the door, but instead of Johnny and the cash it is Val and one of his mobsters. They force their way into the room, expecting to grab the swag for themselves. A shoot-out ensues that leaves everyone in the room dead—except for George, who is mortally wounded. For a moment Kubrick trains his hand-held camera on the pile of corpses spread around the room, recalling for an instant the clump of mannequins in the climactic sequence of *Killer's Kiss*. The room is silent, except for the sound of bouncy Latin music pouring from the radio, providing an ironic counterpoint to the carnage of the scene. As the camera lingers on the bloody bodies, one thinks sardonically that Marvin Unger no longer has to worry about providing for his old age, nor does Randy Kennan have to be concerned about what the captain will think of him. We can picture, too, Mike O'Reilly's bedridden wife waiting for him to return home, as the camera pauses on his remains. It has been quite a killing.

George Peatty has enough life left in him to struggle toward the door. The camera, assuming his point of view momentarily, sways with him in the direction of the door, and George's hand enters the frame to twist the knob. Johnny has just pulled up outside. The camera is now in the back seat of Johnny's car and follows George as he comes out of the building, sprawls across the hood of Johnny's auto, pulls himself together, and forces himself to continue across the street, where he gets into his own car and drives away.

George is moving with the determination of a man who knows he must accomplish something before he takes his last breath. Once home he finds Sherry packing to go away with Val, as he suspected he would. She tries to mollify him with a prefabricated alibi, but for once in his life George is not to be forestalled by his scheming wife. "Why did you do it?" he asks plaintively, already knowing the answer. "I loved you, Sherry." He then blasts away with his pistol, the impotent husband finally penetrating his wife with bullets. As George himself falls forward toward the camera he knocks over the birdcage, symbol of his pitifully narrow existence, which is now at an end.

Johnny, aware that something terrible has happened, drives to the airport to meet Fay as planned. En route he buys the largest suitcase he can find and stashes the loot in it. He finds Fay and they proceed to the check-in counter, passing two men who are quite clearly sizing up everyone who enters the air terminal. With nervous nonchalance Johnny demands that the airline allow him to lug his huge suitcase on board with him rather than stow it in the luggage compartment. Throughout his bickering with the airline personnel, which Kubrick records in a single take, the bulky bag stands inertly in the center of the frame, as Johnny tries to minimize its size.

The scene begins to take on the flavor of black comedy as the obliging clerk suggests that Johnny transfer some of the contents of the valise into some of his other bags and then asks Johnny to consider insuring the suitcase. "Just give me some idea of what is in it and its estimated value," he says with mannered friendliness, "and we'll take care of it." Realizing that he is causing a scene, Clay capitulates and watches apprehensively as the bag is tossed onto a conveyor belt and disappears from sight.

Johnny and Fay arrive at the departure gate just in time to see the baggage truck drive out onto the windy airfield. They watch in

mute horror as the ramshackle case falls off the top of the mountain of luggage and springs open, flooding the airstrip with stolen bills that blow right at the camera. The fate of the money in *The Killing* recalls how the gold dust in John Huston's *Treasure of the Sierra Madre* (1948) blows across the desert sands. In that film the men who have slaved to acquire the gold can only laugh hysterically when they contemplate how it drifted away from them.

But Fay and Johnny are in a daze. She supports his arm as they walk to the street and hopelessly try to hail a taxi before the two FBI agents who have been watching them all along can reach them. Fay tells Johnny to make a run for it, but he can only murmur, almost inaudibly, "What's the difference?" Resigned to their fate, Johnny and Fay turn resolutely around to face the two men advancing toward them through the glass doors of the flight lounge. Like Davy and Gloria in *Killer's Kiss*, Johnny and Fay had hoped to escape the corrosive atmosphere of the big city by flight to a cleaner climate. Earlier Marvin had encouraged Johnny to go away "and take stock of things." But for Johnny, brutalized by a life of crime, it was already too late.

*The Killing* is the kind of crime melodrama that Pauline Kael had in mind when she wrote of the sort of film that has a "sordid, semi-documentary authenticity about criminal activities" and exudes "the nervous excitement of what it might be like to rob and tangle with the law." The occasion of her remarks was the 1968 Jim Brown vehicle *The Split,* which imitated *The Killing* in an uninspired way that makes one appreciate Kubrick's film all the more. When *The Killing* itself was released a decade earlier, Miss Kael saw it as "an expert suspense film, with fast, incisive cutting," and "furtive little touches of characterization." *Time* applauded Kubrick for having shown "more imagination with dialogue and camera than Hollywood has seen since the obstreperous Orson Welles went riding out of town."

"It was a profitable picture for UA," says Kubrick, "and this is the only measure of success in financial terms." But no new offers were immediately forthcoming from any Hollywood studio to Kubrick and Harris as a production team. They then acquired on their own the rights to Humphrey Cobb's angry 1935 novel about World War I, *Paths of Glory,* which Kubrick had read when he was fourteen. He developed a screen play in collaboration with Calder Willingham, as well as with Jim Thompson, who had contributed additional dialogue to *The Killing.* With a script in hand Kubrick and Harris set about finding studio backing for what was to become one of the most uncompromising anti-war films ever made.

# PART TWO:
# THE MATURE
# MOVIEMAKER

**George Macready, Adolphe Menjou and Richard Anderson, PATHS OF GLORY.**

# Chapter Three
# The Unknown Soldiers:

## Paths of Glory (1957)

No major studio showed much interest in financing *Paths of Glory*. "Not because it was an anti-war film about World War I," says Kubrick. "They just didn't like it." Then Kirk Douglas became interested in playing the lead and United Artists agreed to back the project for $935,000. This was still not a big budget by studio standards, but it was astronomical compared to the budgets that Kubrick had previously worked with. The film was released under the banner of Douglas's independent company, Bryna Productions, which was one of the star's stipulations for appearing in the movie. Kubrick points out, however, that "although we had to give Bryna a production credit, it had nothing whatsoever to do with the making or financing of the film."

The title of the story is a reference to Thomas Gray's poem "Elegy in a Country Churchyard," in which the poet remarks that the "paths of glory lead but to the grave." It becomes increasingly clear as the film progresses that the paths of glory that the irresponsible French generals are pursuing lead not to *their* deaths but to the graves of the enlisted men, who are decreed to die in the battles which are fought according to the strategy which the commanding officers manipulate for their own self-advancement.

Kubrick made his movie in the Geiselgasteig Studios in Munich. His two principal location sites, the battlefield and the château where the French officers have set up their general headquarters, were about half an hour's drive away from the studio. The director's budget allowed him to assemble as fine a supporting cast as he had for *The Killing,* notably George Macready as the neurotic General Mireau and Adolphe Menjou as General Broulard, the commander of the French forces.

The story has been told that during shooting Menjou grew im-

51

patient with Kubrick's desire for several retakes on a scene and became angry when the director insisted on doing the scene yet another time after Menjou felt he had already given his best reading. When I asked him about it, Kubrick said that no such incident took place.

For his part, Menjou said after completing the picture that Kubrick reminded him of Chaplin, who directed the actor in *A Woman of Paris* in 1923, because Kubrick, like Chaplin, always took into consideration the actor's suggestions while working out a scene. As far as the number of takes that he requires in order to get a scene as close to perfection as possible, Kubrick believes that the filmmaker must bear in mind that he has to live with a film for the rest of his life once he has made it. If the director cuts corners or makes compromises just to avoid conflicts on the set, he says, "it's still your film to live with the rest of your days."

*Paths of Glory* opens with the "*Marseillaise,*" played in an ominous minor key, accompanying the credits, after which the music gives way to the insistent sound of snare drums (which were similarly used to create tension in the B-52 sequences of *Dr. Strangelove*). A title appears on the screen: "France, 1916." It is superimposed on a shot of the grand château where French army officers live in luxury while the soldiers die amid the mud and the barbed wire of the trenches. Like Joseph Losey's *King and Country* (1964), Kubrick's movie is not really so much an anti-war picture as a study of the way that the class distinctions of the European social system have operated during wartime between officers and men.

Kubrick employs a narrator to set the scene for the audience, though not to the extent that he used this device in *The Killing*. Here the narrator speaks his opening piece and disappears:

"War began between Germany and France on August 3, 1914. Five weeks later the German army had smashed its way to within eighteen miles of Paris. There the battered French miraculously rallied their forces at the Marne River, and in an unexpected series of counterattacks drove the Germans back. The front was stabilized and shortly afterward developed into a continuous line of heavily fortified trenches zigzagging their way five hundred miles from the English Channel to the Swiss frontier. By 1916, after two years of grisly trench warfare, the battle lines had changed very little. Successful attacks were measured in hundreds of yards—and paid for by hundreds of thousands of lives."

While this commentary is being spoken, a squad of soldiers takes its place in two columns at the front door of the château and an open car drives in the front gate, stopping at the door, where

General Broulard gets out. The handsome general's elegant manner belies his calloused and ruthless nature, and therefore foreshadows the equally charming and equally corrupt Minister of the Interior in *A Clockwork Orange*.

Broulard seems to belong to the sumptuous setting that the château provides as he lounges in an ornate chair and toys with the ambitious General Mireau's barely concealed hopes for a promotion. By the most adroit coaxing Broulard is able to manipulate Mireau into agreeing to launch what amounts to a suicidal charge against an impossibly fortified enemy stronghold called the Ant Hill as the first step in an all-out offensive.

Broulard begins by softening Mireau with compliments: "This is a splendid, superb place, Paul. I wish I had your taste in carpets and pictures." Then Broulard gets down to cases, telling Mireau that he has a top-secret matter to discuss with him, a task which he is sure that Mireau can handle for him. Mireau at first hesitates when he hears about the contemplated onslaught on the Ant Hill, though Broulard assures him that he is the only man who can see it through. "You know the condition of my troops," Mireau explains. "My division has been cut to pieces. We are not in a position to hold the Ant Hill, let alone take it."

"I had better not bring up the other thing that was on my mind," says Broulard coyly, preparing to needle Mireau where he is most vulnerable. "If I mention it now you will misunderstand; you might think that I was trying to influence your decision. But as your friend maybe I should tell you. The Twelfth Corps needs a fighting general and you are long overdue for that extra star. If you captured the Ant Hill the Twelfth Corps would be yours."

Having displayed token concern for his troops, Mireau's tone gradually shifts to one of determination: "Nothing is beyond them once their fighting spirit is aroused. We might just do it!" Mireau finally agrees to the Ant Hill attack, for, after all, it is not he but Colonel Dax (Kirk Douglas) who will have to mount the actual attack and watch his men slaughtered.

Mireau marches through the trenches on his way to inform Dax of his mission, stopping awkwardly along the way to buck up the men's spirits as he passes by. He is oblivious to the squalor in which they live, an ugly contrast to the splendor of the château which he has just left. It is a matter of record that the trenches used in the First World War were laid with wooden planks which served as a floor. Kubrick was consequently able to wheel his camera down the length of an entire trench just ahead of George Macready, thereby getting the whole scene in a single take.

"Hello, soldier, ready to kill more Germans?" the general asks

Kirk Douglas, PATHS OF GLORY.

condescendingly each time he pauses en route. "Are you married?" he asks Private Ferol (Timothy Carey). "No? Well then, I bet your mother is proud of you." "Looking over your rifle, soldier?" he inquires of Corporal Paris (Ralph Meeker). "Good; it's a soldier's best friend. You be good to it and it will be good to you." As he moves on he next encounters Private Arnaud (Joseph Turkel) and thus has seen, without realizing it, the three men whose lives he will later seek to sacrifice to save his own reputation.

When he asks another, older soldier if he is married, the man stammers, "My wife—I'm never going to see her again. I'm going to be killed." Mireau's friendly facade immediately cracks and he strikes the man, a gesture that brings to mind General George Patton's controversial slapping of a soldier in an army hospital during World War II. A sergeant who is standing by suggests to Mireau that the man is suffering from shell shock and Mireau—again, like General Patton—bristles in return, "There's no such thing as shell shock! I want the immediate transfer of this baby out of my division. I won't have my men contaminated."

To round out the irony of the scene, Mireau's aide, Major Saint-Auban (Richard Anderson), says to Mireau as they reach Colonel Dax's quarters, "These tours of yours have an incalculable effect on the fighting spirit of the men. In fact their spirit derives from them." Mireau smiles in agreement and, as a shell explodes overhead, fastidiously brushes falling debris from his immaculate cape.

If Mireau is out of place in the world of the trenches, Dax belongs to it in a way that no officer living in the remote world of the château can. Mireau has to stoop to enter Dax's dark, shabby quarters, and quips patronizingly to him, "Quite a neat little spot you've got here." Dax offers Mireau a straight-back chair, but Mireau refuses it, stating grandly that he remains always on the move: "I cannot understand these armchair generals behind a desk, waving papers at the enemy, worrying that a mouse might run up their leg." "With a choice of mice or Mausers," Dax notes, not without sarcasm, "I would take the mice every time."

Mireau looks at the Ant Hill through binoculars, which is as close as he and his fellow generals ever get to the field of battle. "It's not something we can grab and run away with," he mutters, "but it certainly is pregnable." He does not notice the hastily bandaged casualties passing by him at that moment, a portent of the severe losses that will be sustained during the attack on the Ant Hill.

Using the same methods to get Dax to acquiesce to the plan that

Broulard had used on him, Mireau begins by complimenting him on his record in the army and even recalls his success as a criminal lawyer in civilian life. Then he gets down to business and informs Dax that his men are to take the Ant Hill the following morning. He proceeds to outline his estimate of the projected casualties as if he were reeling off batting averages: "Five per cent of the men will be lost going over the top, another five per cent in reaching the enemy's wire; let's say another twenty-five per cent in actually taking the Ant Hill. And we will still have enough men left to keep it."

When the stunned Dax points out that half of his men are calculated to die, Mireau offers him the meager consolation that those who are killed will allow others to advance and that the Ant Hill will at long last change hands. Dax finds condescending the general's exhortation about carrying out the attack in the name of France and tells him so, ending with a reference to Samuel Johnson's renowned observation that patriotism is the last refuge of scoundrels.

Mireau explodes, attacking Dax in his most vulnerable spot, just as Broulard had done to him; in Dax's case, however, it is not the tantalizing suggestion of promotion but rather the threat that he will be separated from his men. Shaken, Dax capitulates: "If anyone can take the Ant Hill, we can." "And when you do," Mireau adds with a flourish, "your men will have a long rest."

Now Kubrick introduces a subplot which demonstrates that officers further down the chain of command think of their men as just as expendable as Mireau and his peers do. As he sits at his desk, Lieutenant Roget (Wayne Morris) is framed by two bottles before him. One has a lighted candle in it and the other contains the whiskey which he imbibes throughout the scene. Roget gruffly informs Corporal Paris and Private Lejeune (Ken Dibbs) that they are all going on a reconnaissance mission into no-man's-land, the sector that lies between the German and French trenches.

Roget is particularly haughty in dealing with Paris because they went to school together and the lieutenant fears that the corporal has little respect for him; he is obviously right. The last shred of respect that Paris might have retained for his superior officer will be torn away in the course of the patrol.

As the trio crawls through the rubble and unburied corpses that litter no-man's-land, Roget sends Lejeune ahead to scout the terrain. When Lejeune does not return immediately, the panicky Roget hurls a hand grenade into the darkness ahead of him and runs back to the French lines. Paris, as if in a trance, proceeds forward and discovers the body of Lejeune, hideously disfigured by the grenade explosion.

When Paris returns to Roget's dugout, the latter grins sheepishly and says, "I'm happily surprised to see you. I thought you were killed." Paris is not to be put off: "You didn't wait around to find out. You ran like a rabbit after you killed Lejeune. No officer would do that. A man wouldn't do it. Only a thing would; only a sneaky, guzzling, yellow-bellied rat with a bottle for a brain would." Roget rises, attempting to regain his lost stature, and cuts Paris off with charges of insubordination, threatening an officer, and disobeying orders. Paris offers countercharges which are, of course, much more serious: "Drunk on duty, wanton murder of one of your men, and cowardice in the face of the enemy."

For the third time in the film we witness an officer cajoling a subordinate for his own personal aggrandizement, and finally browbeating him into submission. "Philip," Roget says ingratiatingly, "have you ever tried to bring charges against an officer? Whose word are they going to believe—or, putting it another way, whose word are they going to *accept*?" By film's end Roget's cynical words are to prove more far-reaching in their application than either he or Paris can imagine at the moment. Paris realizes that his case is hopeless and leaves just as Dax comes in, asking for Roget's report on the night patrol. After Roget fabricates a story about Lejeune's coughing and drawing enemy fire, Dax suspiciously eyes the almost empty whiskey bottle on Roget's desk and leaves.

Just before the battle is to begin at dawn, Mireau once more scans the objective through binoculars and offers his aides a swig of cognac in anticipation of victory. Dax now makes the same journey from one end of the trench to the other which we watched Mireau make earlier, and the contrast is striking. As Kubrick's camera dollies through the trench, sometimes facing Dax as the colonel gives a reassuring glance at his men, sometimes looking ahead of Dax, showing his apprehensive troops making way for him to pass down the narrow corridor opening before him, it is abundantly clear that there is a mutual respect between officer and men of which there was no hint when Mireau made his earlier tour.

Dax reaches the point where he is to wait for the signal to lead his men into battle. He mounts a ladder, ready to take his men over the top. When the time comes, Kubrick shows the men pouring onto the battlefield in a high overhead shot of an entire line of soldiers which reaches from one end of the screen to the other. Then he shifts to a side view of the troops sweeping across the slopes toward enemy lines.

Prior to shooting this sequence, Kubrick spent several days preparing the landscape for the assault by planting explosives, creating bomb craters, placing tangles of barbed wire all over the terrain, and making it look like what one critic called "the rim of hell." On the day that the battle was filmed, the director had six cameras placed at strategic points along the attack route, while he himself used a hand-held camera with a zoom lens to zero in on Kirk Douglas and record his reactions to what was happening around him. These shots of Douglas are a great help to audience identification, drawing the viewer into the battle scenes in a way that mere panoramic shots of the battlefield could never have done.

The German extras in French uniforms were actually members of the police force. At first, Kubrick recalls, they had to get used to the idea of playing the parts of Frenchmen fighting Germans. But eventually they got into the spirit of the movie and played the battle scenes with great gusto. Kubrick assigned various groups of extras to die in different sectors of the battlefield and told them to fall, whenever possible, near an explosion. Watching the battle as it plays on the screen, one can see that Kubrick's German policemen followed his orders to perfection.

Indeed, the effect of all of Kubrick's long-term preparation for the battle sequence is stunning. As bombs explode overhead and shrapnel cascades down on the troops, they crouch, run, and crawl forward, falling in and out of shell holes, stumbling over the corpses of comrades long since dead. The director intercuts close-ups of Dax, a whistle clamped between his teeth, as he sees his men dying on all sides of him and observes the attack turn into a rout and a retreat.

There is a shot of the battlefield as seen through binoculars which provides a transition that leads us back to the command post where Mireau is watching the proceedings. Kubrick once more reminds the audience that field glasses are the generals' only contact with the scene of the hostilities. Mireau searches the horizon for the troops that are supposed to constitute the next wave of the attack. "Miserable cowards, they're still in the trenches!" He calls Captain Rousseau, the battery commander (John Stein), on the field telephone and orders him to fire on the men who are still in the trenches. "They have mutinied," he maintains, "by refusing to advance." On the other end of the telephone line, Captain Rousseau respectfully requests that the general put his order in writing: "Suppose you were killed, General. Then where would I be?" "You'll be in front of a firing squad in the morning. Place yourself under arrest and report to my headquarters," Mireau screams and slams down the receiver. This demonstration of Mireau's madness looks ahead to *Dr. Strangelove* when man's folly will have reached the point where one group of American soldiers will be ordered to attack another group who are dutifully guarding an air base that has been sealed off by a still madder officer, General Jack D. Ripper.

By this time Dax has made it back to the French lines and commands Lieutenant Roget to get the remainder of the men out of the trenches and onto the field. But Roget balks at this, since the retreat is already in progress. As Dax climbs up the ladder out of the trench, exhorting the men to renew their courage and follow him, he is thrown backward into a trench by the body of a French soldier rolling in on top of him. This shot provides one of the many visual ironies that punctuate the film.

Mireau is informed that the attack has failed all along the line. His eyes blaze and light falls across the scar on his face which serves as a symbol of his mutilated personality. He roars apoplectically that he will convene a general court-martial for 3 P.M.: "If those little sweethearts won't face German bullets, they will face French ones!"

For the first time in the movie we see Dax in the unreal world of the château, listening impassively as Broulard and Mireau bicker over the number of soldiers who should be shot to serve as an example to the rest of the troops. Aware that the two generals are bargaining with the lives of his men, Dax tries to reason with them.

On the wall behind Mireau as he talks is a pastoral painting, an emblem of the romantic decor with which he has surrounded himself in his medieval palace, so distant from the harsh realities of trench warfare. This attitude enables him to speak now like a warrior from some heroic epic of yore: "It was the duty of the men to obey orders whether they thought that they were possible or not. If it were impossible to take the Ant Hill, the only proof would be their dead bodies lying in the trenches. The whole rotten regiment is scum; a pack of sneaking, whining, tail-dragging curs. It's an incontestable fact."

Sickened by Mireau's contempt for the fighting men who have been waging his war for him, Dax blurts out, "Then why not shoot the entire regiment? I'm serious. Or take me. One man would do as well to serve as an example. The obvious choice would be the officer responsible for the attack." He says this last sentence looking at Mireau, who turns away from his gaze.

Broulard, who can always be counted on to appear to miss any point that he does not care to acknowledge, ignores Dax's sugges-

tion and enters the fray by directing Mireau to settle for a token number of soldiers to be shot and be done with it. He is delighted with Mireau's concession to have each company commander select one man from the first wave of the attack, three in all. Despite Mireau's protests to the contrary, Broulard appoints Dax to defend the accused, and closes the conference by demurring from making an appearance at the court-martial in order to let Mireau handle the whole affair. In reality Broulard is shrewdly keeping his white-gloved hands from getting soiled by having any official connection with the proceedings.

Dax, intent on getting the scapegoats acquitted, visits the three prisoners in their cell to discuss the court-martial. They turn out to be three of the men to whom Mireau had imparted his perfunctory encouragement during his tour of the trenches. With righteous indignation all three of the men express their resentment about being executed to save a general's vanity.

The prisoners are escorted by guards into the enormous room in the château where the trial is to be held. They enter in extreme long shot from the opposite end of the room, dwarfed figures who have no control over the forces that are now determining their destinies. The checkered pattern on the highly polished floor makes the room look like a gigantic chessboard, further underscoring the feeling that the three defendants are but pawns in the power plays of their superiors.

The tone of the trial as a mere formality is set at the outset by the president of the court-martial (Peter Capell), who says casually that because the indictment is lengthy it therefore will not be read. Dax's protest that his clients have a right to know what the charges are against them is met with a testy reply from the president: "The charge is cowardice during the attack on the Ant Hill."

Major Saint-Auban, a sycophant of Mireau's, has been appointed prosecutor. He has no difficulty in confusing the first defendant to take the stand, Private Ferol, into admitting that he retreated when he should have advanced.

Arnaud is better able to field the major's questions than Ferol had been. Asked by the prosecutor if he urged his comrades forward, he snaps back without hesitation, "Most of them died as they left the trenches. The rest of us advanced until Captain Renoir ordered us to fall back." "Aside from your sad failure to utter battle cries," Dax inquires sarcastically, "was your behavior different from that of the others? Is it not true that you were designated a coward by drawing a slip of paper marked with an X?"

The president of the court-martial, who always addresses Dax as if he were a recalcitrant schoolboy, reminds the defense attorney that it is accepted practice in the French army to choose one enlisted man by lot to serve as an example for the rest of the soldiers; since not one of the troops succeeded in reaching the German lines, any man who was so chosen could be convicted fairly. He consequently refuses to allow Dax to introduce testimony on behalf of Arnaud's past bravery, saying that the only evidence he will entertain as attesting to the private's courage is proof that he reached the German lines.

Corporal Paris is quickly disposed of by the prosecutor, who does not accept the corporal's story that an officer who was shot fell on him as he tried to leave the trench and knocked him out. Paris's only way of substantiating his contention is to point to the abrasion on his forehead, which the president dismisses as having possibly been self-inflicted.

Now that the prisoners have been hustled through their testimony, there remain only the final pleas by the two attorneys. As Saint-Auban paces back and forth during his summation speech, the camera is placed behind the row of five judges whom he is addressing, so that they are in the foreground of the frame and he is only visible between them. This visual composition implies that the major is making a grandstand play not only to win his case but to impress the judges with his subservient loyalty to the military establishment by seeing that the scapegoats are convicted, all done with a view to future promotion.

"I submit that the attack on the Ant Hill was a stain upon the flag of France," he intones melodramatically as his voice echoes through the great hall, "and that it has dishonored every man, woman, and child in the French nation. I ask you to find the accused guilty."

When Dax sums up his case he moves back and forth with his hands in his pockets, as if thinking out loud. This time the camera is shooting from behind the three prisoners so that they dominate the frame, and Dax can be seen between them. This composition indicates that it is concern for them that is in the forefront of Dax's consciousness and not the favor of his superior officers before whom he is pleading the case.

"Sometimes I am ashamed to call myself a human being and this is one of them," he begins. "I protest that the prosecution introduced no witnesses to support its case and that no stenographic record of these proceedings has been made. The attack was no stain on the flag of France; but this trial is such a stain." The camera is now slightly below Dax, shooting up at him in a way which makes his figure more imposing as he finishes his statement: "Gentlemen, to find these men guilty will be a crime to haunt each

George Macready and Kirk Douglas, **PATHS OF GLORY.**

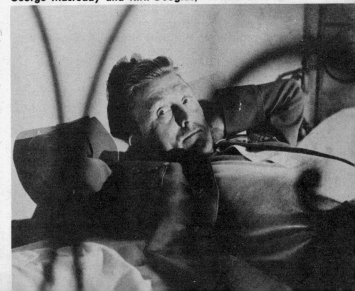

of you to the day you die. I can't believe the noblest impulse in man, his compassion for another, can be completely dead here. Therefore I humbly beg you to show mercy to these men."

In his book *The Cinema of Joseph Losey,* James Leahy contrasts the final plea of Colonel Dax in *Paths of Glory* to that of his counterpart, Captain Hargreaves (Dirk Bogarde), in Losey's *King and Country,* who is defense attorney in an equally unfair military court-martial. To Leahy the difference between the two summation speeches in the two films is that Dax makes an "indulgently theatrical" speech right to the audience, whereas Hargreaves directs himself to his fellow officers on the court-martial panel, leaving the audience "free to observe and judge the nature of Hargreaves's emotionalism."

Having seen both movies several times over the years, I am at a loss to see that the two directors handle the parallel scenes any differently. In both cases Kubrick and Losey intend that the defense attorney's plea be directed, in the context of the dramatic situation, to the judges before them, but by extension to the film audience as well, since both Kirk Douglas and Dirk Bogarde at times address their remarks to the camera. In both films the tribunal which condemns the innocent is confident that it is upholding the traditional code of military honor. Yet how different the court's action in each film seems to the audience when viewed through the critical cameras of Kubrick and Losey. Both directors clearly want to elicit an emotional response from the audience as it witnesses the tragic miscarriage of justice on which each picture turns, for both moviemakers extend the action of their respective films beyond the verdict of the court-martial to make the moviegoer share the last hours and deaths of the convicted.

In *Paths of Glory,* after the president of the court-martial announces that the hearing is closed and that the court will deliberate, Kubrick cuts immediately to a sergeant already issuing instructions to the men who are to patrol the execution ceremonies. No one, it is evident, has had any doubt as to what will be the outcome of those deliberations.

In their dark, depressing cell, the three convicted prisoners are greeted by a soldier who bursts in on them with their last meal, a duck dinner, "compliments of General Mireau." Kubrick shot this crucial scene fifty-six times before he got all of the details precisely right. The condemned men are not allowed to have utensils, so they must accept the degradation of eating the sumptuous fare with their hands. The gloomy cell is lit only by a window at the back of the room, which lends an almost eerie atmosphere to the setting.

The three men speculate about the possibilities of escape or a last-minute reprieve. By this means Kubrick keeps the suspenseful tone of the film from slackening even after the verdict has been rendered. In addition, the verbal and visual ironies continue to mount up throughout the scene. Paris spies a cockroach on the table and complains sullenly, "It will have more contact with my wife and child after today than I will because I'll be dead and it will still be alive." Ferol smashes the cockroach with his fist, commenting morosely, "Now you've got the edge on him."

The chaplain (Emile Meyer) now enters and lugubriously advises the men to prepare for death. Like the Anglican minister in *A Clockwork Orange,* this representative of religion makes a more favorable impression on the viewer as the film goes on. At first he seems an ineffectual dispenser of pious platitudes, but as the sequence continues his genuine compassion for these unfortunates is clearly seen to be as strong as that of Dax. Both men must stand by helplessly and witness a travesty of justice which they cannot avert. The priest hears the confession of Ferol, who by now has begun to weep and whine uncontrollably in the face of his imminent death. Paris gives the chaplain a letter for his wife and prepares to make his confession.

Suddenly Arnaud, who could be seen in the background of the previous shot taking generous swigs from a whiskey bottle, attacks the chaplain: "You say we should have faith in our creator; death comes to us all. That's really deep!" Holding up his bottle, Arnaud proclaims, "This is my religion." With that, Arnaud lunges at the priest and Paris slugs him, sending him careening backward against the wall. He slides to the floor unconscious.

The doctor who is summoned to examine him pronounces that he has a skull fracture and may not live through the night. He gives Arnaud an injection and directs that if he is still alive in the morning someone should pinch his cheeks to wake him up: "The general wants him to be conscious during the execution," he says, politely overlooking the chaplain's contention that the execution should be delayed.

Dax has not been able to save the lives of his men, but he is able to mete out some poetic justice of his own. He orders Lieutenant Roget to preside over the execution, knowing that it will be intolerably painful for the lieutenant to have to be immediately responsible for the killing of Paris. Roget begs Dax to be excused from the assignment, but Dax, savoring every word, describes the procedure to be followed in commanding a firing squad, winding up with, "Your request is denied. You've got the job. It's all yours."

Dax, exhausted after the trying events of the day, lies down on his cot to rest when Rousseau, the captain of artillery, intrudes with information that he feels has some bearing on the court-martial. Startled, Dax is jolted into alertness. This new development serves as yet another injection of suspense into the action, once more allowing the audience to hope that justice may yet be done. Kubrick cuts to a glittering military ball being held at the château, apparently in the same gigantic room where the court-martial had taken place only a few hours earlier. Mireau is waltzing with a lady in a grand gown and Broulard is chatting with a couple when Dax asks to see him in the library.

Never without his ready smile, Broulard greets Dax with the news that the records of casualties show that Dax's men must have acquitted themselves well in the battle for the Ant Hill. This factor, however, is no reason why the execution should not go ahead as scheduled. With his customary mixture of charm and duplicity, Broulard tries to win Dax to his point of view:

"We think we're doing a good job running this war. The general staff is subject to all kinds of pressure from the press and from politicians. Perhaps it was an error of judgment to attack the Ant Hill. But if your men had been a little more daring, you might have taken it. We'll never know. Why should the general staff have to bear more criticism than we have to? Besides, these executions will be a tonic for the entire division. There are few things more fundamentally encouraging and stimulating than seeing someone else die. Troops are like children; just as a child wants his father to be firm, so troops crave discipline. In order to maintain discipline you have to shoot a man now and then."

The towering illogic of these remarks is matched only by those of the president of the court-martial earlier about choosing scapegoats by lot. If the context in which both speeches are made was not obviously serious, one might have thought that they were bits of black comedy reminiscent of *Catch-22* or some similar anti-war story which has the flavor of farce. Consequently, it is not difficult to see why in making *Dr. Stangelove* Kubrick later turned to black comedy as a suitable forum in which to embody an anti-war theme.

The general turns to leave the room and Dax follows him. Both men recede into a long shot as they walk toward the door at the far end of the library. Dax nonchalantly mentions that he happens to have with him sworn statements by the men who witnessed Mireau's command that the artillery gunners fire on their own trenches. As Broulard hears this he slams shut the door through which he was about to exit and, in close-up, has a look of shock on his face that he cannot conceal, an expression which was signaled by the jolting bang of the door.

Broulard is already considering the wide-ranging implications of Dax's revelation before the colonel can point out to him that the high command would not let the execution proceed if they knew that the same man who ordered the court-martial had already, earlier the same day, ordered his own soldiers to be shot in the trenches. "What would your newspapers and politicians make of that?" Dax concludes pointedly, employing Broulard's own propensity for understatement. Typically, Broulard excuses himself with a noncommittal phrase about a host being too long away from his guests.

Because we cannot as yet guess what steps Broulard will take to prevent Dax's charges against Mireau from erupting into an international scandal, the execution sequence which follows opens with an air of suspense: will Broulard cancel the execution in order to keep the whole affair from coming to light? The condemned men, however, know nothing of what has recently transpired, and so they see the bleak light of dawn streaming through their cell window with manifest foreboding.

The camera pans from the unconscious Arnaud tied to a stretcher in the background, to Ferol kneeling in the corner sobbing out a prayer, to Paris in the foreground with a look of resignation on his face. This shot exemplifies Kubrick's deft use of "cutting inside the camera." In a situation in which another director might have used three separate shots to introduce each of the three prisoners on the morning of their deaths (a long shot of Arnaud, a medium shot of Ferol, and a close-up of Paris), Kubrick instead places them at different distances from the camera and thus fluidly transforms a long shot into a close-up without the need of editing.

The sergeant in charge of the patrol which is to lead the prisoners to the place of execution offers Paris a drink to fortify his spirits. Taking it, Paris grins cavalierly, "Do you know, I haven't had one sexual thought since the court-martial began?" His smile turns into a grimace and he bursts into tears, falling at the feet of the sergeant, who whispers to him, "Pull yourself together. There are dignitaries and newspapermen out there. How do you want to be remembered by your wife and children? A lot of us will be joining you in death before this is over."

To the incessant throbbing of drums the prisoners are led to face the firing squad down the same avenue that stretches before the château where the film began. The camera falls back before the advancing procession: Paris has regained his composure; Arnaud is being carried on a stretcher; and the whimpering Ferol clutches a rosary with one hand and clings with the other to the sleeve of the priest, who whispers to him kindly but firmly to get hold of himself as the sergeant had done with Paris in the death cell a few moments before.

Timothy Carey at this point puts the finishing touches on his masterly portrayal of Ferol, a cowardly yet somehow sympathetic man. Kubrick has always had the knack of sensing the range of roles that an actor can play, regardless of the kind of parts he has had in the past, and this holds true with Carey. After his fine performance as the cool master marksman in *The Killing*, one would not immediately have thought of casting him as Ferol, whose personality is at the other end of the spectrum from that of the sharpshooter in *The Killing*. As it turned out Carey is equally good in both parts.

Now Kubrick turns his constantly moving camera toward the officers and men who line the path of the execution party: the drummers, a photographer, Colonel Dax, and then Broulard. This last shot is the viewer's tip-off that Broulard has taken no action against Mireau. The audience now knows for certain that no last-minute rescue of the prisoners is to take place and can therefore enter fully into the intensely realistic depiction of the execution which is at hand.

The camera tracks forward relentlessly toward the three stakes against which the men are to be shot and the drums halt as they are tied to these posts. The sergeant, dutifully following out Mireau's orders to the last detail, duly pinches Arnaud's cheeks so that he will regain consciousness long enough to be aware of his own death. Major Saint-Auban, seemingly comprehending for the first time the enormity of the injustice in which he has taken part up to this point with relish, now reads the official decree of execution in a weak voice that is barely audible. The words of the indictment (which were never heard at the court-martial) evaporate into the morning air as soon as the major utters them, as if already giving the lie to Broulard's pompous assertion the night before of the profound and lasting effect that the execution will have on army morale and discipline.

There is a final shot of Mireau and Broulard looking on in stern dignity and then the restless camera moves behind the members of the firing squad to record their blast of bullets as the three victims in the distance crumble forward in death. Kubrick cuts from the barrage of gunfire to the clatter of silverware as Mireau exults at breakfast about the wonderful way that the men died, for he is the god on the altar of whose ego the three hapless soldiers were sacrificed. "I'm glad you could be there, George," he says to Broulard.

"These things are always grim but this one had a kind of splendor." Mireau even feels expansive enough to compliment Dax, who has just arrived, on how well his men died.

"By the way, Paul," Broulard remarks in the most offhand way imaginable, "Colonel Dax here has come to me with a story that you ordered your artillery to fire on your own men during the attack." Mireau, shattered that Broulard has found out, sputters about the falsity of the charges and Dax's efforts to discredit him.

Broulard continues, still urbane and smiling, "You can't imagine how glad I am to hear that there is no truth at all in the charge, Paul. I'm certain that you'll come through the hearing all right. The public soon forgets these things, and you deserve the chance to clear your name." As the specter of a public hearing rises before Mireau, he realizes that his career is ruined, regardless of the cheery terms in which Broulard has informed him of it.

Like the Minister of the Interior in *A Clockwork Orange,* Broulard is always careful to arrange everything so that the blame for whatever might go wrong can be placed on someone other than himself. Broulard was willing to indulge even the neurotic Mireau's ruthless tactics so long as they brought success in battle and no embarrassment to himself. In order to save his own position, therefore, Broulard is completely prepared to let Mireau take the rap while he goes scot-free. "I have one last thing to say to you, George," says Mireau, throwing down his napkin. "The man that you stabbed in the back is a soldier." He retreats from the camera, stalking toward the door at the opposite end of the room, his diminishing figure a visual metaphor for his irretrievable loss of status. Presumably he will do the "proper thing" and blow his brains out, once more vindicating the inflexible military code of honor.

"It had to be done," shrugs Broulard. "France cannot afford to have fools guiding her military destiny." He then offers Dax Mireau's command, jovially adding with a knowing look, "Don't overdo the surprise, my boy; I know you've been maneuvering for his job from the start." That Broulard considered Dax an opportunist like himself was suggested the first time they met, when Broulard chided Mireau for not bringing such an up-and-coming young officer to his attention before. Hence Broulard has consistently mistaken Dax's opposition to Mireau for a calculated attempt to take over his job. Broulard's vision has been so totally corroded that he is no longer capable of recognizing integrity when he sees it.

"I am not your boy," Dax rejoins in contempt. "I certainly didn't mean to imply any biological relationship," Broulard returns defensively, commanding Dax to apologize instantly for telling him what he can do with the promotion. "I apologize," Dax smolders; "I apologize for not revealing my true feelings sooner; for not calling you a degenerate, sadistic old man."

Regaining his veneer of charm, which never deserts him for more than a second, the general replies smoothly, "Colonel Dax, you are a great disappointment to me. You've spoiled the keenness of your mind by sentimentality. You really did want to save those men, and you were not just angling for Mireau's command. You are an idealist—and I pity you as I would the village idiot. We're fighting a war that we've got to win. Those men didn't fight, so they were shot. You bring charges against General Mireau and I insist that he answer them." Finally, appealingly, he asks, "What have I done wrong?" Dax searches the elderly, distinguished-looking man's face and gasps, "If you don't know the answer to that question, I can only pity you."

Adolphe Menjou's Broulard is one of the most subtle portraits of evil in all of cinema. The filmgoer has all he can do to resist being taken in by the general's suave, engaging manner in order to be able to realize that Broulard is no less ruthless than Mireau, only shrewd enough never to overplay his hand as Mireau has done; and he is for that reason more insidious. In a *Saturday Evening Post* interview Alfred Hitchcock once explained why he always has made his villains charming and polite (in the way that Broulard is): "It's a mistake to think that if you put a villain on the screen, he must sneer nastily, stroke his black mustache, or kick a dog in the stomach. The really frightening thing about villains is their surface likableness."

By the same token Major Saint-Auban, as essayed by the handsome Richard Anderson, appears to be a likable young officer until we infer that, in contrast to Dax, he is using the court-martial as part of his campaign for promotion. Indeed, *he* will probably get Mireau's position, after having patronized the general throughout the film, and prove a fitting crony for Broulard.

Despite the unflinching picture of human misery and moral depravity that Kubrick has given us in *Paths of Glory,* the film nonetheless ends on a note of hope for humanity. Walking back to his post, Dax hears some of his men whistling and shouting in a nearby tavern, blowing off steam after the ordeal of witnessing the senseless death of their comrades earlier in the day. He stands in the doorway and sees that they are coaxing a timid German girl prisoner to sing a song to them (she is played by German actress Susanne Christian, who is now Mrs. Stanley Kubrick). To make her feel more at ease, the host gives her a merry introduction, presenting her as "a little diversion."

He drags the frightened girl onstage amid a raucous ovation from the troops. Slowly, tentatively, her lips begin to move in a German song that is not yet audible because of the general noise. Then the soldiers, most of whom seem either overage or underage (a telling comment on the state of the French army), begin to listen to the melody. Though they understand not a syllable of the German words, the plaintive tune stirs memories of home and loved ones, and they commence humming along with her.

Kubrick's camera passes over their faces, finally pausing on perhaps the youngest recruit, whose cheeks are streaming with unabashed tears that match the ones shimmering on the girl's face. Dax turns away, convinced that his men have not lost their humanity, despite the inhuman conditions in which they live and die.

His moment of reverie is quickly dispelled, however, by a messenger who delivers his orders to prepare his men to move back to the front. An afternoon in a village tavern is as close as they have come to the extended rest which Mireau had promised them after the Ant Hill engagement. Dax, who has been made aware by recent events that he is not much less of a pawn of the general staff than his men are, extends to them what scant consolation he can. "Give them a few minutes more," he instructs his messenger, and enters the post, slamming the door behind him as a roll of snare drums drowns out the tavern singing and builds to a climax as the film ends.

*Paths of Glory* has lost none of its power in the years since it was made. Its examination of the moral dilemmas that are triggered by war, and which are sidestepped in the film by the very men at the policy-making level who should be most concerned about them, has become more relevant than ever in the wake of the Vietnam War. Reassessing the movie in *TV Guide* at the time it was released to television, Judith Crist judged that "this 1957 film has grown in stature through the years, not only as an example of the filmmaker's art but also as an ultimate comment on the hypocrisies of war." The French army in World War I is the subject of the film, she continues, but any army in any war could serve for this story. This statement recalls that in his first feature film, *Fear and Desire,* Kubrick deliberately did not specify the actual war during which the story was set in order to underline the universal implications of the plot. "It is a bitter and biting tale, told with stunning point and nerve-racking intensity in eighty-seven brilliant minutes. Kirk Douglas has never been better than as the human colonel caught between generals and privates."

Because Douglas gave one of his best performances ever in *Paths of Glory,* he wanted to work with its director again. He got the chance when Kubrick took over as director of *Spartacus,* a spectacle about slavery in pre-Christian Rome. But this time their association would prove to be less amicable and less fruitful than it had been while they were making *Paths of Glory.*

**Kirk Douglas and Stanley Kubrick, SPARTACUS.**

# Chapter Four
# Decline and Fall:

# Spartacus (1960)

After finishing *Paths of Glory,* Kubrick wrote two scripts, neither of which was accepted for production in Hollywood. Marlon Brando engaged him to direct the actor's own production *One-Eyed Jacks,* but after six months of desultory script conferences with the star, Kubrick left the picture and Brando decided to direct the film himself. Considering the fiasco that *One-Eyed Jacks* turned out to be, Kubrick was well rid of that commitment.

John Baxter, in *Hollywood in the Sixties,* confers on Brando the "prize for prodigality": "Delays because of Brando's insistence that actors improvise (rewards up to $300 were offered to extras, out of Brando's own pocket, for the most effective reactions in key scenes like the hero's flogging and mutilation), and his insistence on 'perfect' waves in the seacoast sequences that kept the crew waiting for weeks (at $50,000 a day) made *One-Eyed Jacks* a commercial disaster." The disciplined Kubrick simply could not have functioned in that kind of situation.

Meanwhile Kirk Douglas had begun production on *Spartacus,* of which he was executive producer as well as star. "Anthony Mann had begun the picture and filmed the first sequence," Kubrick recalls, "but his disagreements with Kirk made him decide to leave after the first week of shooting. The film came after two years in which I had not directed a picture. When Kirk offered me the job of directing *Spartacus* I thought that I might be able to make something of it if the script could be changed. But my experience proved that if it is not explicitly stipulated in the contract that your decisions will be respected, there's a very good chance that they won't be. The script could have been improved in the course of shooting, but it wasn't. Kirk was executive producer. He and Dalton Trumbo the scriptwriter and Edward Lewis the producer had it their way with the script and the casting.

"Of course I directed the actors, composed the shots, and edited the picture. But *Spartacus* remains the only film over which I did not have absolute control. I have since involved myself more and more in the administrative side of film production because it is in this area that many artistic battles are won and lost." Because Kubrick did in fact direct the actors, compose the shots, and edit the film, *Spartacus* deserves more scrutiny as a Kubrick film than it has received in the past, and I shall try to fill that lacuna here.

As to the source of the friction between Douglas and Kubrick while *Spartacus* was being made, there has been much speculation, about which Kubrick maintains a tactful reticence. I recounted to Kubrick the most plausible explanation that I had heard, and he, quite understandably, had no comment. Someone who was involved with the production of the film has said that initially Douglas was disposed to accept Kubrick's suggestions about revising the script and about other aspects of the production. When Howard Fast, the author of the novel on which the film was based, saw some of the rushes, he reportedly told Douglas that he was lucky to have found such a talented director on such short notice. Douglas was offended by this remark, however well meant, because it seemed to imply that the success of the film, with which he had been so deeply involved for months, would depend largely on the director who had arrived at the eleventh hour.

However accurate the foregoing account may be in explaining why Douglas did not have the same rapport with Kubrick while collaborating with him on *Spartacus* which they had enjoyed while shooting *Paths of Glory*, the fact remains that Douglas's recent references to Kubrick's contribution to *Spartacus* have smacked of condescension. Recalling Kubrick's first day on the *Spartacus* set with Laurence Olivier, Charles Laughton, Peter Ustinov, and Jean Simmons, Douglas is quoted by *Newsweek* as saying, "It was a funny scene. Here was Kubrick with his wide eyes and pants hiked up looking like a kid of seventeen. [Kubrick was actually thirty.] You should have seen the look on their faces. It was as if they were asking, 'Is this some kind of joke?' "

Douglas's anecdote seems hardly fair in retrospect, especially since he had enough confidence in his young director at the time to entrust him with the job of steering a $12 million production with a cast of ten thousand extras. Still, Douglas's comments are in keeping with the fact that he chose a picture of Kubrick for the film's souvenir program in which the star-producer was pictured in the foreground standing over the director. (Today Kubrick smiles when this is pointed out to him and, again, has no comment.)

In any event, the reviewers of the finished film later paid court to the director's success in raising *Spartacus* above the level of the average spear and sandal epic, and Peter Ustinov as Batiatus the slave trader went on to win an Academy Award under Kubrick's direction.

*Spartacus,* like *Paths of Glory,* opens with a narrator who creates the historical context of the film for the audience. As we watch a band of slaves toiling in a stone quarry, we hear:

"In the last century before the birth of Christ, which was destined to overthrow the pagan tyranny of Rome and bring about a new society, the Roman Republic stood at the very center of the civilized world. Yet, even at the zenith of her power, Rome lay stricken with the disease called human slavery. The age of the dictator was at hand, waiting in the shadows for events to bring it forth. At that time a slave woman added to her master's wealth by giving birth to a son named Spartacus, a proud, rebellious boy. He lived out his youth and young manhood dreaming of the death of slavery. It was two thousand years before it finally would die."

By this time the camera is trained on Spartacus (Kirk Douglas) as he helps a fellow slave to rise after he has fallen under the weight of the load of rocks he is carrying. A Roman guard orders Spartacus to get on with his own work and lashes him to the ground for good measure. Spartacus sinks his teeth into the soldier's leg and is beaten by several guards before he will let go.

He is then chained to a wall as further punishment. While he is manacled there, Batiatus examines him with a view to including Spartacus in the new batch of slaves which he is gathering for training at his gladiatorial school. The fat, foppish slave trader is impressed when he learns that Spartacus is strong enough to have hamstrung a soldier not an hour before. "Marvelous," he mutters. "I wish I'd been here."

When Spartacus and his new companions arrive at the training center, Marcellus, the chief trainer (Charles McGraw), delivers his orientation speech: "You will be trained to fight to the death. If you cooperate you will be given privileges, even the companionship of a woman. Cheer up. Some of our graduates live five, even ten years, or become trainers like me." The inductees are then branded on the leg, making clearer than ever their status as animals who are to be fattened for the kill.

Spartacus tries to make friends with his fellow gladiators. One of them, an Ethiopian named Draba (Woody Strode), discourages him: "You don't want to know my name and I don't want to know your name. Don't try to make friends with me. I may have to kill you someday." Almost in spite of himself, however, Draba does make friends with Spartacus, emphasizing the brotherhood theme that is at the heart of the movie.

Because they are responding well to their training, the new students are granted female companionship for an evening. Spartacus draws Varinia (Jean Simmons). "I've never had a woman before," he whispers as she enters his cell. But he is overheard by Batiatus and Marcellus, who leer down voyeuristically at him through the barred window in the ceiling of his cell. Feeling more than ever like a caged beast, Spartacus grabs at the bars overhead and shouts, "I am not an animal!" "You may not be an animal," chortles Batiatus, "but this sorry show gives me little hope that you'll ever be a man." Batiatus's mincing mannerisms lend a touch or irony to his quip.

But Spartacus is indeed a man, as he demonstrates in the course of the practice sessions with his fellow gladiators. Kubrick's camera roves among them as they joust with each other and dodge their way through the obstacle course that Marcellus has devised to test their alertness.

The training school is stirred with excitement when a messenger reports that Marcus Licinius Crassus, the distinguished Roman general and senator, is going to pay the school a visit in order to observe some exhibition matches. The agitated Batiatus commands a slave, "Serve my best wine—in small goblets." It is Ustinov's deft handling of such witty lines, in this case showing how Batiatus's desire to please the visiting dignitary is in conflict with his innate stinginess, that no doubt contributed to the actor's winning an Oscar for his performance.

Crassus (Laurence Olivier) arrives with three companions: Helena, a Roman matron (Nina Foch); Claudia, a younger woman (Joanna Barnes); and Claudia's fiancé Glabrus (John Dall), who is also Crassus's protégé. The general orders two matches and Helena adds pointedly, "to the death." Batiatus is once more in a dither: "We don't fight to the death here; it would cause ill feeling among the students; that is for later." "Name your price," snaps Crassus; Batiatus does. The camera photographs the gladiators through the bars of the slave compound as Crassus's party chooses the combatants. "I feel sorry for the poor things in all this heat," Claudia says with a show of sympathy.

While the four gladiators, among them Spartacus and Draba, prepare for their ordeal, Batiatus entertains his guests with his best wine (in small goblets). Crassus pulls a veil from the bust of his archenemy in the Senate, Gracchus, which the host had diplomatically covered. "How far do I have to go to escape from that face?" Crassus laughs. Glabrus grabs Varinia by the ankle as she fills his cup and the slave girl dumps the remainder of the pitcher's contents on his head. Here is an independent spirit chafing under the confinements of servitude; she will prove a kindred spirit for Spartacus. Crassus too is drawn to her: "I like her; she has spirit. I will buy her." In this jovial atmosphere Crassus informs Glabrus that he has arranged—through bribery—to have Glabrus appointed commander of the garrison of Rome, the only power strong enough to checkmate Gracchus and the Senate.

The first exhibition match gets under way while Spartacus and Draba wait anxiously for their turn to come. They sit in a stifling enclosure next to the arena listening to the clashing steel beyond the door, not daring to look each other in the eye. Draba's prediction that one day they might have to fight each other to the death has come true sooner than anyone would have imagined. Meanwhile the four patricians for whom this spectacle is being staged sit on the veranda overlooking the arena, absorbed in chitchat.

When Spartacus and Draba take to the field, the Ethiopian lunges at his opponent with a trident and a net. The net at one point is thrown over the camera which then must shoot through it—an inventive way for Kubrick to make the spectator feel that he is right in the middle of the contest. Draba, having thrown Spartacus to the ground, turns his eyes pleadingly toward the guests of honor. Helena, temporarily distracted from her conversation, jabs her thumb downward. Draba, enraged, refuses to acknowledge the signal for him to kill Spartacus. Instead he pulls the triple-pointed spear away from his friend's throat and hurls it toward the quartet on the balcony. As he climbs up the wall toward Crassus, a guard spears him in the back and his blood spatters Crassus's immaculate white boots as his body slides into the dust below.

As the gladiators march in silence to their cells after a meal, the body of Draba, hung upside down, is in the foreground of the shot. "It will remain there until it rots," says Marcellus. Then he directs Spartacus's attention through the barred window to Varinia, riding in a cart as part of Crassus's entourage, on her way to Rome. "Take a look at her," Marcellus gloats; "she has been sold." When the stricken Spartacus asks where she is going, the slave trainer swats him across the face with a whip: "No talking in the kitchen, slave!"

Spartacus goes berserk and throttles Marcellus, and thus ignites a spasm of violence in the room. Now the leader of an impromptu insurrection, Spartacus drowns another of his captors by forcing his head into a kettle of stew, while other gladiators take up the kitchen cutlery and slash their way into the courtyard and scale the wall that stands between them and freedom. The blue sky suddenly appears overhead as they reach the top of the wall and then drop to the other side.

This sequence is as good as any in the film to demonstrate Kubrick's assured handling not only of the wide-screen frame, but also of color, with which he had worked only once before. Regarding the wide-screen ratio, Kubrick comments that he has never been unduly concerned about composing shots in this format. "The first thing you do is make sure you have the action in the front of the frame blocked out properly," he says, "and then what is taking place on either side and in the background of the shot will almost take care of itself."

So in this scene: as Spartacus and his men latch onto the spear-pointed gate which they are climbing like a ladder to reach the top of the wall, the camera looks down on them in their grubby slave vesture, which is the same muddy color as the earth below. When they go over the top the camera turns upward to give them the brilliant blue sky, symbol of the freedom they have just won, as a background. The camerawork here was obviously calculated to take advantage of the vast expanse of space provided by the wide screen and employ it as a backdrop against which the action is being played.

"They have forced other slaves to join them, fighting, looting," a Roman senator proclaims to his colleagues as they debate what action is to be taken to halt the slave revolt. "Each day their numbers swell." "The garrison of Rome has nothing to do," intervenes Gracchus (Charles Laughton). "Why bring back legions from the wars to put down this rebellion? Not even the whole garrison will be needed. Six corps should be enough. I propose Julius Caesar as temporary commander here while Glabrus is away crushing the slaves." In a single stroke the shrewd Gracchus has managed to separate Glabrus from his mentor Crassus and install his own protégé Caesar (John Gavin) in command at home.

Charles Laughton, who gives his usual strong performance as Gracchus, was always an intractable actor for directors to deal with. Indeed, the reason that another historical epic, *I Claudius* (1937), was abandoned after a month of shooting was due largely to the friction between Laughton and the film's equally strong-minded director, Josef von Sternberg. Kubrick remembers Laughton as living up to his reputation for being difficult to direct during the making of *Spartacus*.

Laughton was one of several British actors cast by Douglas in the film. Douglas's idea was to use British actors like Laughton and Olivier to play the Roman patricians and Americans like himself and Tony Curtis (who appears later in the movie) to enact the slaves. The polished accents of the English actors make a neat contrast with the more pedestrian voices of the Americans in the cast and nicely reflect the class barrier between the two types of characters being portrayed. Douglas did not carry through this concept of casting with total consistency, however, since the British Jean Simmons plays a slave girl and the American John Gavin is Julius Caesar. But by and large Douglas's international casting works.

Lounging in the splendor of his villa, which recalls the luxurious château in which the generals lived in *Paths of Glory*, Crassus receives a gift of some slaves from the governor of Sicily. One of them, Antoninus (Tony Curtis), strikes his fancy. "You shall be my body servant," Crassus says. It is a matter of historical record that Roman generals indulged their proclivities for young specimens of their own sex as well as for members of the opposite sex. After the road-show engagements of *Spartacus* were completed, Universal permanently eliminated from the film a scene in which Crassus subtly attempts to seduce Antoninus. The studio probably felt that the general audience would find any hint of homosexuality offensive, for this topic was not to be treated forthrightly on film for another decade, when movies like *The Boys in the Band* (1970) and *The Music Lovers* (1971) appeared. With this scene de-

leted, however, Crassus's later behavior toward Antoninus is simply inexplicable, as we shall see.

Spartacus and his men are still in possession of the gladiatorial school. Walking by chance into the arena, he sees his followers applauding a battle to the death between two middle-aged captive Romans. The slave leader intervenes with manifest disgust. "I swore that if I ever got out of here I would never watch two men fight to the death again. What's happening to us? Are we becoming like the Romans? Are we just a band of drunken looters? We are an army of gladiators. There never has been one before. We shall march to the sea, where Cilician pirates have ships that are willing to carry us out of Italy for a price. They will take us away from Rome forever!"

As Spartacus and his men make forays over the countryside, gathering ever greater numbers of slaves to their cause, they come upon a group of slaves waiting to join them, among whom is Varinia. She has run away from Batiatus, who was conducting her to Rome. "He was too fat to catch up with me," she laughs. "No one will ever sell you again," says Spartacus, overjoyed at their reunion. He sweeps her onto a horse and they gallop off into an incandescent sunset—another example of Kubrick's mastery of color and wide screen.

Meanwhile the corpulent Batiatus is conferring with the equally obese Gracchus about his loss of Varinia. This scene affords a fine opportunity for two British actors of skill to play together. Batiatus confides his hatred of Crassus to his friend, blaming the general for causing the rebellion, which began with Crassus's insistence that the exhibition matches be to the death. The slave trader further bemoans the fact that Varinia escaped before Crassus had paid for her, so it is he who has had to bear the financial loss. Gracchus, ever looking for ways to annoy Crassus, offers to buy Varinia from Batiatus when she is caught.

In his villa Crassus is being helped out of his bath by Antoninus. As both men stand nearly naked by an open window, Crassus points to some soldiers marching by in the distance. "That, boy, is Rome; the might, the majesty, the terror that is Rome. You must serve her, abase yourself before her, grovel at her feet; you must love her." In the context of the homosexual inferences of the scene that is now missing from the film, Crassus in this scene is probably making another veiled pass at his body servant. Since he is a powerful general, Crassus symbolizes the might and majesty of Rome of which he has just spoken. Therefore, it is himself whom he is suggesting that Antoninus must serve, grovel before, love. Very likely Antoninus has not missed this meaning in Crassus's

remarks, for when the general turns to see what effect his grandiose speech has had on the young man, he discovers that he has been addressing an empty room.

Meeting Spartacus for the first time at the slave encampment to which he has fled, Antoninus tells his new leader that he is, among other things, a magician and a poet. "But I came here to learn how to fight," Antoninus tells Spartacus. "You know things that can't be taught," Spartacus counters. The two men are quickly becoming close friends in the way that Spartacus had befriended Draba earlier, and the sad end of that relationship already casts a shadow over this new friendship.

An emissary of the Cilician pirates seals the agreement to transport Spartacus and his ever growing family of men, women, and children out of Italy as soon as Spartacus's army can fight its way to the sea. "But first you must face the six cohorts of Roman soldiers that are on their way here now," the merchant says. Stunned at this news, Spartacus immediately regains his composure and announces confidently, "We don't have to march on Rome. Rome has come to us."

Spartacus and his men make a surprise attack on the Roman camp by night and the ineffectual Glabrus is quickly brought literally to his knees. The representative of Rome now grovels in the dust before his conqueror, the Roman tents ablaze in the background. Spartacus holds Glabrus's imperial baton in his hand and says with contempt, "I found this in your tent, Glabrus. It is the symbol of the Senate and all the power of Rome." Snapping it in two, he returns it to its owner. "Take that back to your Senate. Tell them that you and this broken stick are all that are left of the garrison of Rome. Tell them that we want our freedom. We hate Rome and mean to leave her."

Standing now in the Senate, encircled by its members, Glabrus delivers Spartacus's ultimatum. He is forced to admit to Crassus that he failed to take the usual precautions to safeguard his campsite against a surprise attack. "After all," he explains with manifest embarrassment, "they were only slaves." "Crassus sponsored this young man," Gracchus notes smugly. "Let him name the punishment." "The punishment of banishment is known to all," the exasperated Crassus rejoins. "And I will not dissociate myself from his disgrace. I shall retire to private life."

Gracchus, a corrupt politician of the same stamp as Crassus, already divines Crassus's long-term strategy. The general wants to bide his time until the threat of Spartacus grows to the point that the Senate will give him dictatorial powers to end the slave revolt. "I won't take the dictatorial of Crassus," Gracchus shouts to the assembly. "That is what he is out for and that is why he'll be back." As the narrator told us in the film's spoken prologue, "The age of the dictator was at hand, waiting in the shadows for events to bring it forth."

The slaves continue their endless trek to the sea through winter sludge and spring rains, uphill against the wind. This montage serves as a visual metaphor of their uphill fight for freedom, with all of the obstacles they have to face. In another montage sequence the slaves are pictured at rest at one of their temporary camping places: Antoninus is learning to fight, a child is watching his elders milking the cows and gets squirted in the face with milk.

Kubrick's focusing on individuals in the welter of people that make up the numberless army of slaves has an affinity to the way that Cecil B. DeMille personalized the epic scenes in his films. It is easier for an audience to identify with individuals than with a crowd, and DeMille implemented this idea, for example, in *The Ten Commandments* (1956), in the scene in which Moses and the Israelites depart from Egypt. As they leave the capital city and head for the desert that is waiting for them, DeMille focuses not only on the mass of people pouring out of the city, but on some children trying to get a recalcitrant mule to budge, a baby crying in its mother's arms, and other personalizing, homely images. So too in *Spartacus* Kubrick uses the same kind of technique for the crowd scenes involving the slaves' army. At one point his camera moves silently across the endless rows of sleeping slaves in a night scene, pausing on an aged couple sleeping in each other's arms, children curled up together, etc.

(Several of these scenes involving masses of extras portraying either the slave army or Roman soldiers were shot on the grassy hillsides on the edge of the Universal lot in Hollywood. Suburbanites who live near the studio still remember being awakened early on several mornings as troop movements took place almost in their back yards. There are other reminders of *Spartacus* at Universal as well. The Cinema Pavilion Museum houses a glass case containing a Roman sword and helmet used in the film, while preliminary sketches for some of the scenes are framed and hung close by. These are interesting indications of the esteem in which the studio itself holds the film.)

**Stanley Kubrick, Tony Curtis and Laurence Olivier.**

While steaming in the Roman baths, Caesar learns that nineteen thousand men have been lost in a recent engagement. Crassus, who has since his "retirement" remained on the fringe of senatorial gatherings such as this in order to keep in touch with what is transpiring, overhears Caesar's conversation with Gracchus about the recent military setback. He bargains with them to allow him to lead the legions against Spartacus.

After Crassus departs, Gracchus whispers to Caesar that he has made a deal with the Cilician pirates: "We won't interfere with them while they are transporting Spartacus and his tribe out of Italy. With Spartacus out of the way there will be no need to make Crassus dictator." "Is the Senate to bargain with pirates?" Caesar chides, apparently trying to retain the shred of integrity he still has left. "If a criminal has what you want, you do business with him" is the sum of Gracchus's political philosophy.

Just as in *Paths of Glory*, in which the possibility of the pardon of the condemned prisoners on the eve of their execution generated suspense, so in *Spartacus* Gracchus's deal with the pirates allows the viewer to hope for a while that Spartacus and his people may yet escape being crushed under the iron heel of Rome. And, as in the previous film, these hopes are doomed. Spartacus is informed that the Cilician pirates have set sail without him and his army. Crassus, it seems, has outbid Gracchus, and bribed the mercenary pirates to depart ahead of schedule. His jaw set, Spartacus says, "Crassus is inviting us to march on Rome so he can confront us and become the savior of the city; that would be his final victory over the Senate. That is why he wants to meet us."

Spartacus goes out of his tent to address the slaves, and Kubrick intercuts his speech with Crassus's oration to the Senate and the people of Rome, recalling the manner in which Shakespeare in his history plays has opposing generals addressing their respective troops in parallel fashion before a major battle. Spartacus tells his people, dressed as they are in their ragged, weatherworn garments, "The Romans hope to trap us here with our backs to the sea. We have no choice but to march toward Rome and face Crassus and end this war the only way it could have ended: by winning this battle and freeing every slave. I'd rather be here, free among brothers, than be the richest citizen of Rome. We've traveled a long way together. Now we must fight again. Maybe there is no peace in this world for anyone. As long as we live we must stay true to ourselves. We are brothers and free. We march tomorrow!"

Crassus, for his part, stands before an endless formation of soldiers, all gleaming helmets and spears. He speaks in a clipped, haughty tone very different from Spartacus's calm, affectionate manner: "I have been elected commander in chief of the armies of the Senate and the people of Rome. I promise a new Italy and a new empire. And I promise you the body of Spartacus. I have sworn!"

At his battlefield headquarters Crassus lays plans with his general staff. "I'm not after glory," he says, "I'm out to kill the legend of Spartacus." The ubiquitous Batiatus is then summoned to the general's presence and asked for a physical description of Spartacus. The slave trader surprises the commander in chief by telling him that he has seen Spartacus before: "He once trained under your auspices. You and your friends saw him when you visited my gladiatorial school. If it isn't subversive to say it, I made him what he is today." (This quip about subversion is undoubtedly a reference by scriptwriter Dalton Trumbo to the investigations of the House Committee on Un-American Activities in the time of the Red scare of only a few years before. Trumbo had been blacklisted at that time and *Spartacus* was his first major screenplay after his period of forced inactivity.) In exchange for the franchise to auction off the slaves who survive the battle, Batiatus, ever the opportunist, agrees to finger Spartacus for Crassus.

In contrast to Crassus, who is aloof from his troops, Spartacus walks among his men to enliven their spirits before the battle begins, just as Colonel Dax did in *Paths of Glory*. Kubrick and Douglas might easily have had that scene from the earlier film in mind while shooting the present one, for it is built up in a similar fashion: the camera cuts from Douglas's friendly face to reaction shots of admiration and affection from the people whom he passes.

Spartacus comes upon Varinia, who has been pregnant for some time. "He hits me with his fist sometimes," she says with maternal pride. "He wants to see his mother," Spartacus returns. Then, thinking of the dim future, he adds, "No matter how often we beat the Romans they always have yet another army. We've started something that has no ending. I pray for a son who will be born free."

As the Roman army begins its advance across the battlefield toward the slave army, Kubrick photographs them in extreme long shot in order to encompass the entire formation. The director holds his camera steady and still to let the enormity of the might of this almost limitless force which the slaves are facing sink into the audience's consciousness. When the Romans are within range, however, the redoubtable slaves release burning bundles of straw that roll down the slopes toward the enemy, scattering the first line of soldiers.

But the Romans are reinforced instantly by the next line of troops, who engage Spartacus and his men in combat. As in his filming of the key battle scene in *Paths of Glory,* Kubrick's cameras seem to be everywhere at once, burrowing into the bloody pileups of combatants who fight furiously, until at the end of the day the carnage is complete. Corpses, heaped one on another, mutely testify to the brutal battle that has just ended. This shot of the dead brings to mind the image of the battlefield casualties in D. W. Griffith's *Birth of a Nation* (1915), which its director labeled "War's peace."

Crassus rummages around among the bodies in a fruitless effort to find Spartacus's corpse, while a tribune announces that the surviving slaves will be spared crucifixion if they will identify their leader's remains. In what is one of the most moving scenes in the entire movie, Antoninus, who has been sitting next to Spartacus, stands up and shouts, "I am Spartacus!" and is joined by a whole host of his comrades who stand up with the same cry. Crassus stares in amazement at this demonstration of devotion to a leader.

Angry and desperate, Crassus has Batiatus flogged out of camp when the latter does not find Spartacus among the prisoners. As the slaves file by him on their way to crucifixion, the victorious general spies Antoninus and Spartacus walking side by side. "Hold this man to the end," he says, staring vindictively at his former body servant, "and that one too," he adds, motioning toward Spartacus. Since the crucial scene that established the general's sexual interest in Antoninus has been removed from the film, the motive for Crassus's peculiar hatred for Antoninus is not altogether clear. In reality it is Crassus's humiliating sense of rejection by the young man, and not just that the slave had escaped from his household, that prompts him to single Antoninus out for special punishment. As for his choosing Spartacus to join Antoninus in being the last to die, perhaps Crassus has at last recognized him.

Batiatus, smarting under the flogging he received by Crassus's order, has taken refuge with Gracchus, his old ally, and is tempted to help him make life uncomfortable for Crassus. Batiatus tells Gracchus that Varinia's child has been born and that she and the baby have been taken into custody by Crassus. "Let's steal this woman," Gracchus suggests with a wicked gleam in his eye. "I can no longer hurt Crassus in the Senate, but I can hurt his pride" (as in fact Antoninus has already done).

Gracchus knows that Crassus's victory spells his defeat. Summoned to the Senate, he sits sullenly in the darkened, almost empty chamber as Crassus snarls, "If your rabble falter in loyalty to the State, they will be imprisoned. Lists of the disloyal have

**Tony Curtis and Kirk Douglas, SPARTACUS.**

**Kirk Douglas and Jean Simmons.**

been compiled." There is little doubt that this statement too was inspired by Dalton Trumbo's bitter personal experiences with the House Committee on Un-American Activities. "Is my name on such a list?" Gracchus inquires, already sure of the answer. Crassus grandly responds that he intends to let Gracchus live as long as he is willing to help acclimate his former followers to the new regime.

Kubrick's chief complaint about working on *Spartacus* was that Douglas would not accept his suggestions about improving the script, which, he felt, was saddled with a weak story line. In general the plot seems to hold up well, however, until we approach the end of the film, where the story begins to slow down instead of gaining momentum as it should. Perhaps it is these later scenes that the director has in mind when criticizing the film's script. Surely no other Kubrick film grinds to a halt the way *Spartacus* does.

The following scene is the worst offender in the whole movie in terms of being awkward, overlong, and in the end unnecessary, for it tells us little that has not already been established with more taste. In it Crassus tries to seduce Varinia with jewels and finery, finally threatening to kill her child if she does not acquiesce. Varinia verbalizes what the filmgoer is already thinking, that threats are hardly calculated to win Varinia's love. When Crassus asks her about Spartacus, she says in so many words what had been skillfully implied in the foregoing scenes in which Crassus arranged to take custody of Varinia and the child: "You are afraid of him," she taunts. "That's why you want his wife, to soothe your fear by having something that he had. When you're so afraid, nothing can help you. We shall win."

"Could we ever have won?" Antoninus muses as he sits shackled to Spartacus, awaiting their turn to die. "We won something just by fighting," Spartacus answers, "If one man says no to Rome, Rome begins to fear. Yet tens of thousands of us said no. That was the wonder of it." Now Crassus unveils his insidious plan to torture the two slaves in a way that they had not suspected. He has them unchained and commands them to fight to the death before him; the victor is to be crucified: "We will test this myth of slave brotherhood." Once more Spartacus has to face a friend in a deadly encounter as he did with Draba at the school.

"Don't give him the pleasure of a contest," Spartacus whispers to his companion. "Lower your guard and I'll kill you. It is my last order." Antoninus, whose arduous attempts to learn to fight will now be tested against his best friend, grimly refuses to obey Spartacus's last command. He is determined not to allow Crassus to crucify Spartacus if he can help it. But Spartacus overpowers him, murmuring, "Forgive me," as he plunges his dagger into his friend. They exchange words of love, Spartacus attesting that he loves Antoninus like the son whom he will never see. Putting their relationship on a paternal rather than a fraternal level seems to be yet another unnecessarily fervid effort on the part of the studio to quash any suggestion of homosexuality in the movie, an implication that would not have been present in this scene in any case.

"I wonder what Spartacus would say if he knew that Varinia and her child were slaves in my household," Crassus says, playing his trump card to make Spartacus give away his identity; and so Spartacus does. "Crucify him," the general orders, now secure in his final victory over the slave leader. "I want no grave or marker. His body is to be burned and his ashes scattered in secret."

Batiatus brings Varinia and the baby to Gracchus, who gives them all senatorial passes to leave the city, along with articles of freedom for her and the child. "I'm going on a journey too," Gracchus says, almost thinking out loud. After they all have gone, he picks up a sword and walks slowly down a corridor away from the camera, a diminishing figure like that of General Mireau as he made his last exit near the end of *Paths of Glory*. In both cases a formerly powerful man is pictured as metaphorically reduced in stature by canny camera placement. Gracchus goes through a doorway and draws a curtain behind him. The curtain has closed on his career and his life.

While Batiatus is presenting their papers to the guard at the city the defeat of the slave revolt. Hence it is the fate of Spartacus's son and not merely "Miss Simmons's postwar predicament" that free." Spartacus looks down, his symbolic identification as a crucified Christ figure now complete, and repeats the one word *free* as his head falls back against the cross. "He'll remember you, Spartacus, because I'll tell him who his father was and what he dreamed of." Then she gets into the cart and Batiatus drives down the avenue lined with crosses which leads them beyond the gates of Rome.

Pauline Kael dismissed Bosley Crowther's review of *Lolita* by saying that Crowther "can always be counted on to miss the point." In the case of *Spartacus* he certainly did. "A great deal more is made of Miss Simmons's postwar predicament than of the crucifixion of six thousand slaves," he wrote in his *New York Times* review of the film. On the contrary, the movie has gone to great pains to make it clear that the survival of Spartacus's only

96

son as a free man will serve as an inspiration that will overshadow the defeat of the slave revolt. Hence it is the fate of Spartacus' son and not merely "Miss Simmons's postwar predicament" that matters at the end of the film.

Spartacus is ultimately defeated by the superior forces of Rome, but the might of the empire is already weakening from within, as evidenced by the skulduggery that generals and senators alike practice throughout the movie in an effort to use the crisis that Spartacus has precipitated to their own political advantage. Now that the age of the dictator has arrived, as the film's prologue foretold that it would, the Romans have in effect enslaved themselves to Crassus in exchange for his delivering them from Spartacus.

In representing the rebellious slaves as a concretization of man's efforts to resist dehumanization throughout human history, *Spartacus* fits thematically into Kubrick's total canon of films better than most critics of his work are prepared to admit. Spartacus was vanquished by the technological superiority of Roman military tactics, and man will continue in Kubrick's films, particularly his trio of science-fiction films, to resist being overpowered by his own ever increasing technological advances.

Moreover, *Spartacus* has a further thematic affinity with Kubrick's other pictures, in that once more a man has devised an apparently foolproof plan which fails in the end through a mixture of unforeseen chance happenings and human frailty. Crassus's crass bribery of the Cilician pirates is just as decisive in bringing about Spartacus's defeat as the might of the Roman army. In a Kubrick film human weakness and/or malice along with chance are always standing in the wings ready to disrupt the best-laid plans that his heroes or anti-heroes can devise.

Hence *Spartacus* seems to be more than a marginal film in Kubrick's career, although it could well have been a better picture all around had Kubrick been allowed to exercise the artistic control that he has enjoyed on all of his other films. Nevertheless, as Henry Herx wrote in *The Catholic Film Newsletter,* "With *Spartacus* Kubrick proved that he could handle commercial subjects with distinction."

Yet Kubrick does not remember the film with any great satisfaction. Perhaps the most significant thing about the movie in terms of Kubrick's career as a whole is that his experience in making the picture served to strengthen his resolve to safeguard his artistic independence in making future films. Director John Schlesinger (*Midnight Cowboy*), who shares Kubrick's independent cast of mind, says that film companies "will go to enormous lengths to keep a director from having final say over a film he makes with their backing, so that other directors won't ask for it too. For this reason they even try to append their granting of artistic control over the film to a letter rather than put it in the contract. But you must have the assurance of final cut in writing; otherwise you haven't got it, no matter what they say." Kubrick's experience in making *Spartacus* for Douglas bears this out; for, as he has said, more artistic control was promised him verbally than ever materi-

**Charles Laughton, Peter Ustinov and Jean Simmons, SPARTACUS.**

alized while he was working on the film.

To ensure total control on his next film, he joined forces with his former producer, James Harris, with whom he acquired the rights to Vladimir Nabokov's *Lolita*. Kubrick is not happy that critics tend to place *Lolita* only ahead of *Spartacus* in terms of quality. *Lolita* is perhaps his most underrated film, and deserves the attention that we are now going to give it.

James Mason and Peter Sellers, LOLITA.

# Chapter Five
# Child's Play:

# Lolita (1962)

With the collapse in the 1950s of Hollywood as the center of world filmmaking, many of America's independent filmmakers moved to Europe, where they could make films more economically, and therefore more easily obtain financial backing. Kubrick settled in England to make *Lolita* (1962) because M-G-M had funds frozen there. As I mentioned in Chapter One, he has remained in England and made all of his subsequent films there.

Nonetheless he still considers himself an American director, for it was not until the fourth film he directed in England, *A Clockwork Orange,* that he used a British setting and a predominantly British cast. In this respect Kubrick can be sharply contrasted with Joseph Losey, another American-born director who migrated to England. Losey's films, such as *The Servant* and *The Go-Between,* have become so thoroughly British in concept and character that one can easily forget that they were made by a director who hails from Wisconsin.

*Lolita* was the last film Kubrick made in association with James Harris, who later became a director himself (notably of *The Bedford Incident,* 1965). When Kubrick and his partner announced that they had acquired the rights to Vladimir Nabokov's controversial novel, there was much speculation in the trade press as to how the team would tackle a story that deals with the perverse love of an older man for a pubescent girl.

Part of their problem was rooted not so much in the novel itself, which has great artistic merit, but in the sensational reputation the book had acquired since its publication and still retained to some extent, especially in the minds of those who had never read it. In the afterword which he wrote for the novel, Nabokov recalls that it was turned down by several publishers, none of whom, he suspects, read the manuscript to the end. It was finally brought out by the Olympia Press in Paris, which specialized in erotica. Only recently has Nabokov's novel been reexamined and recognized as the superb piece of fiction that it really is. At the time Kubrick undertook to film it, however, the novel was still something of a *succes de scandale*.

Andrew Sarris in his review of the film accused Kubrick of losing his nerve and underestimating his audience by not treating the story with more candor, because "there is nothing new about nymphet worship on the screen." He points to Shirley Temple, whose appeal, "even more shockingly, was that of a prenymphet (adults always liked Shirley more than children did, anyway)"; and to Ginger Rogers, who "charmingly impersonated a wartime Lolita in *The Major and the Minor*." Neither of these cases, nor the others which Sarris cites, for that matter, provided a favorable precedent on which Kubrick could stake his filmization of *Lolita*.

While he was reviewing films for a London weekly called *Night and Day* in 1937, Graham Greene made the same point that Sarris did about Shirley Temple in treating her performance in John Ford's *Wee Willie Winkie*. Greene was summarily sued for libel by the child star's studio. In his notice of the film Greene had said that "her admirers—middle-aged men and clergymen—respond to her dubious coquetry . . . only because the safety curtain of story and dialogue drop between their intelligence and their desire." Greene's magazine was fined close to $10,000 for this playfully satiric review and had to shut down.

The "safety curtain" of story and dialogue provided in *The Major and the Minor* is that the Ginger Rogers character is really a mature woman masquerading as a child. This takes the edge off any potentially shocking implications that the movie might otherwise have had. This sort of plot gimmick is reminiscent of the way that Shakespeare would undercut such implications in his comedies. The possible homosexual overtones of a hero's falling in love with an attractive young man were averted by having the latter turn out to be a beautiful lady in disguise. No one—then or now—bothered to speculate about the fact that for a while at least the hero really thought the girl was a boy.

In the case of *Lolita* Kubrick had no such ploys or detours in which to take refuge. Hence Sarris's condescending suggestion that Kubrick was unnecessarily diffident in approaching the subject matter of *Lolita* is just a bit too facile.

The book is narrated by Humbert Humbert (who has changed all of the names in the story, including his own, to protect the

guilty), as he commits the tale to his diary. He is a college professor who falls hopelessly in love with twelve-year-old Dolores Haze, known to her friends as Lolita. Nabokov has always insisted that he chose that name for his heroine simply because he found it appealing, and denies that it is a reference to Charlie Chaplin's second wife, actress Lolita McMurry, who was known professionally as Lita Grey. (Lolita McMurry was sixteen when she married Chaplin and nineteen when she divorced the hapless comedian after a spectacularly sensational divorce trial in which she contended that she was too young to be married to a "demanding" husband like Chaplin. The papers, however, played up both the marriage and the divorce as if Lolita were a pubescent nymphet. Hence it is just possible that this well-known scandal could have contributed to the germination of Nabokov's story.)

Humbert in the novel calls himself a "nympholept," a word by which Nabokov sought to suggest the term "lepidopterist," a butterfly specialist, something which Nabokov himself has been for years. The metaphor works perfectly in the story, since Humbert, in trying to snare his butterfly, is enmeshed in the net himself and never possesses for long the object of his obsession. Furthermore the word "nympholepsy" had already come to mean a frustrating attachment to an unattainable object, lending universal implications to Humbert's plight. Novelist John Updike has written that Nabokov has "the lepidopterist's habit of killing what he loves; how remarkably few, after all, of Nabokov's characters do evade the mounting pin." Humbert certainly does not.

Despite the difficulties attendant on making a movie of *Lolita,* the novel fairly begged to be committed to celluloid. On one page, while eyeing the "wanted" posters in a post-office lobby, Humbert says in an aside to the reader, "If you want to make a movie out of my book have one of these faces gently melt into my own while I look at it." On another page he reflects, while recalling Lolita and himself engaging in horseplay, "A pity no film has recorded the curious pattern . . . of our simultaneous or overlapping moves." Elsewhere Humbert muses on watching Lolita play tennis and says that he regrets that he had not immortalized her in "segments of celluloid" which he could then run in "the projection room of my pain and despair."

With so many cinematic references in the novel, it is not surprising that Kubrick engaged Nabokov to write the screenplay of *Lolita.* Kubrick vividly recalls his consternation when he received Nabokov's first draft and discovered that it would run for several hours if all of its four hundred pages were filmed as they stood. The novelist then prepared a shorter version, of which he speculates that Kubrick finally used about twenty per cent.

In 1974 Nabokov published *Lolita: A Screenplay,* his version of the script. Even this published version, however, is not an exact replica of Nabokov's shortened script, for he has restored some scenes that he originally deleted and has in other ways altered it further. Reading through Nabokov's published screenplay, however, does give us some idea of why Kubrick revised the novelist's script so extensively.

For one thing, Nabokov includes a scene in his scenario depicting the death of Humbert's mother, to which he refers in the novel: after she is struck by lightning at a picnic, "her graceful specter floats up above the black cliffs holding a parasol and blowing kisses to her husband and child who stand below, looking up, hand in hand." This is the kind of background material that helps enrich a character in a novel, but which must be sacrificed in the interest of keeping a film to a practical length.

In addition, Nabokov added other scenes in his script, such as the burning down of the house where Humbert was to have stayed before he moved in with Lolita and her mother, which are based on unused material that he had regretted discarding from the published novel, and which he therefore reinstated in the screenplay. Again, these incidents would have complicated further a film which eventually was to run a full two and a half hours in its final version.

When Nabokov finally saw *Lolita* at a private screening, he recalls in his foreword to the screenplay, he found that Kubrick was "a great director, and that his *Lolita* was a first-rate film with magnificent actors," even though much of his version of the script had gone unused. Alfred Appel of Northwestern University, who has had several interviews with Nabokov, told me that the novelist has never had anything but good comments to make about Kubrick's film of his book, largely because after the writer had spent six months working on the scenario himself he came to realize vividly how difficult adapting a novel to the screen really is.

Nabokov has said, for example, that "the four main actors deserve the highest praise." Sue Lyon childishly pulling on her sweater during the scenes in which she and Mason travel cross-country, he notes, "are moments of unforgettable acting and directing. The killing of Quilty is a masterpiece, and so is the death of Mrs. Haze." He still feels, however, that had he had more to do with the actual shooting of the movie he would have stressed certain things that were not emphasized in the film, and hence his decision to publish his revised version of his screenplay. Still, he also admits that "infinite fidelity may be an author's ideal but can prove a producer's ruin," and so offers his published screenplay "not as a pettish refutation of a munificent film but purely as a vivacious variant of an old novel."

Nabokov's final script conference with Kubrick was held on September 25, 1960, in Kubrick's home in Beverly Hills. Kubrick and Harris locked themselves in an office for a month to work Nabokov's script into shape for filming, and further changes were made in the course of the shooting period. "What finally came out on film was a tremendous improvement over the script," says Harris. "Stanley does his writing in the making of the film." Kubrick has developed the habit over the years of encouraging his cast to improvise during the course of the rehearsals that precede the filming of each scene, a procedure that would prove particularly fortuitous in the case of *Dr. Strangelove* and *A Clockwork Orange*.

James Mason, who played Humbert Humbert in the film, feels that the rehearsal periods during the production of *Lolita* afforded the cast an excellent opportunity to explore the significance of each scene. Kubrick found that Sue Lyon, who played the title role, had learned all of her lines before filming started, says Mason, "and she had to be induced to think of the lines in a particular scene as something that came out of the feeling of the character in that scene. So we started improvising during rehearsals and forgot the lines we had learned and got to grips with the situation instead, finding that this helped us to understand much more quickly what each scene was basically about. Sue made a considerable contribution to many of the scenes because she spoke the same language as the character she was playing."

Peter Sellers as Quilty does several comic impersonations in the course of the movie, as he endeavors to badger Humbert, by various ruses, into giving up Lolita to him. Because of Sellers's brilliant flair for improvisation, these scenes are among the best in the movie and portend his playing of three separate roles in *Dr. Strangelove*.

At the time that Kubrick made *Lolita* the freedom of the screen had not advanced to the point it has reached today. He therefore had to be more subtle and indirect in the movie than Nabokov had been in his book in suggesting the sexual obsession of an older man for a nymphet. "I wasn't able to give much weight at all to the erotic aspect of Humbert's relationship in the film," says Kubrick. "And because I could only hint at the true nature of his attraction to Lolita, it was assumed too quickly by filmgoers that Humbert was in love with her. In the novel this comes as a discovery at the end, when Lolita is no longer a nymphet; and it is this final encounter, and the sudden recognition of his love for her, that is one of the most poignant elements of the story."

Since the erotic aspect of the narrative had to be soft-pedaled (Andrew Sarris notwithstanding), Kubrick decided to emphasize the black comedy inherent in the story. Pauline Kael writes in *I Lost It at the Movies,* "The surprise of *Lolita* is how enjoyable it is; it's the first *new* American comedy since those great days in the forties when Preston Sturges re-created comedy with verbal slapstick. *Lolita* is black slapstick and at times it's so far out that you gasp as you laugh."

Kubrick has often expressed his admiration for Chaplin, and it is therefore fitting that he can trace the cinema heritage of black comedy back to films like Chaplin's *Monsieur Verdoux* (1947), in which the Little Fellow was turned into a lady-killer in the literal sense of the term. In 1947 audiences were not prepared to appreciate black comedy, that genre of storytelling that finds humor in situations usually reserved for serious treatment. It has only been in the wake of later cinematic essays in black comedy like *Lolita* and *Dr. Strangelove* that filmgoers have been able to appreciate in retrospect Chaplin's earlier mastery of that genre.

Kubrick strikes this note of black comedy at the very beginning of the film and maintains it throughout. The first image of the movie, seen behind the credits, is Humbert's hand reaching across the wide screen to caress Lolita's foot as he begins to paint her toenails, thus making a wry comment at the outset on the subservient nature of his infatuation for the girl.

After the credits there is a prologue in which Humbert arrives at Quilty's musty mansion for a decisive showdown with him about Lolita. This sequence firmly establishes the air of black comedy that permeates the picture. Humbert stumbles about among the cluttered rooms, brandishing a revolver and shouting Quilty's name. In the novel Humbert bumps into Quilty as the latter emerges from the bathroom. In the film Kubrick introduces Quilty by having him begin to stir under the dust cover of one of the sheeted chairs in the living room, which is strewn with empty bottles and other remnants of the previous night's orgy.

The disheveled Quilty, dressed in pajamas and slippers, and trying vainly to cope with a hangover, wraps the sheet around himself like a toga and says with a lisp, "I am Spartacus. Have you come to free the slaves or something?" This jibe at the unpleasant experience that making *Spartacus* had been for Kubrick must have given him some consolation. More importantly, Quilty's quip also indicates that he is not taking Humbert's threats to kill him very seriously. Taking his cue from the Spartacus remark and the toga effect, Sellers suggested during the rehearsals for the scene that Quilty challenge Humbert to play a game of "Roman ping-pong, like two civilized senators."

Quilty bats the ball at Humbert, who lets it dribble across the table. "Okay," says the challenger, trying to be congenial, "*you* serve." Humbert, perhaps without being completely aware of what he is doing, returns the ball when Quilty hits it toward him again and continues his aimless patter. "It's absurd how people invade this house without knocking and even make a lot of long-distance phone calls." Quilty's frivolous and erratic behavior is an arch counterpoint to Humbert's single-minded, broken-voiced despair: "Do you remember a girl named Dolores Haze? Lolita?" "Maybe she made some phone calls," shrugs Quilty. Eyeing Humbert's gun he makes a remark which ostensibly refers to Humbert's lack of dexterity at ping-pong, but which really is Quilty's way of saying that Humbert should accept his loss of Lolita as inevitable: "Gee, you're a bad loser, Captain. I never had anyone pull a gun on me just for losing a game."

"I want you to concentrate," says Humbert. "You are going to die. Try to understand what is happening to you." But Quilty, wrapped in the haze of his hangover, is beyond grasping the situation. He glides into an imitation of an old sourdough, reminiscent of countless sagebrush epics. "That's a durlin' gun you got there, mister. How much do you want for a durlin' gun like that?" Making every effort to ignore this horseplay, Humbert forces Quilty to read from a confession that he has penned for him, but Quilty blithely carries on the charade. "What's this, the deed to the ranch? Can't read, mister. I never had any of that there book larnin'." Nevertheless Quilty takes up the paper and focuses his bleary eyes. " 'Because you took advantage of a sinner,' " he reads haltingly; " 'because you took advantage of my disadvantage when I stood Adam-naked—' Adam-naked! You should be ashamed. '—before a federal law; because you cheated me and took her at an age when young girls—' It's getting smuttier, mister."

Fed up, Humbert snatches back the paper and Quilty dons boxing gloves, announcing that he wants to "die like a champion." (Following the earlier reference to *Spartacus,* this could be another satirical jibe at Kubrick's previous association with Kirk Douglas, one of whose first starring roles was in *Champion*.) Humbert opens fire and grazes Quilty's boxing glove, prompting the latter at last to try to reason with Humbert a little more seriously. "Listen, Captain, stop trifling with life and death. I'm a playwright. I now all about this sort of tragedy and comedy and fantasy and everything. I have fifty-two successful scenarios to my credit, added to which my father is a policeman."

As he dramatically sits down at a piano, like a composer in some forgotten Hollywood musical biography, Quilty seeks to distract his tormentor from his set purpose by saying, "You look like a music lover to me. Why don't I play you a little thing I wrote last week." He launches into a Chopin polonaise. "We could dream up some lyrics, share the profits. 'The moon is blue and so are you. She's mine tonight'—I mean 'She's *yours* tonight' . . ."

Finally bedeviled beyond endurance, Humbert fires again and Quilty runs toward the camera and up the grand staircase. Humbert nicks him in the leg, and the wounded man drags himself farther up the steps. "Gee, you hurt me, you really hurt me. If you were trying to scare me you did a pretty good job. My leg will be black and blue in the morning," he says, still unable to drop his playful tone completely. Humbert follows his prey up the stairs as Quilty scrambles behind a painting of a genteel eighteenth-century noblewoman which is propped up against the wall. The camera lingers on the painting and we watch it fill up with bullet holes as Humbert empties his gun into it. The rest of the film will unfold in flashback.

Much critical ink has been spilled over whether Kubrick should have transferred Quilty's murder from its place at the end of the novel to the opening of the film. In his preliminary discussions with Nabokov about the screen adaptation of the book, Kubrick saw that much of the interest in the novel centered around Humbert's machinations to possess Lolita and at the same time preserve an air of surface propriety in his relationship with her. When Lolita later disappears and he tracks her down, Humbert learns that Quilty had snatched her from him after playing several grim tricks to get Humbert to relinquish his hold on the girl.

By shifting Humbert's final encounter with Quilty to the beginning of the film, Kubrick exchanged the surprise ending of the novel for the suspense of making the moviegoer wonder how and when Humbert will realize what Quilty is up to. Of course we still do not get the full explanation of what Quilty has done until Lolita fits the pieces into place for Humbert in their last meeting. Nonetheless, the film audience has the satisfaction of being aware all along about Quilty's ingenious bamboozling of Humbert at every turn.

In tipping off the viewer at the outset of the movie that Quilty is the immediate architect of Humbert's ruin, Kubrick has opted for sustained suspense over momentary surprise. Alfred Hitchcock has often said that he prefers suspense to surprise, as he once explained in a *Saturday Evening Post* interview with Pete Martin. Hitchcock says that he gives the audience all of the facts as early as

possible because that way he can build up tension. When the viewer knows that one character constitutes a threat to another he wants to scream out, "Watch out for so-and-so." "There you have real tenseness," Hitchcock concludes, "and an irresistible desire to know what happens." In choosing to let the audience know that Quilty is Humbert's nemesis right from the start, therefore, Kubrick has followed Hitchcock's recipe for suspense just as the master himself describes it.

Telling the story this way also gives Quilty a much meatier role in the film than he had in the book, where he remains behind the scenes for the most part. It furthermore gives the audience the delight of wondering where and in what disguise the multi-talented Sellers will turn up next.

With a title that reads "Four Years Earlier," the story proper gets under way. Humbert, acting as narrator, explains on the sound track how he came to meet Lolita. "I had recently arrived in America, where many Europeans have found a haven. Because I had done some translations of French poetry which had gained some attention in literary circles, I was given a lectureship at Beardsley College in the fall. But I decided to stay in Ramsdale, a small resort town, for the summer and was looking for a place to stay."

Charlotte Haze (Shelley Winters), a bumptious, dowdy widow approaching middle age, guides Humbert on a tour of her house, pretentiously waving a cigarette holder at him and calling him Monsieur. "Culturally we are a very advanced group and very progressive intellectually," she says. "I'm chairman of the Great Books Committee. Last season I had Clare Quilty lecture on Dr. Schweitzer and Dr. Zhivago." She pairs the names as if both were equally noted physicians.

In opening her campaign to win Humbert's attentions, she ever so casually makes it clear that she is a widow, pointing to her husband's picture (it looks like a photo of a younger Nabokov) and to the urn containing his ashes. Humbert retrieves his hand just as he is about to touch the urn, which he had taken to be a vase. As Charlotte yammers about her congenial home, she leads Humbert into the back yard, where he sees Lolita for the first time and is obviously bedazzled. The girl lounges languidly in the sun in an abbreviated swimsuit, exuding a sex appeal far beyond her years.

Several critics have questioned the casting of Sue Lyon in the title role, saying that she looked too old for the part and accusing Kubrick of copping out by giving the impression that Humbert was infatuated not with a twelve-year-old nymphet but with a teen-ager. "She was actually the right age for the part," Kubrick counters. "Lolita was twelve and a half in the novel and Sue was thirteen. I suspect that many people had a mental image of a nine-year-old."

Pauline Kael laid this objection definitively to rest in her notice of the film in *I Lost It at the Movies*: "Have reviewers looked at the schoolgirls of America lately? The classmates of my fourteen-year-old daughter are not merely nubile; some of them look badly used." She complimented Kubrick and company for not dolling Sue Lyon up in childish clothes and pigtails since "the facts of American life are that adolescents and even pre-adolescents wear nylons and makeup and two-piece strapless bathing suits and have *figures*." In effect Kubrick opted for accuracy over the film-goer's preconception of how Lolita should look.

By the next scene Humbert, Lolita, and Charlotte have taken to going out together. They are watching a horror film in a drive-in theater. The domineering Charlotte is behind the wheel of the car, an indication of how she always seeks to be in the driver's seat when dealing with others, especially her daughter and would-be lover. Humbert, significantly, is sitting between the two females. Registering fright, Charlotte shrewdly grabs Humbert's hand. He in turn just as shrewdly takes Lolita's hand and slips his first hand out of Charlotte's grip to scratch his nose. Lolita, absorbed in the horror movie, puts her other hand on top of his. He places his remaining hand over hers, and Charlotte, never to be outdone, slaps her hand on top of them all.

Humbert's obsession for Lolita is growing, we infer from a montage of images, such as the one in which Lolita twirls a hula hoop around her hips and Humbert slyly leers at her across the top of the book he is pretending to read.

At a high school dance which Humbert and Charlotte are helping to chaperone, Humbert is content to feast his eyes on Lolita from his vantage point behind a floral decoration, but Charlotte spies him out and insists that they socialize. She introduces him to John and Jean Farlow, a young couple who like to think of themselves as the apex of small-town sophistication. "John and I are very—broad-minded," Jean confides to Humbert with a wink. Humbert smiles, perhaps wondering if their liberated attitudes would encompass his fascination for Lolita.

Clare Quilty makes his first appearance in the movie proper at the dance. "Hello *again*," Charlotte greets him meaningfully, dancing into his arms. "I've been the local authority on you ever since that afternoon that changed my life—when you lectured to us." Finally recognizing her, Quilty grins knowingly, "Don't you have a daughter with a lovely, lilting name?" In retrospect the viewer will later infer from this interchange that Quilty had seduced Charlotte to gain access to Lolita, just as Humbert will marry the hapless Charlotte for the same reason.

After the dance Lolita goes off to a party and Charlotte dragoons Humbert home for a "cozy supper." Humbert has been dreading the moment when Charlotte will drop her posture as the sedate widow and make an overt play for him, and it is now at hand. She slips into something more comfortable—and seductive: a gown with a leopard-skin design. Then she switches on some Latin music with an emphatic beat and offers to teach the middle-aged professor the latest steps. Pretending not to notice the possible sexual connotations of her invitation, Humbert demurs politely, "I don't even know the old ones."

Not to be put off, at least not just yet, Charlotte steers Humbert around the living room floor, in the driver's seat as usual, and finally backs him up against the wall, passionately protesting that, although she swore she would never marry again, she now feels that "life is for living. Take me in your arms. I can't live in the past any longer." Lolita picks just this moment to return from the party and Humbert is saved from submitting to his landlady's blandishments. Tears of frustration in her eyes, Charlotte coaxes Humbert to go for a drive, but he courteously bows his way out of the room and goes to bed, leaving Charlotte alone. She dumps an unopened champagne bottle back into an ice bucket and begins to weep.

This is perhaps Shelley Winters's best scene in the film and points up the consistently fine performance which she turns in as Charlotte. She demonstrates her ability to make us laugh at Charlotte's frowsy gentility and dreams of youthful romance and at the same time she stirs our compassion for the young widow's vulnerability and loneliness. As she whimpers and cries at the end of the scene we realize for the first time just how deeply the actress has made us understand Charlotte.

In the novel Humbert quotes copious passages from the diary which he kept while staying with the Hazes. In the film we do see him occasionally committing his experiences to its pages. At one point he begins to expound on "the twofold nature of the nymphet: the mixture of tender, dreamy childishness and a kind of eerie vulgarity. . . . I know it is bad to keep a diary, but it gives me a strange thrill to do so." Presumably Humbert's occasional narrative comments on the sound track are quotations from this diary.

Still piqued at the way Lolita's presence makes it difficult for her to pursue Humbert with the gusto she would like, Charlotte tells Humbert that she is going to pack her irritating daughter off to summer camp so that they can spend more time together. As always, James Mason's immaculately understated performance is perfectly attuned to the demands of the scene. When he hears this piece of news, a look of consternation steals across his face that faultlessly mirrors Humbert's feelings at the moment. "Is something wrong with your face?" Charlotte inquires, noticing his pained expression. He excuses himself on the pretext of going upstairs to nurse a toothache.

The next morning Humbert sulks in Lolita's room while she and her mother pack her things in the Haze station wagon for the trip to the girls' camp. When the car has pulled away Humbert hurls himself on her bed and sobs into her pillow, for he believes that he will never see her again, since he is to depart for Beardsley College before she returns from camp. He has to pull himself together, however, when the Haze maid unexpectedly presents him with a hastily scribbled note that may be from Lolita.

"This is a confession," it begins; "I love you." But as he reads on it is clear that the missive is from Charlotte. "Last Sunday in church the Lord told me to act as I am now doing and write you this letter. I am a passionate and lonely woman. You are the love of my life. And now will you please go. Scram! *Departez!* Your remaining would mean that you are ready to link your life with mine and be a father to my little girl." At that last line Humbert bursts out laughing uncontrollably, understanding as he does that he will have to accept Charlotte's marriage proposal if he is to remain in a position to carry out his designs on Lolita.

The camera pans away from Humbert clutching at the letter and rests on a poster of Clare Quilty on Lolita's bedroom wall. The picture could be a mere sign of teen-age hero worship, but by film's end the image of Quilty's photo looking with bland detachment on Humbert's grief will, in retrospect, take on much more significance.

Humbert accepts his fate and the marriage takes place, he informs us in a voice-over. Since he no longer enjoys the same kind of privacy that he had when he was a boarder, Humbert must now take refuge in the bathroom to commit his thoughts to his diary. While he is busy making his entry about the wedding, Charlotte, as possessive as ever, knocks on the bathroom door, solicitously pining, "Dear, the door is locked. Sweetheart, I don't want any secrets between us." Through the door she prattles at him about the past. "Were there a lot of women in your life before me?" Nettled, Humbert shouts back through the door that symbolically stands between them, "I'll make you a complete list. Will that satisfy you?" "I don't care about any of the others. I know that our love is sacred; all of the others were profane," she proclaims operatically.

Sue Lyon and James Mason, LOLITA.

She shows Humbert her dead husband's revolver, which in this context takes on a phallic significance, especially when she says as she fondles it, "This is a sacred weapon, a treasure. But don't worry, it isn't loaded." He had bought it when he learned that he was ill. "Happily he was hospitalized before he could use it." Pursuing Humbert's affections with the savagery of a cavewoman, Charlotte embraces him on the bed. Humbert slyly looks beyond his wife to a photograph of Lolita on the bedside table. Even an amateur psychologist could deduce that he is referring his sexual encounters with Lolita's mother to the girl herself. To say that Humbert's sexual obsession with the nymphet has to be implied by looks in the film, therefore, is still saying quite a bit.

Charlotte abruptly interrupts Humbert's reverie by informing him that she intends to send Lolita straight from camp on to boarding school and then to college, ending with what sounds to Humbert like a death sentence: "It's going to be me and you alone forever." He looks wistfully at the photo of Lolita which now seems so desperately out of reach. Charlotte goes off to the bathroom and Humbert thoughtfully contemplates his predecessor's gun, toying with the idea of ridding himself of his unwanted spouse once and for all.

He advances toward the bathroom, where he can hear the bathtub filling with water; the door is slightly ajar. "She splashed in the tub, a clumsy, trusting seal. What do you know, folks; I just couldn't make myself do it." Humbert points the gun at the camera, then lowers it and stares helplessly ahead. He slowly pushes the door open—and she is not there.

The "trusting" Charlotte, he discovers, is in his study, busily prying into his diary. " 'That Haze woman,' " she repeats hysterically, " 'that cow, the obnoxious mama!' You are a monster. I am leaving you and you are never going to see that miserable brat again." She locks herself in the bedroom and this time it is Humbert who is outside knocking beseechingly at the door. She holds up the book to her husband's urn and blubbers, "Harold, look what happened. Darling, forgive me."

Downstairs Humbert mixes a batch of martinis, still hoping to mollify his distraught wife and not lose Lolita for good. The phone rings; he listens incredulously, and then calls upstairs, "Charlotte, there's a man on the phone who says that you've been hit by a car." The wind blows the front door open and he sees an ambulance race by the front of the house. We see the aftermath of the accident as Humbert arrives at the scene.

In the book at this point Humbert says, "I have to put the impact of an instantaneous vision into a sequence of words; their physical accumulation on the page impairs the actual flash, the sharp unity of impression" which the camera can give in a single image: the milling crowd of neighbors, the driver of the car that has overrun Charlotte, and finally the corpse underneath a blanket that someone has placed over it.

As Charles Barr has commented on this passage in *Film Quarterly,* there is no literary equivalent for "getting things into the same shot" as a director can do in filming a scene which may take many words to describe on the printed page. As a result a scene like Charlotte's death gains in impact in being translated from page to screen. Kubrick has gotten all of the details which Humbert described in the novel "into the same shot" as Humbert in the movie approaches the site of the accident. The director tells me that when he composed this shot he was not consciouly thinking of Humbert's aside in the novel about how the written description would look on film. "How else would you do it?" he says.

One of the best examples of black comedy in the whole film, after the prologue in Quilty's mansion, is the scene in which Humbert, like an ex-convict savoring the first moments of his parole, floats dreamily in the bathtub sipping a martini, drinking in the realization that Lolita is completely his now that Charlotte, the

last obstacle (as far as he knows) to his possessing her, has been removed like a captured chess piece from the board.

The Farlows, concerned for Humbert's morale, burst into a bathroom. "Broad-minded" Jean averts her eyes when she sees that Humbert is in the tub, although he has pulled the shower curtain partway closed. They mistake his mellow alcoholic detachment for a severe state of shock. "Try to think of Lolita," says Jean, ladling out unneeded consolation. "She is all alone in the world and you must live for her." As if Humbert had been doing anything else!

To make things even more farcical, the father of the driver of the car that struck Charlotte down comes to intercede for his son, and he too squeezes into the crowded bathroom, flipping the lid of the toilet down and seating himself in order to discuss the funeral arrangements. Humbert hardly listens, his thoughts already preoccupied with his plans to spirit Lolita away from summer camp.

As he drives the Haze station wagon into the campgrounds he passes a huge sign that welcomes him to Camp Climax. The place is aptly named, we later learn, when Lolita tells Humbert that Charlie, a relative of the proprietors, has made it his business to initiate several of the girls into the mysteries of sex. While they drive along the highway, Humbert assures Lolita that her mother's sudden illness is not serious and that they will see her soon.

The pair stop for the night at a large hotel where Quilty too is staying with his constant companion, a glum young woman about whom Quilty jokes with the desk clerk, Mr. Swine. Quilty and his girl then stand inconspicuously at the opposite end of the front desk and listen as Humbert and Lolita sign in. Quilty overhears Humbert's ensuing conversation with the desk clerk, who has only a single room left. To maintain a surface propriety Humbert asks for a cot to be installed in the room, an item which he has no intention of using. Humbert's plans to seduce a minor, however, abruptly founder when a stranger introduces himself on the shadowy terrace and mentions that a police convention is currently staying at the hotel.

When Humbert feigns nonchalance and asks the man whom he is with, the response is unsettling: "I am not with someone, I am with you." Quilty is the stranger on the terrace and he will in fact stay right with Humbert all the way to the time when he will at last win Lolita away from him. Leaning on the porch railing with his back to Humbert, Quilty says that he is a state trooper and Humbert immediately starts to bow out.

"No, you don't have to leave at all," Quilty says, launching into a seemingly casual but really coldly calculated monologue. "I get the impression that you want to leave but you don't like to leave because you think you would look suspicious, and I'm a policeman. You don't have to think that, because I haven't really got a suspicious mind at all. I'm not suspicious, but other people think I'm suspicious, especially when I stand around on street corners. One of my boys picked me up the other week because he thought I was too suspicious." Humbert does not know what to make of Quilty's stream of chatter and finds it all the more threatening for that reason.

"I couldn't help notice when you checked in tonight," Quilty continues. "It's part of my job. I noticed your face, and I said to myself when I saw you, 'That's a guy with the most normal face I have ever seen in my life.' Because I'm a normal guy and it would be great for two normal guys like us to get together and—talk about world events, you know, in a normal sort of way." Now Quilty bears down a bit more on his victim. "Let me say one other thing. I noticed you had a lovely little girl with you. As a matter of fact she is taller rather than little, a lovely, sweet girl. Your daughter? I figured you might want to get away from your wife. If I was married I would want to get away from my wife."

Now completely flustered, Humbert blurts out that his wife was in an accident but that she is coming on later. "How, in an ambulance? I am sorry about that remark, sir. Listen, I am friends with George Swine. I can help you by putting a word in his normal ear. Let me see the accommodations that you have and then I can have a word with George. We could get you and your daughter a lovely little bridal suite." With that last thrust Humbert is completely undone by Quilty and hastily goes upstairs to his room.

The relevance of Quilty's monologues to the film as a whole has been questioned by some commentators, as if they were mere comic interludes in which Peter Sellers has the opportunity to show off his dexterity at improvisation and impersonation. On the contrary, each of Quilty's comic turns grows out of the action and has a strong influence on what develops next. So here: as a result of his encounter with the policeman-Quilty, Humbert scraps his elaborate plans to seduce Lolita on that occasion.

Humbert's troubles for the night are not yet over. There is a hilarious slapstick sequence in which Humbert, with the aid of a bumbling bellboy, tries to set up the recalcitrant rollaway bed that he had ordered earlier. Their grappling with the cot represents one of the first incidents in a Kubrick movie of a mechanical apparatus refusing to submit to man's presumed dominion over it. This theme will recur again, most especially in *Dr. Strangelove* and *2001*. As Humbert wearily climbs into the apparently vanquished rollaway, the vindictive bed once more collapses, signaling the complete collapse of Humbert's plans to possess Lolita that night.

In the morning Lolita awakens Humbert and asks him coquettishly if he would like to play a game that she learned from Charlie at camp. As she whispers the details in his ear, a look of lecherous anticipation crosses Humbert's face and the scene discreetly fades. Very tactfully Kubrick has managed to get across to the audience that, in spite of all of Humbert's intricate plans to seduce Lolita, she has in effect finally seduced him.

Afterward, as they continue their trip in the station wagon, Lolita insists on stopping to call her mother in the hospital. Just before shooting this scene Kubrick called for a Coke and a bag of potato chips for Sue Lyon in order to add just the right flavor of incongruity to the scene in which Humbert is forced to tell Lolita that her mother is dead—an example of how some nice touches occur to the director just before the cameras roll. When Humbert finally convinces the girl that he is not fooling about her mother's death she stops munching and bursts into tears.

Her crying carries over into the next scene in a motel room, where she sobs, "Everything has changed between us. Everything was so normal." Without being aware of it she has used the word *normal,* which popped up incessantly in Quilty's policeman monologue. Lolita has obviously been around Quilty often enough to pick up his jargon. The clues to her involvement with an older man other than Humbert are beginning to mount up.

"Accompany us now to Beardsley College," says Humbert, voice-over, "where my poetry class is in its second semester." By this time the relationship of stepfather and stepdaughter has become increasingly stormy. He is jealous of her younger male companions and accordingly refuses to allow her to be in the school play. "You don't love me," she screams. "You just want to keep me locked up with you in this filthy house."

Later when Humbert returns from class he finds an uninvited visitor awaiting him in his dark study. When he switches on the light Quilty, disguised as Dr. Zempf, the school psychiatrist, materializes like an apparition. He is wearing thick glasses and a moustache, and speaks with the smooth German accent which Sellers will call upon again in the title role of *Dr. Strangelove.* In the novel an authentic member of the school faculty intercedes with Humbert to let Lolita appear in the play. It is much more effective to have Quilty perform this function in the film to nudge the viewer with the suspicion that Quilty has some sinister purpose of his own for being interested in Lolita's appearing in his play.

"Dr. Humbert, do you mind if I am putting to you a blunt question?" Quilty begins. "We are wondering if anyone has instructed Lolita in the facts of life. The onset of maturity seems to be giving her trouble. She gets a lot of notice. She has poor concentration and sighs a good deal in class and seems to be suffering from some acute repression of the libido of her natural instincts. She wrote yesterday an obscenity on a health pamphlet. We Americans are progressively modern and believe it is important to prepare the majority of young people for satisfactory mating and successful child rearing."

With disarming illogic Dr. Zempf winds up his spiel with the proposition that all of Lolita's problems will be solved if "you, Dr. Humboldt [sic], definitely unveto that girl's participation in the schoolplay," adding for good measure, "You should also loosen up on the dating and the dancing. Otherwise a quartet of psychologists will have to come and inspect the home situation. We don't want these people fiddling around in the home situation, do we?" Humbert of course agrees. At his wit's end, he does not notice that when Quilty prepares to light a cigarette he has to lift his thick glasses furtively in order to see what he is doing, giving away his disguise.

Kubrick shot Sellers's monologues in long takes without much camera movement or cutting. In fact the camerawork throughout the film is markedly unobtrusive. Asked about this, Kubrick points to Chaplin's ability to create his films with a minimum of camera dexterity. "If something is really happening on the screen," says Kubrick, "it isn't crucial how it is shot. Chaplin had a simple cinematic style, but you were always hypnotized by what was going on." Certainly Sellers's monologues in the film deserve this kind of treatment.

On the night of the play's performance, Lolita stands backstage waiting to go on and exchange smiles with Quilty, who is also in the wings. He later observes Humbert dragging Lolita out of the auditorium after the play is over. Humbert has discovered in the course of a conversation backstage with Lolita's music teacher that she has not appeared for a lesson for weeks. Humbert assumes that she has been seeing one of her male classmates but we suspect that it may be Quilty.

Still wearing her stage makeup and gaudy costume, Lolita looks like a garishly dressed kept woman as she sulks on the couch and argues with Humbert. Fed up with the strain of trying to conceal his sordid relationship with his stepdaughter, Humbert proposes that he and Lolita go away for a long trip around the country "so we can get back the way we were before." Lolita screams at Humbert the way she used to yell at her mother, "No! I hate you! Why don't you leave me alone?" After making a phone call, however, she sweetly agrees to the extended journey. Humbert is so relieved that it does not occur to him, as it does to the filmgoer, that she has probably gotten advice from Quilty to string along with Humbert for a while.

Our suspicions are confirmed when Humbert says ruefully over the sound track as he and Lolita spin along the highway, "I cannot tell you when I first knew that a strange car was following us. Queer how I misinterpreted the designation of doom." He fears that yet another policeman is tailing him and wants to have it out with him. Lolita tries to dissuade Humbert from doing so but the problem is solved, for the moment at least, by the disappearance of the other car.

Lolita falls ill and is committed to a hospital in the nearest town. When Humbert visits her with flowers and other gifts, a new crisis arises with his finding a note from a male admirer and a mysterious pair of sunglasses in her room. Lolita maintains that both belong to a friendly nurse who stops by to see her. Back in the motel where he is staying Humbert is roused from a sound sleep by a telephone call in the middle of the night. It is Quilty's last and most menacing impersonation:

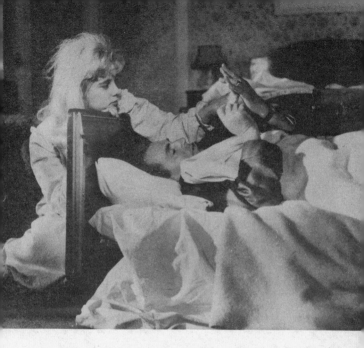

"Is this Professor Humbert? Just wondering how you are enjoying your stay in our lovely little town. My department is concerned with the bizarre rumors about you and that lovely, remarkable girl. You are classified in our files as a white widowed male. I wonder if you would be prepared to give us a report on your current sex life, if any."

Completely unhinged, Humbert dashes frantically to have Lolita released from the hospital, only to find that she left earlier in the evening in the company of her "uncle." As Humbert rages down the corridor to Lolita's empty room he is tackled by two hospital attendants who send him sprawling to the floor toward the camera. A doctor examines the pupils of Humbert's eyes and calls for a straitjacket with evident relish. This is more than even Quilty had bargained for: Humbert being committed to a mental ward. Humbert musters all of his English reserve and says quietly, "I really ought to be moving on now," as if he were taking leave of a boring hostess. "Uncle Gus came for her. I forgot about him. He's very easy to forget." He is set free and walks down the hall away from the camera, a sad, defeated character retreating into the distance.

The novel chronicles Humbert's fruitless efforts to track down Lolita, but Kubrick wisely bypasses this episode and cuts immedi-

ately to an unseen Lolita laboriously typing a note to Humbert asking him for money to help her and her husband prepare for the coming of their baby. Following this lead, Humbert drives through a slum neighborhood in a big city and stops at a dead end in front of a tawdry bungalow. He takes Harold Haze's revolver from the glove compartment with a view to shooting the man who took Lolita away from him on that fateful night two years earlier.

Wearing horn-rimmed glasses, her hair askew, and showing every day of her six months' pregnancy, Lolita is no longer the sleek, sensual girl that Humbert had enshrined in his memory. Humbert decides against using his gun as soon as he learns that Lolita's husband is not the man who spirited her away from the hospital. "Do you remember Dr. Zempf?" she asks. "That car that followed us around? Mother's old flame at the school dance? That cop you talked to at the hotel? And that guy that called you at the motel?" Humbert concedes that he has never been a good guesser. For his benefit, and for those members of the audience who also are not good guessers, Lolita explains:

"All of them were Clare Quilty. I had had a crush on him ever since he used to visit Mother. He wasn't like you and me; he wasn't a normal person." Quilty's word again. "He was a genius. He had a kind of beautiful Oriental philosophy. I guess he was the

only guy I was ever crazy about." Humbert is hurt by this but, characteristically, Lolita does not notice. "Oh, my husband Dick is very sweet, but it's just not the same. Quilty took me to a dude ranch near Santa Fe. He had a bunch of weird friends staying with him: painters, writers, nudists, weight lifters. But I figured I could take anything for a couple of weeks because I loved him. He promised to get me a movie contract, but it never turned out that way. Instead he wanted me to cooperate with the others in making some kind of art movie. No, I didn't do it," she snaps, flaring up for a second like the old Lolita, not to say like her mother, whom she is beginning to resemble more and more. Indeed Lolita, paunchy with pregnancy and wearing a seedy maternity dress, is already becoming a slatternly matron very much like her dead mother. Humbert realizes regretfully that he has helped to rob her of her youth.

Her husband Dick now enters this domestic scene. He is a friendly young man, not particularly handsome, who wears a hearing aid. She had met him in Phoenix, where she was working as a waitress after Quilty abandoned her. He invites his stepfather-in-law to stay with them for a few days. "He can't stay, Dick," says Lolita emphatically in the direction of his hearing aid. As the ultimate irony Dick smilingly calls Humbert "Professor Haze."

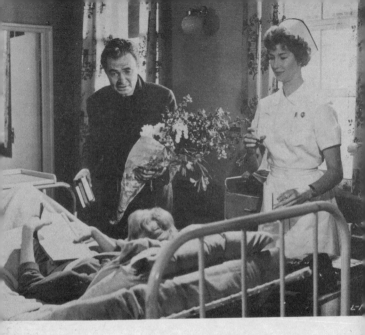

After Dick leaves the room Humbert makes his final plea to Lolita to allow him to rescue her from what he sees as her present shabby circumstances. "Lolita, between here and that old station wagon is twenty-five feet. Come with me now, just the two of us. I want you to leave your husband and this awful house and live with me, die with me, do everything with me. We'll start fresh. It's not too late."

Lolita begins to understand that Humbert's sexual obsession with her has at last turned into genuine love. "It is this last encounter," Kubrick comments, "in which Humbert expresses his love for Lolita, who is no longer a nymphet but a pregnant housewife, that is one of the most poignant elements of the story." Lolita also understands that she still must decline Humbert's invitation. She has wrecked too many lives and she will not hurt Dick. Humbert turns over to her the money from her mother's estate and makes for his car, trying to avert the tears that have already started to course down his cheeks.

He proceeds immediately to Quilty's mansion, intent on shooting him, we now understand, not just because Quilty had lured Lolita away from him but because, after he had done so, Quilty had merely used her for a while and then coldly discarded her. Kubrick repeats footage from the prologue and we see Humbert enter Quilty's lair searching for him. The film ends with a shot of the portrait behind which Humbert had finally trapped Quilty, riddled with bullet holes. A printed epilogue informs us that "Humbert Humbert died in prison of coronary thrombosis while awaiting trial for the murder of Clare Quilty."

The ending of *Lolita* is unique; I know of no other movie that creates as much compassion for the tragic end of its obsessed hero by employing a simply worded epitaph on the screen at the fade-out. One cannot help feeling somewhat sorry for a man who organized his whole life around the pursuit of a goal that would be short-lived in any event, the love of a nymphet who could never remain a nymphet for long. It is Humbert's recognition that he has used Lolita and must suffer for it, however, that humanizes him in our eyes to the point where he is worthy of whatever pity we wish to give him.

For those who appreciate the black comedy of *Lolita* it is not hard to see that it was just a short step from that film to Kubrick's masterpiece in that genre, *Dr. Strangelove*, which expands Kubrick's study of human folly in *Lolita* to cosmic proportions.

# PART THREE:
# TRILOGY:
# THINGS TO COME

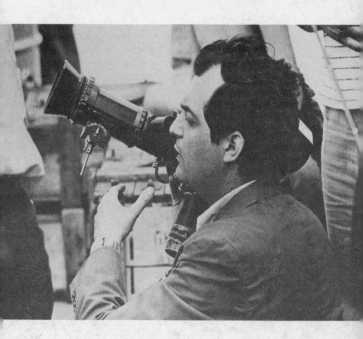

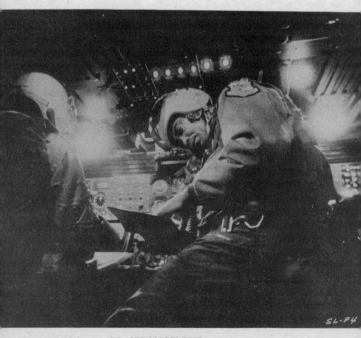

James Earl Jones, DR. STRANGELOVE.

# Chapter Six
# Stop the World:

# Dr. Strangelove
# or
# How I Learned to Stop
# Worrying and Love the Bomb
# (1964)

In his treatment of the *film noir* cycle in American cinema, which I referred to in Chapter One, Paul Schrader pointed out a triple theme inherent in these films: "a passion for the past and present, but also a fear of the future. The *noir* hero dreads to look ahead, but instead tries to survive by the day, and if unsuccessful at that, he retreats to the past. Thus *film noir*'s techniques emphasize loss, nostalgia, lack of clear priorities, insecurity."

This analysis of *film noir* could well serve as a description of the way that *Dr. Strangelove, 2001,* and *A Clockwork Orange,* in crystallizing man's fears of the future, are rooted in Kubrick's earlier pictures. They show how the unpleasant, tough world of today (*Fear and Desire, Killer's Kiss, The Killing, Lolita*) had developed from the equally corrupt world of yesterday (*Paths of Glory, Spartacus*), and will lead to the dark, forbidding world of tomorrow. For, as I mentioned earlier in analyzing *Killer's Kiss,* Kubrick's vision suggests that man's failure to cooperate with his fellow man in mastering the world of the present can only lead to man's being mastered by the world of the future. And this is precisely what happens in *Strangelove* and the other science-fiction films which follow it.

Kubrick had originally planned *Strangelove* as a serious adaptation of Peter George's novel *Red Alert,* which is about the decision of the psychotic general who orders his troop of B-52 bombers to launch an attack inside Russia. As he developed the script with Peter George, however, his approach to the material changed: "My idea of doing it as a nightmare comedy came in the early weeks of working on the screenplay. I found that in trying to put meat on the bones and to imagine the scenes more fully, one had to keep leaving things out which were either absurd or paradoxical

135

in order to keep it from being funny; and these things seemed to be close to the heart of the scenes in question."

Kubrick asked Terry Southern to add some further comic touches and continued to revise the script while the film was in production, during what Kubrick calls "the crucial rehearsal periods." For a scene which might require three days of shooting the director will often spend the first day working out details of the action, listening to all of the suggestions which the cast and anyone else around have to offer. He weighs all of these carefully against his own ideas and finally decides on how the scene should be handled. "Stanley is a very quiet person and a brain picker," says Slim Pickens, who appeared in *Dr. Strangelove.* "He surrounds himself with a bunch of bright people and when anybody comes up with a bright idea Stanley uses it."

This period of rehearsal is one of maximum tension and anxiety, Kubrick explains, "and it is precisely here where a scene lives or dies." The subsequent choice of camera angles, he feels, is relatively simple by comparison with the working out of the scene with the actors in rehearsal. "During the shooting of *Dr. Strangelove*," he recalls, "many substantial changes were made in the script, sometimes together with the cast during these improvisations. Some of the best dialogue was created by Peter Sellers himself." In fact, Dr. Strangelove's "resurrection" from his wheelchair at the end of the movie was the product of one of the crucial rehearsal periods.

In the film Sellers plays not only the title role of the eccentric scientist, but also the President of the United States, Merken Muffley, and Group Captain Lionel Mandrake, the British officer who tries to dissuade General Jack D. Ripper from initiating the bombing attack. In his review of the film in *The Village Voice,* Andrew Sarris notes that Kubrick had also intended Sellers to play Major "King" Kong, the commander of the only bomber to get through to its Russian target. Sarris expresses disappointment that, because of an injury, Sellers was not able to play this fourth part since, in his view, that would have meant that "almost everywhere you turn there is some version of Peter Sellers holding the fate of the world in his hands."

Nevertheless, as things stand, Sellers enacts the roles of the three men behind the scenes who are most deeply involved in trying to keep Major Kong from carrying out the mission that he has been led to believe by Ripper's orders is his duty. In any case, Slim Pickens gives the performance of his career as Kong, the good-natured, benighted Texan.

*Dr. Strangelove* recalls *The Killing,* not only because it shows

**Slim Pickens, DR. STRANGELOVE.**

how a supposedly foolproof plan of action can go awry, but because once more Kubrick is telling a story that takes place in several places at once. Instead of turning back the clock to show an action that has been developing elsewhere while the previous scene was in progress, as he did in *The Killing,* however, Kubrick develops the parallel lines of action in *Strangelove* by cutting abruptly back and forth from one place to another in mid-scene. This lets the audience know how what is happening in another location is influencing what is taking place in the scene now before them, and vice versa. Consequently the script of *Strangelove* is one of the most tightly knit, brilliantly constructed screenplays ever devised. Only repeated viewings can indicate the subtlety and skill with which it has been put together.

The tone of the screenplay neatly straddles the line between straightforward realism and straight-faced farce. The flight deck of Major Kong's B-52, for example, was constructed at Shepperton Studios in authentic detail in what one visitor to the set described as an area about the size of a packed linen closet. It is just this air of realism and the inexorable plausibility with which the story unfolds that led Columbia Pictures to add a printed preface at the beginning of the film which reads:

"It is the stated position of the United States Air Force that their safeguards would prevent the occurrence of such events as are depicted in this film. Furthermore it should be noted that none of the characters portrayed in this film are meant to represent any real persons living or dead."

Once this official disclaimer is disposed of, the film gets under way. An expanse of clouds is seen stretching across the screen with mountain peaks poking through in the distance. Over the soft whirring of the wind a narrator says, almost furtively: "For more than a year, ominous rumors had been privately circulating among high-level Western leaders that the Soviet Union had been at work on what was darkly hinted to be the ultimate weapon, a Doomsday device. Intelligence sources traced the site of the top-secret Russian project to the perpetually fog-shrouded wasteland below the Arctic peaks of the Zhokhov islands. What they were building, or why it should be located in such a remote and desolate place, no one could say."

The picture will be more than half over before further reference is made to the top-secret Doomsday machine, which will in the end reduce the world to the trackless waste pictured in the very opening image of the film.

The credit sequence begins with a close-up of the nose of a plane protruding proudly toward the camera like an erect phallus. To the strains of "Try a Little Tenderness" played softly on the sound track, a nuclear bomber is refueled in mid-flight by a tanker aircraft. This symbolic coupling sets the tone for the sexual metaphors that are spread throughout the movie, underscoring the sexual obsessions of various characters, chiefly General Ripper. Over this scene the credits unfold, looking as if they were chalked on the fuselage of a plane in the manner of air force pilots who chalk morale-boosting slogans on their planes before going into combat. When the refueling is finished, the B-52 flies off on its own, the credits end, and the music fades.

Now it is night; landing field lights wink in the darkness in which Burpleson Air Base is wrapped. A radar detector spins relentlessly on the airfield. Inside the computer room an officer stands immersed in an endless sheet of data that is coming out of one of the computers. Already, it seems, man's machinery has begun to master him, as it will continue to do in the film until the final triumph of the Doomsday machine over the whole of humanity at the end of the picture.

Group Captain Mandrake extricates himself from the data sheet to take a phone call from his immediate superior, General Ripper, the commander of the base (played by Sterling Hayden, who organized the ill-fated robbery in *The Killing*). Ripper is first pictured in a long shot sitting at his desk, with only a fluorescent lamp overhead to pierce the darkness by which he is engulfed.

"The base is being put on Condition Red," he informs Mandrake. "This is not an exercise. It looks like we are in a shooting war. My orders are to seal this base tight. I want all privately owned radios to be impounded; otherwise they might be used to transmit instructions to saboteurs."

The narrator makes his second and final intrusion on the sound track to explain that, in order to guard against the possibility of surprise attack, the U.S. Strategic Air Command (SAC) maintains a force of planes airborne twenty-four hours a day, spread out from the Persian Gulf to the Arctic Ocean. "But they all have one geographic factor in common. They are all two hours from their targets inside Russia." Hence Ripper has placed the planes in his command on Plan R, according to which they will all proceed to bomb their specifically allotted primary and secondary targets within the Soviet Union.

Inside one of the bombers, the crew sits around lackadaisically as they fly their routine mission. Major Kong pages through *Playboy,* pausing at the centerfold; one of the crew members performs card tricks for his own amusement; the radio operator, Lieutenant Goldberg, munches a candy bar until he receives the transmission of Wing Attack Plan R. Major Kong thinks Goldberg is playing a

**Tracy Reed and George C. Scott, DR. STRANGELOVE.**

practical joke and insists on having the message confirmed by Burpleson.

"Goldie, how many times have I told you guys I don't want no horsing around on the airplane," he says irritably, as if he were addressing the unruly occupants of a school bus. Here is an example of how much of the humor—and horror—of the movie is rooted in the fact that the individuals most seriously involved in the crisis around which the film turns either do not grasp the enormity of what is happening or fall back on patterns of behavior that would be perfectly acceptable under normal circumstances, but which become madly incongruous given the situation. "General Ripper wouldn't give us Plan R unless them Rooskies had already clobbered Washington and a lot of other places," Kong says over the intercom.

When the orders are duly confirmed, Kong dramatically opens the book of instructions labeled *Plan R,* clamping on his trusty ten-gallon hat just as the insistent strumming of "When Johnny Comes Marching Home" commences on the sound track. This melody will continue to be heard in every one of the flight deck scenes, its incessant snare drum accompaniment building tension in a manner akin to Ravel's *Bolero.*

"Well, boys, I reckon this is it," Kong says solemnly; "nuclear combat toe to toe with the Rooskies." Like a cavalry officer in some forgotten Civil War film, Kong reminds his men that the folks back home are counting on them and that "there will be some important promotions and citations when we come through this. And that goes for every last one of you," he concludes generously, "regardless of your race, your color, or your creed!"

The phone rings in the bedroom of General Buck Turgidson (George C. Scott) and is answered by his secretary/mistress Miss Scott (Tracy Reed). She has just come out from under a sunlamp and we recognize her as the subject of the *Playboy* centerfold that Major Kong was studying earlier. (Miss Scott is referred to in publicity layouts for the film as "Miss World Affairs," though she is never called that in the film.)

She tells the caller, General Butridge, that General Turgidson is in the powder room and cannot come to the phone. Turgidson finally appears, first seen coming toward the phone in the wall mirror behind Miss Scott (a composition similar to the telephone sequence in *Killer's Kiss* described earlier). Turgidson is wearing shorts and a sport shirt open down the front: he obviously considers himself a he-man and sexual athlete. Butridge explains that General Ripper has implemented Plan R and sealed off Burpleson so that he cannot be reached even by phone.

With forced nonchalance Turgidson tells Miss Scott that he is going "to mosey over to the War Room" to see what is happening. Turgidson's two obsessions are war and sex—a connection already established in the credit sequence—and he constantly is talking about one in terms of the other. Hence he consoles Miss Scott; "I'm sorry, baby. Start your countdown without me and I'll be back before you can say 'Blast off!'"

At Burpleson the guards and enlisted men stand in little groups around the base tensely listening to Ripper's proclamation of the Red Alert over the public-address system. A jeep filled with commandeered radios backs up toward the camera. In several of these shots the motto of SAC can be seen posted prominently in the background: "Peace is our profession." This banner appears on the wall behind General Ripper as he sits at his desk making his speech, grasping a cigar in one hand and a slender hand microphone in the other. Ripper, who we shall shortly learn has severe sexual problems, is here shown sporting a phallic symbol in each hand.

"Your Commie has no regard for human life, not even for his own," Ripper announces with foreboding. "The enemy may even come in the uniform of our own troops." Later on, when the President orders American troops to break into Burpleson and put Ripper in telephone communication with him, this is precisely what the general thinks has happened. He continues, "In the two years I have been your commanding officer you have always given me your best." As Mandrake listens to these lugubrious remarks he absentmindedly picks up a transistor which had been overlooked in the general confiscation of radios. He switches it on and is amazed to hear rock music pouring out of it.

The beat of rock 'n' roll gives way to that of "When Johnny Comes Marching Home" as we return momentarily to the B-52. Kong has ceremoniously distributed the Attack Profile to the crew and orders all of the transmission receivers aboard the aircraft to be adjusted so that only messages preceded by the emergency code prefix O.P.E. will get through. Therefore the viewer already knows the emergency code prefix call letters that Mandrake will now try to wrest from the demented Ripper in order to radio the bomber wing to call off the attack.

Mandrake bursts into Ripper's office, the transistor radio music twanging nasally in his hand, and tells the general that if a real Russian attack were under way there would be no regular civilian broadcasting on the radio. The camera, which is behind Ripper's desk, remains stationary as the general rises, walks to the other end of the room, locks the door and returns to his desk. It is now

**The War Room, DR. STRANGELOVE.**

painfully clear to Mandrake that the orders to put Plan R into effect did not come from the President but originated with Ripper himself.

Standing at attention, Mandrake formally demands that Ripper give him the code prefix by which he can radio the bomber wing to turn back from their Russian targets. "Our fellows will be inside Russian radio cover in about twenty minutes," he points out to Ripper, adding with his customary British penchant for understatement, "We don't want to start a nuclear war unless we really have to, do we?" When Ripper refuses, Mandrake marches to the door at the opposite end of the room and finds that it is locked. Seen in long shot, he is a tiny figure standing helplessly alone as he realizes that he is imprisoned with a madman.

Alexander Walker has noted that *Dr. Strangelove* is basically about a crisis of communication. The film takes place in three locations, each of which is totally shut off from the others: the air base where the crazed Ripper sits in a locked room; the B-52 (aptly named *The Leper Colony*) which is presided over by a pilot obsessed with carrying out what he thinks is his duty; and the War Room, soon to enter the film, which is ultimately dominated by the mad nuclear scientist of the film's title.

"A decision is being made by the President and the Joint Chiefs of Staff in the War Room of the Pentagon," Ripper says to Mandrake, referring to this third critical location, "and when they realize that there is no possibility of recalling the wing, there will be only one course of action open: total commitment." Ripper condescends to reveal to Mandrake some of his reasons for putting Plan R into action. "Clemenceau once said that war was too important to be left to the generals. But today war is too important to be left to the politicians. They have neither the time, the training, nor the inclination for strategic thought. I can no longer allow Communist infiltration, Communist indoctrination, Communist subversion and the international Communist conspiracy to sap and impurify all of our precious bodily fluids."

As Ripper describes in this and later scenes his fears about preserving his male potency, to which he refers as his precious bodily fluids or his bodily essence, Kubrick photographs him in close-up from below, with a huge phallic cigar between his lips all the while he is talking. As we stare at close range at his face, we almost feel that Kubrick is taking us into the twisted mind of the man.

We now get our first glimpse of the War Room, a murky, cavernous place, where President Muffley sits at a vast circular table with his advisors, reminiscent of King Arthur and his Knights of the Round Table. Overhead is a bank of lights which bathes the

**George C. Scott and Peter Sellers, DR. STRANGELOVE.**

men below it in an eerie glow similar to that in which Ripper sits. At one end of the room is the Big Board, a huge map with twinkling indicators that show the progress of the bomber wing toward their Russian objectives. "The aircraft will begin penetrating Russian radar cover in about twenty-five minutes," Turgidson informs the assembly, summing up the situation.

The President indignantly inquires how Ripper could have managed to exceed his authority in such a spectacular way, since only the President can authorize the use of Plan R. Almost sheepishly Turgidson reminds Muffley that he himself had approved the emergency clause in the procedures governing nuclear attack, according to which a lesser official could invoke Plan R in the event of a sneak attack by the enemy.

Turgidson then reads Ripper's memo to SAC, urging all of the other base commanders to follow his lead in executing Plan R: "My boys will give you the best kind of start, 1400 megatons worth, and you sure as hell won't stop them. So let's get going; there's no choice." Turgidson seems swept along by Ripper's spurious rhetoric until he stumbles into the last sentence: "God willing, we will prevail, in peace and freedom from fear, and in the purity and essence of our natural fluids."

It is now evident to all that the very existence of life on this planet is in jeopardy because a psychotic general has been able to manipulate according to his own paranoid fantasies the presumably foolproof U.S. security measures governing nuclear attack. This situation reminds me of the musings of one of the characters in Federico Fellini's *La Dolce Vita* (1960). The philosopher Steiner reflects somberly, "Sometimes I think of the world that my children will know. They say that the world of the future will be wonderful. But what does that mean? It needs only the gesture of a madman to destroy everything." This is exactly the prospect facing the characters in *Strangelove*.

Kubrick himself has said that the serious threat remains that a psychotic figure somewhere in the command structure could start a war. Even if it involved only a limited exchange of nuclear weapons, he believes, it could devastate large areas. "I'm not entirely assured that somewhere in the Pentagon or Red Army upper echelons there does not exist the real-life prototype of General Jack D. Ripper."

Muffley asks about the reliability of the psychological tests that approve a man like Ripper for high command, and Turgidson responds meekly, "I wouldn't be too hasty, Mr. President; I don't think it's fair to condemn a whole program because the human element has failed us." Of course, in the context of Kubrick's total vision, as gleaned especially from his later films, this remark is ironic. For Kubrick often suggests in these movies that it is not the human element that is ultimately at fault but man's increasing tendency to place more and more faith in his "infallible" machines, even to the point where the human element can no longer intervene to set things right when they go askew.

Turgidson, with his rabid military mind, gleefully maintains that things have already gotten to the point where the only recourse possible is to back Ripper's attack with an all-out nuclear

offensive against the Russians before they can retaliate. "If we attack now," he exclaims with typical crudity, "we have a good chance of catching the Commies with their pants down." The President, who is not quite the ineffectual simp that some reviewers have made him out to be, counters sensibly that it is the avowed policy of the United States never to strike first with nuclear weapons and that General Ripper's action was not an act of national policy; furthermore, he contends, there are still other alternatives to the acts of aggression which Turgidson is proposing.

Turgidson nevertheless forges on, respectfully maintaining that the President must decide between the lesser of two evils: one in which 20 million people will die as a result of his plan to back up Ripper's attack on Russia; the other in which 150 million people will be annihilated because of Russian retaliation to Ripper's bombing of Russian targets. "I'm not saying we wouldn't get our hair mussed," Turgidson concedes with thinly concealed disdain for the casualties involved. "I'm saying ten to twenty million people killed—tops—depending on the breaks."

Muffley nonetheless orders a detachment of soldiers to invade Burpleson Air Base and constrain General Ripper to phone him.

Turgidson warns, however, that any force trying to enter Burpleson once it has been sealed off will encounter severe casualties. General Faceman, who is to dispatch the force, is not impressed: "I think my boys can handle any opposition without too much difficulty." Since probably only a few hundred lives are likely to be lost, the engagement probably does not even qualify as "hair mussing" to the military mind. In the course of all of this speculation about soldiers killing their own comrades and the expendability of those who will become the casualties in the confrontation with the enemy, the specter of General Mireau from *Paths of*

**Stanley Kubrick and Peter Bull, DR. STRANGELOVE.**

*Glory* seems to be brooding over the scene.

Inside the B-52, Kong and his men are opening their survival kits while over the intercom the major itemizes the incongruous contents. There are, among other things, one drug issue containing morphine pills and vitamin pills; pep pills and tranquilizers; one miniature combination Russian phrase book and Bible; one issue of prophylactics; three lipsticks; and three pairs of nylon stockings. "Shoot," Kong comments, "a fellah could have a pretty good weekend in Vegas with all that."

The Russian ambassador, Alexei de Sadesky (Peter Bull), has

been summoned to the War Room by the President in spite of Turgidson's objections that the Commie will see the Big Board. De Sadesky's first act is to select some delicacies from an elaborate buffet table laden with goodies. Kubrick had originally included a scene in the film in which the War Room personnel engage in a free-for-all with pastry from the buffet table.

Kubrick devoted five days to shooting this sequence and had even thought of having the final scene in the War Room end with the President and the Russian ambassador still immersed in a mountain of goo. During a rehearsal period, however, a different ending—that of Strangelove's "miraculously" rising from his wheelchair—was worked out as the final image of the War Room in the film. But Kubrick retained the bulk of the pastry-throwing scene until he had the movie previewed. After watching this segment with an audience he decided to delete it completely from the final print of the picture because "it was too farcical and not consistent with the satiric tone of the rest of the film." This was a wise decision, since the humor in *Strangelove* is basically of the tongue-in-cheek variety, not slapstick.

Peter Bull still remembers the look on the face of the proprietor of the dry cleaning establishment near Shepperton Studios when the pile of costumes that had been saturated with pastry in the course of shooting the fight was delivered one Friday evening and requested to be ready for shooting the following Monday.

When the President fails to reach the Russian premier on the hot line, the ambassador suggests the phone number of what must be a Moscow brothel, judiciously noting that "our premier is a man of the people but he is also a man." While the President is trying to get through, a scuffle develops between the Russian envoy and Turgidson, who has caught him taking pictures of the Big Board with a camera concealed in a matchbox. De Sadesky is indulging in espionage just as Turgidson had predicted he would. The President intervenes, in one of the countless moments of irony that abound in the film: "Gentlemen," he scolds, "you can't fight in here. This is the War Room!"

With that, we switch to Burpleson Air Base, where a real battle is about to begin. Through binoculars the soldiers guarding the base see trucks of soldiers approaching in the distance. The latter are pictured on the screen with black masking around the edges of the frame to give the impression that the filmgoer is also peering at them through the binoculars. "Those trucks look like the real thing," one soldier says to his buddy, and the other man replies that the invaders must have obtained them as war surplus.

A machine gun in the foreground of the frame begins firing at

the troops in the distance and they begin to scatter, while Kubrick photographs them with film that approximates the grainy quality of newsreel footage. This kind of cinematography adds a naturalistic flavor to the battle sequence.

Once he has gotten through to Premier Kissoff, the President diffidently tries to explain the critical state of affairs in such a way that the latter will not go into a rage that will prompt him immediately to initiate retaliatory measures against the United States. The situation is not helped by the fact that "the man of the peo-

SL-9876

ple" is drunk. What follows is a brilliant comic monologue in which Sellers once more proves, as he did in *Lolita,* that he is the master of improvisation and of black comedy. Kubrick says that Sellers is always at his best in dealing with grotesque and horrifying circumstances which other actors would not think playable at all. This makes him the perfect ally for the director, of whom Alexander Walker has written, "Comedy, for Kubrick makes it possible to deal with issues that would be unbearable in any other form."

After asking the inebriated premier to turn down the music that is blaring in the background, Muffley continues: "Well, it's good that you're fine, and I'm fine too. I agree with you, it's great to be fine. Now then, Dimitri, you know how we've always talked about the possibility of something going wrong with the bomb. The *bomb,* Dimitri. The hydrogen bomb. Well now, what happened is that one of our base commanders . . . went a little funny in the head, and did a silly thing . . . He ordered his planes to attack your country. Well, let me finish, Dimitri. . . . Well, can you imagine how *I* feel about it? Why do you think I'm calling you, just to say hello?"

The President goes on to say that the bombers will not reach their objectives for another hour, and this statement is accompanied by a shot of their positions on the Big Board. Then Muffley haltingly offers to give to the Russian air staff a complete run-

154

down of the targets, both primary and secondary, for which the B-52s are aiming, along with their flight plans and defense systems. "If we can't recall them," he says, dreading the sound of his own words, "we are just going to have to help you destroy them."

After assuring the Russian premier that he is even sorrier about the calamity than Kissoff himself is, the President turns the phone over to de Sadesky, who is stunned by what he hears. "The fools," he gasps in a hoarse whisper; "the Doomsday machine—a device that will destroy all human and animal life on earth for one hundred years." If one of the bombers succeeds in dropping a nuclear bomb inside Russia the Doomsday machine will be set off automatically. "In ten months," laments the ambassador, "there will be so much fallout that the earth will be as dead as the surface of the moon. A Doomsday cloud of radioactivity will encircle the earth for ninety-three years!"

The Doomsday machine, he replies to the President's anxious inquiries, was created as a deterrent to possible nuclear attack and once it has been triggered it is designed to go off anyhow, even if someone tries to untrigger it. Once again in the film we see that man has forfeited his power of choice and placed himself at the mercy of his own mechanical creations, in which he has more faith than in himself.

At this point Dr. Strangelove comes forward in his wheelchair

to enter the discussion. He is Kubrick's vision of man's final capitulation to the machine: he is more of a robot than a human being, his mechanical arm spontaneously saluting Hitler, his former employer, his mechanical hand, gloved in black, at one point trying to strangle the flesh and blood that still remains in him. Strangelove is, moreover, reminiscent of Dr. Rotwang, the insane inventor in Fritz Lang's *Metropolis* (1926). To such a personage does Muffley now turn for advice.

Asked by the President if the U.S. had ever contemplated anything like a Doomsday mechanism, Strangelove concedes that plans for such a device were abandoned because he and his colleagues agreed that this idea would not be a *practical* deterrent to nuclear attack "for reasons that should now be obvious. It would have to be automatic in order to rule out the possibility of *human* error," he says with manifest disdain. Then he turns on the Russian envoy and demands to know why the machine was kept a secret: "The whole point of it was lost when you didn't tell the world." "It was to be announced at the party congress on Monday," de Sadesky responds with no little embarrassment. "The premier loves surprises."

Meanwhile, back at the base, Ripper sits forlornly listening to the approaching gunfire outside his citadel, which is proving more and more pregnable by the minute, and talking to Mandrake, who

**Above, Sterling Hayden, Peter Sellers and Stanley Kubrick, DR. STRANGELOVE.**

is at a loss to know how to reach his commanding officer, sunk as he is in the depths of his psychosis. Mandrake adopts a tentative, patronizing manner, seeking to ingratiate himself with Ripper to the point where the general will confide to him the secret code prefix that will enable him to recall the wing. Instead Ripper begins to reveal to him the full range of his paranoid psychosexual complex:

"Mandrake, do you realize that the Commies drink vodka but never water? Yet water is the source of all life. Seventy per cent of you is water, and we need fresh water to replenish our bodily fluids. I drink only distilled water or grain alcohol or rainwater. Fluoridation is the most monstrously conceived Communist plot we've ever had to face." Ripper is interrupted by a volley from the soldiers outside who are fighting their way into the building. It leaves his office a shambles. After blasting away with a few rounds of ammunition at the advancing troops that he thinks are Communist soldiers disguised in American uniforms, Ripper continues his explanation of his decision to launch a nuclear attack, all the while sucking on a cigar:

"Do you realize that there are studies under way to fluoridate salt, flour, milk, even children's ice cream, Mandrake?" Ripper first became aware that there was an international Communist plot to poison the drinking water "during the physical act of love. A profound sense of fatigue, a great sense of emptiness followed. Luckily I was able to interpret these feelings correctly as a loss of essence." In other words, in his frantic effort to explain away his impotency, Ripper has applied his ongoing paranoid suspicions of Russian conspiracies to his situation and convinced himself that the blame even for his sexual inadequacy can be laid at the door of the Russians.

By now Burpleson's defense force has surrendered. "My boys have let me down," Ripper moans, sitting in the middle of the chaos that was once his office. His cigar, which has, significantly, gone out, wilts limply between his tight lips; his sickly face is covered with perspiration. "They are going to be in here soon," he mumbles. "I don't know how I would stand up under torture. They might force the code out of me." "Give me the code and I'll keep it from them," says Mandrake spiritedly, snatching at any possibility of getting Ripper to confide in him.

But the general only lumbers on, in the grip of his madness: "I believe in a life hereafter, and I know I can answer for what I have done." Having relinquished his cigar, Ripper takes yet another phallic symbol in hand, a loaded pistol, and retreats into the bathroom, where he blows his brains out, as if he were unconsciously aping Adolf Hitler to the last. His body apparently has fallen against the door, for Mandrake has difficulty in pushing it open.

Aboard the bomber, the navigator reports that a missile is tracking the aircraft, so Kong institutes evasive action which results in the plane's being damaged but not destroyed. The Russians have evidently begun using the information that the President had passed on to them about the whereabouts of the bomber wing.

Kubrick creates a marvelous "you are there" sense of realism when the missile strikes: the voice of the navigator grows more and more apprehensive as he watches on his indicator the distance between the missile and the plane rapidly closing and announces this over the intercom. The shock of the explosion follows and the plane is filled with smoke and debris as it rocks under the impact of the missile's force. Radio operator Goldberg discovers as the plane settles back on course that the radio mechanism is out of commission: "I think the auto-destruct apparatus was hit and it blew itself up."

Because of all of those World War II films in which the viewer was supposed to root for the bomber to complete its mission in the face of enemy attack, one gets so caught up in the scenes on the flight deck that he momentarily catches himself empathizing with

Major Kong's satisfaction that the bomber can still reach both its primary and secondary targets, despite the damages the plane has sustained. Then the filmgoer is jolted into realizing that if *The Leper Colony* reaches either target, it will irreversibly ignite the Dooms-day machine. Kong, of course, does not know this, and so he reassures his crew, "Well, boys, we got three engines out and we got more holes in us than a horse trader's mule. The radio's gone and we're leaking fuel, and if we were flying any lower we would need sleigh bells on this thing. But at this height the Rooskies won't spot us on no radar screen."

Meanwhile Mandrake is studying the doodles left behind on Ripper's scratch pad. P.O.E. appears several times, sometimes spelled out as "Purity of Essence" or as "Peace on Earth." These two phrases represent two concepts that were connected in the warped mind of the lately deceased general.

Colonel Bat Guano (Keenan Wynn) shoots the lock off the office door and enters, his rifle poised for further use. Sizing up Mandrake in a uniform that is unknown to him, Guano asks caustically, "What kind of suit is that?" Mandrake, deeply offended that his rank has been questioned, replies icily, "This happens to be a Royal Air Force uniform. I am General Ripper's executive officer. I think I know the recall code; it's a variation of the letters

159

P.O.E. I have to call the Strategic Air Command immediately."

Guano, who has kept his rifle trained on Mandrake all this time, has sexual preoccupations of his own. He thinks that sexual "preeverts" are responsible for the current crisis and in that he is closer to the truth than he realizes. His assessment of the situation: "I think you are some kind of deviated preevert and that you were organizing some kind of mutiny of preeverts and that General Ripper found out about it." Mandrake's retort is swift, and implies that our proper Englishman is still nettled by Guano's slur on his uniform: "If you don't let me call the President, a court of inquiry will give you such a trimming that you'll be lucky to get to wear the uniform of a bloody toilet attendant." He convinces Guano to allow him to phone the President from a nearby booth since all of the other phones in the building are dead. Guano gives his permission with a warning that has become one of the most often repeated comic lines from the film: "If you try any preeversions in there, I'll blow your head off."

In another of the long string of ironies with which the film is filled, Mandrake discovers that he lacks the correct change for the coin telephone and that the White House will not accept a collect call. He demands that Guano fire into a Coke machine in order to obtain the necessary money. Guano reluctantly agrees, ruefully warning his prisoner that it is Mandrake who will have to answer to the Coca-Cola Company. This reverence for property is extraordinary coming from a man who has just successfully blasted his way into Burpleson Air Base with a tommy gun.

Guano shoots into the machine, bends down to scoop up the cascading coins and is squirted full in the face with Coke by the vindictive machine. Not only does this final comic touch bring the scene to a hilarious close; but it further symbolizes that the mechanical devices in the movie are beginning to turn against man, as if in anticipation of the final triumph of the Doomsday machine. Referring to Dr. Strangelove's mechanical arm in the same vein, Alexander Walker describes it as a piece of mechanism "in collusion" with all of the other rebellious mechanical apparatus in the picture.

In the War Room there is general rejoicing over the announcement that the recall code, which Mandrake has been able to transmit to the wing, has been acknowledged by all but the four planes that have been shot down. In a moment of pseudo-religious sentiment, Turgidson summons the assembly to attention while he addresses the Almighty as if He were a superior officer: "Lord, we have heard the wings of the Angel of Death fluttering over the Valley of Fear." The camera focuses on Dr. Strangelove, surrounded by darkness, as the general rumbles out these words.

Turgidson is interrupted by a call on the hot line from Premier Kissoff, who stormily informs President Muffley that one of the planes previously thought to have been shot down is still airborne and headed for its target. "I'm afraid they're jamming your radar," Muffley apologizes. "I'm sorry, Dimitri, but they are trained to do that. I guess you're just going to have to get that plane. Put everything you've got into those sectors and you can't miss."

Turgidson looks aghast as he listens to Muffley's words to Kissoff. When the President asks the general if that plane might possibly reach one of its targets, Turgidson replies with mindless euphoria, "If the pilot's really good he can barrel that baby in so low—you just got to see it sometimes—a big plane like a B-52, its jet exhaust frying chickens in the barnyard. Has he got a chance of reaching his target? Why, hell, yes, he has!" Finally grasping the implications of what he has just said, Turgidson, for once, is struck dumb.

The navigator of *The Leper Colony,* however, is much less sanguine than Turgidson about the plane's potential to carry out its mission. He advises Kong that because the rate of fuel loss is accelerating, the aircraft can no longer reach either its primary or its secondary target. With a determination that increases in inverse proportion to the obstacles that are mounting to bar his way, Kong fumes, "Well, shoot! We didn't come this far to dump this thing in the drink. What's the nearest target?" The navigator sets a new course and the plane is on its way to the only target it can hope to reach before it runs out of gas.

As the airship approaches its new objective, the bombardier finds that the bomb doors will not open. "Stay on the bomb run, boys; I'm going to get those doors open," Kong vows. The drumming musical theme associated with all of the scenes on the flight deck becomes steadily louder and more persistent as Kong drops into the bomb bay, moving toward the camera between the two huge nuclear bombs in the foreground. He sits astride one of the bombs and fusses with wires on the bomb door circuits, which spit and flare at him defiantly, while the navigator overhead announces on the intercom that the plane is approaching its target.

As the navigator says anxiously, "Target in sight! Where the hell is Major Kong?" the bomb bay doors swing open. With the immensities of space yawning beneath him, Kong manages to dislodge the bomb on which he is seated from its chamber and he begins to plummet with it toward earth. Kong waves his stetson in the air and gives out with a rodeo shout as he hurtles downward.

The bomb between his legs looks like a gigantic symbol of potency, thus rounding out the sexual metaphors which permeate the film. Specifically the immense phallic image recalls General Ripper's fear of impotency, which had triggered the bombing mission in the first place. The screen turns a dazzling white as the bomb lands on target, and we return for the last time to the brooding shadows of the War Room.

In this moment of utter desolation, Dr. Strangelove speaks up. He is never at a loss for a plan for the survival of himself and his colleagues, whatever may happen to humanity at large. He suggests that it would be quite easy to preserve a small nucleus of the human species at the bottom of some of the deeper mine shafts. "It would not be difficult, mein Führer," he says, in spite of himself. "Nuclear reactors could provide power. Greenhouses could produce plant life. Animals could be bred and slaughtered." "People could stay there for years?" the President muses. "I'd hate to decide who goes down and who stays up."

Strangelove responds with maniacal glee, "It could easily be decided by a computer programmed for youth, health, sexual fertility." As the middle-aged men around him stare at Strangelove menacingly, he hastily adds, "Of course, our top government and

military men must be included. With a ratio of ten women to every man, I estimate we could reattain the present gross national product in twenty years." Dr. Strangelove's calculations are plainly teaching his listeners to "stop worrying and love the bomb" with the strange love he has had for it all along.

The sexual implications of Strangelove's plan appeal particularly to Turgidson, who asks with feigned detachment, "Doctor, wouldn't this necessitate the end of the so-called monogamous sexual relationship?" Indeed it will; because the male survivors will have to breed many offspring, "the women will be selected for their sexual characteristics, which will have to be of a highly stimulating nature," the doctor answers. Life in the mine shaft, as pictured by Strangelove, will involve assembly-line sex, which is just the kind of mechanical process that would appeal to him.

The survivors will not even be depressed by the loss of so many of their loved ones, he points out: "When they go down everyone will be alive. The prevailing emotion afterward should be one of nostalgia for those left behind, combined with a spirit of bold curiosity for the adventure ahead."

Even in the midst of cosmic calamity, man remains true to his perverse inclinations. The Russian ambassador surreptitiously takes pictures of the Big Board with a camera concealed in his watch. He disregards the fact that these photos will be of no earthly use for normal espionage purposes now that life on this planet is doomed to extinction for a century. And Turgidson, with his abiding paranoia about Russian conspiracies, which is surpassed only by General Ripper's, begins yammering at the President that the Soviets may try "an immediate sneak attack to take over our mine shaft space. Mr. President, we cannot allow a mine shaft gap!"

Just at this moment Strangelove miraculously rises from his wheelchair. "Mein Führer," he exclaims, "I can walk!" Strangelove, with all of his false limbs, is more of a machine than a man. Therefore once the Doomsday machine has been detonated, he experiences a surge of energy, a sympathetic vibration, as it were, with this ultimate and decisive triumph of the machine over man.

There follows a series of blinding explosions while on the sound track we hear a popular ditty which Kubrick resurrected from the Second World War: "We'll meet again, don't know where, don't know when. . . ." (Kubrick told me that he used the original recording by Vera Lynn, which served not only to bring the song back to popularity but Miss Lynn as well.)

In the context of the film's ending the song becomes an anthem of the millions who will be extinguished by the radioactive fallout precipitated by the Doomsday machine. The singer fondly reflects that the survivors "will be happy to know that as you saw me go I was singing this song." Another verse speaks of the future, when the blue skies will drive the dark (radioactive) clouds away. This is illustrated by the vision of a distant sunset amid the black clouds now enveloping the earth.

This final touch of black comedy emphasizes the fact that the humor which Kubrick had originally thought to exclude from *Strangelove* provides some of its most meaningful moments. They are made up, as one reviewer wrote, of the incongruities, the banalities and the misunderstandings that we are constantly aware of in our lives. "On the brink of annihilation they become irresistibly absurd." As Charlie Chaplin once said of black comedy with reference to his own *Monsieur Verdoux* (1947), "I saw a chance to take a tragedy and satirize it. It is a phenomenon of life that, thank God, a thing when it is overstated becomes ridiculous. This is the salvation of man's sanity."

One of the humorous elements of *Strangelove* is the collection of absurd names with which Kubrick and his co-scripters have blessed their major characters. Many of the names have sexual connotations, such as General Jack D. Ripper, named for the notorious sexual psychopath. Ripper reveals his fears of impotency to Captain Mandrake, who is named after the mandrake root, a plant which in mythic lore is said to encourage fertility. General Buck Turgidson's last name is made up of an adjective meaning swollen (referring in this case to the male member) and the word for male offspring. The bald Merken Muffley's first name is a reference to female pubic hair.

Other names in the movie have connotations other than sexual. There are the two Russians, Ambassador de Sadesky and Premier Kissoff, whose names speak for themselves; and Colonel Bat Guano, whose last name is defined by Webster's as bird manure. And, of course, the weird scientist of the film's title, whose strange love of death and destruction, nurtured by a lifetime spent in perfecting instruments of destruction, enlivens him in a way that nothing else can. All of these names contribute to the black comedy of the film.

Critic Pauline Kael, however, who adored the black comedy of *Lolita,* was not happy with *Strangelove*'s further foray into the same territory. "*Dr. Strangelove* opened a new movie era. It ridiculed everything and everybody it showed," she wrote in *Kiss Kiss Bang Bang.* "*Dr. Strangelove* was clearly intended as a cautionary movie; it meant to jolt us awake to the dangers of the bomb by showing us the insanity of the course we were pursuing. But artists' warnings about war and the dangers of total annihilation never tell us how we are supposed to regain control, and *Dr. Strangelove,* chortling over madness, did not indicate any possibilities for sanity."

Kubrick's own response to this kind of criticism would be to point out, as he did in *Playboy,* that "in the deepest sense I believe in man's potential and in his capacity for progress. In *Dr. Strangelove* I was dealing with the inherent irrationality in man that threatens to destroy him; that irrationality is with us as strongly today, and must be conquered. But a recognition of insanity doesn't imply celebration of it; nor a sense of despair and futility about the possibility of curing it."

Miss Kael's criticism of the movie seems to presuppose that a motion-picture director is somehow obligated to suggest solutions to the problems with which he deals in his films. On the contrary, what a serious filmmaker like Kubrick hopes to do in a movie like *Strangelove* is to explore a problem as accurately as possible in a visual medium in order to provide the viewer with what another director, Stanley Kramer, has termed "a climate of examination" in which the filmgoer can consider the problem for himself. Kramer continues: "I'm convinced that you can't change anyone's mind with a movie. However, I do believe that you can stimulate people to think about a problem, to perhaps consider it from another angle. It's my hope that people can come out of a theater thinking, 'Well, I never thought of it in just that way before!' I try to throw a searchlight on a problem. We can't pretend to solve it, but we can illuminate it from one angle." Or, as Kubrick himself puts it, "Works of art affect us when they illuminate something we already feel; they don't change us."

In *Strangelove,* then, Kubrick has turned the searchlight of satire on the "balance of terror" that the nuclear powers seek to maintain to hold each other in check. In so doing Kubrick has illuminated the common foibles of ordinary humanity as well, human flaws that are all the more obvious when they come to the surface in the context of a cosmic catastrophe.

It is an unquestioned tribute to Kubrick that *Strangelove* has proved more durable than later black-comedy satires of the same type, such as *Catch-22* (1970). The unsettling theme that we have watched emerging from *Strangelove* is the plight of fallible man placing himself at the mercy of his infallible machines and bringing about his own destruction by this abdication of moral responsibility. These sentiments are very close to those which Chaplin expressed in his closing speech in *The Great Dictator* (1940): "We think too much and feel too little. More than machinery we need humanity. More than cleverness we need kindness and gentleness. Without these qualities, life will be violent and all will be lost."

Kubrick further explored his dark vision of man in a mechanistic age in *2001: A Space Odyssey,* which would take us still further into the future and pose even more searching questions about man's destiny to the film audience. As Arthur C. Clarke, the co-author of *2001,* has commented, "What makes *2001* so unique is that it poses metaphysical, philosophical and even religious questions. I don't pretend that we have the answers. But the questions are certainly worth thinking about."

# Chapter Seven
# From Here to Infinity:

# 2001: A Space Odyssey (1968)

In recalling how the initial notion for *2001* came to him, Kubrick says, "Most astronomers and other scientists interested in the whole question are strongly convinced that the universe is crawling with life; much of it, since the numbers are so staggering, equal to us in intelligence, or superior, simply because human intelligence has existed for so relatively short a period. I therefore think it is presumptuous for us to suppose that we are the only occupants of the cosmos. The chemical and biological processes of forming life are not so extraordinary that they should not have occurred countless times throughout the universe. So I became interested in man's response to his first contact with an advanced world. As someone once said, 'Sometimes I think we're alone, and sometimes I think we're not. In either case, I find the idea quite astonishing.' "

After reading Arthur C. Clarke's science fiction short story "The Sentinel," Kubrick got in touch with its author. He told Clarke that he thought the story could serve as the basis of a screenplay, and the rest is movie history. They first turned the short story into a novel in order to develop completely the potentialities of the plot, and then transformed that into a movie script. M-G-M bought their package, originally entitled *Journey Beyond the Stars,* and financed the color, Cinerama film for $6 million. After four years of work on the film, the budget eventually rose to more than $10 million.

The procedure of writing a novel that can be used as the source of a screenplay is not as unorthodox as it may sound. Graham Greene utilized the same technique when he was creating *The Third Man.* "My approach to writing a screenplay is to write a treatment of the story which is then turned into a script," Greene

**Stanley Kubrick and Arthur C. Clarke, 2001.**

has told me. "I write the treatment like a novel. What today is known as the novel of *The Third Man* is really the treatment which I did before writing the script." As Greene explains it, he finds it almost impossible to capture characterization and atmosphere "in the dull shorthand of a script. One must have the sense of more material than one needs to draw on." Similarly, *2001* started as a novel-length treatment that could serve as the raw material for the screenplay which Kubrick and Clarke were going to write.

The novel called *2001: A Space Odyssey* which Arthur Clarke published shortly after the release of the film is basically his re-working of the prose treatment which he and Kubrick had constructed prior to working on their finished screenplay, and I shall refer to it throughout this chapter as the treatment for the movie script of *2001*. It is a great help in detecting how Clarke and Kubrick's ideas changed in the course of their developing the treatment into a screenplay.

Clarke and Kubrick began to compose *2001* in the spring of 1964, only a couple of months after the premiere of *Dr. Strangelove*. By the end of the year the first draft of the prose treatment was completed. As the co-authors revised their work, the "female" computer named Athena became the "male" computer Hal; the

170

"Dawn of Man" sequence, which had at first been inserted into the plot as a flashback, was moved back to the beginning of the story as a prologue; and the monolith, which began in "The Sentinel" as a pyramid, became a black rectangular block.

Even while they were still writing the script under the tentative title of *Journey Beyond the Stars*, Kubrick and Clarke were aware of parallels between their story and Homer's epic poem *The Odyssey*. To the ancient Greeks, Kubrick said at the time, the vast stretches of the sea must have had the same sort of mystery and remoteness that space has for man in the space age. Moreover, the islands that Homer's Ulysses visited "were no less remote to his readers than the planets that our astronauts will be encountering are to us. *Journey* also shares with *The Odyssey* a concern for wandering, exploration and adventure." With all of these resonances of Homer's *Odyssey*, it is not surprising that Kubrick changed the name of the film on which he was working to *2001: A Space Odyssey* before shooting began in December 1965.

Filming began at Shepperton Studios outside London, which had sound stages big enough to accommodate the largest sets needed for the movie. Then the production moved in January 1966 to the smaller Borehamwood Studios, which were near Kubrick's home (and which have since been converted to a refrigeration storage center). By May 1966, Kubrick had finished shooting with the cast and then went on to spend another year and a half creating the 205 separate special effects process shots which comprise about half of the total film, and account for more than half of the movie's budget. Kubrick did everything possible to make each special effect completely authentic, seeing to it that it conformed to what scientists projected, on the basis of known data, that space travel would be like in the twenty-first century.

When the script called for a process shot that no known cinematic technique could provide, Kubrick and his technical staff would have to devise ways of creating the effect in question. Jeremy Bernstein, who visited the set while *2001* was in production at Borehamwood, remembers watching a group of Kubrick's special effects staff working on minutely detailed scale models of spacecrafts that would be made to look, through the wonders of process photography, like the real thing. Kubrick referred to their working area in the studio as "Santa's Workshop."

Each special effects shot might include several elements, each of which had to be photographed separately. For example, one shot might include a scale-model spaceship sailing through the atmosphere with drawings of the various planets in the background which would be visible at this point in its flight. The shot of the spacecraft would have to be superimposed on the shots of the planets in order to create a single image on the screen.

It is not surprising that Douglas Trumbull, one of the supervisors of the special photographic effects, later got the chance to direct a science fiction film of his own, *Silent Running* (1973), with Bruce Dern.

The special effects work, however, was also the principal cause of the escalation of the film's budget, and Kubrick has an abiding gratitude for Robert O'Brien, who was in charge of production at M-G-M when *2001* was being made. "He realized," says Kubrick, "that it was necessary for us, somehow, to overcome the previously unsolved problems of making the special effects in the film look completely realistic, and he understood that new techniques were being devised. There were probably great pressures on him from the other studio executives, but he never mentioned them to me."

*2001* began with a short story, the essence of which was preserved throughout every version of the script. Hence it would be interesting to begin our consideration of the film with "The Sentinel." This tale, originally published by Clarke in 1948, is narrated by a geologist who is part of a lunar expedition in 1996. In the course of the investigation party's stay on the moon he notices a distant object atop a mountain peak, glittering as it catches the sunlight. When he induces his assistant to climb the mountain to examine the artifact, he discovers that it is a pyramid-shaped object, twelve feet high, which he takes to be a shrine of some sort. He conjectures that perhaps some lunar civilization, long since extinct, placed it there.

On further investigation, however, he comes to realize that "it was as alien to the moon as I myself." The shining pyramid is surrounded by an invisible shield which the geologist and his assistant are able to break through only after two decades of experiments. They then dismantle the artifact only to find that its advanced technology is completely incomprehensible to them.

The narrator theorizes that millions of years before, representatives of a civilization that perhaps even then had surpassed the present evolution of our own left the pyramid on the moon as a token of their passage. It was a sentinel designed to signal to them when it was discovered that the human race had achieved a sufficient degree of civilization to have conquered space and reached the moon. The story ends on a tense note of expectancy: "We have set off the fire alarm and have nothing to do but wait. I do not think we will have to wait for long."

With this neat little open-ended episode as a starting point, Clarke and Kubrick set to work developing a fully realized story that would explore all of the implications hinted at in "The Sentinel." When they finished the prose treatment, they incorporated some of the explanatory narration from the treatment into the shooting script. In addition, Kubrick appended a ten-minute prologue to the film, consisting of edited interviews with several scientists about their speculations on extraterrestrial life elsewhere in the universe.

After screening *2001* for M-G-M executives in March 1968, however, Kubrick decided to cut the entire prologue (a partially edited transcript of which can be found in Jerome Agel's *The Making of Kubrick's 2001*). By this time he had already eliminated all of the film's narration, most of which occurred in the "Dawn of Man" prologue.

Since Kubrick had used narration in his films from the very beginning of his career, it is significant that he removed every trace of explanatory narration from the final version of *2001*. In the past Kubrick had turned to narration as the most simple and direct way to telegraph exposition to the audience. There is, for instance, the foreboding spoken prologue of *Dr. Strangelove* and the narrator who keeps the viewer posted on developments throughout *The Killing*.

When he came to *2001*, however, Kubrick decided that "the feel of the experience is the important thing, not the ability to verbalize or analyze it." He wanted to elicit a response from his audience at a deeper level than that of narration and dialogue. Here for the first time was a superspectacle that did not depend on a strong plot line to carry its audience along. Indeed, the same set of characters do not even persevere throughout the entire film. This makes the movie seem, superficially at least, to be a series of episodes that are only remotely connected. It is principally through images rather than words, then, that the film unfolds. "Less than half of *2001* has dialogue," Kubrick notes. "It attempts to communicate more to the subconscious and to the feelings than to the intellect."

It is true that in the past some films have been freighted with spoken commentary which only served to stand between the moviegoer and his experience of the film itself. A classic example of supremely unnecessary narration occurred in the case of Fred Zinnemann's 1948 film *The Search,* about displaced persons after the Second World War. Without the director's knowledge or consent, a narrator was added at the beginning of the film to explain the situation in postwar Europe, already obvious from the telling images on the screen. James Agee rightly complained in *The Nation,* "While starving children grab for bread, a lady commentator informs us that they are hungry and that the bread is bread."

More recently, when Joseph Losey's *Secret Ceremony* (1968) was released to television, Universal added a plodding narration spoken by a psychiatrist who pointed out to the audience that the two emotionally tortured women played by Elizabeth Taylor and Mia Farrow were psychologically disturbed. This robbed the viewer of the chance to infer the sinister implications that lay beneath the surface of the story. Understandably, Losey had his name removed from the credits of the TV version of the film.

A film director must decide, therefore, when a narrator's commentary is going to add depth to the story he is telling and when it is going to be simply in the way. Kubrick opted for the second possibility in *2001*, but there were those who were associated with the film who did not agree with him. Dr. Frederick Ordway, who served for eighteen months as a technical consultant on the film, wrote Kubrick after seeing it that the director should restore "the splendid words of narration." Kubrick stuck to his original decision, however, and more and more critics have come to agree with him.

In her *Filmguide to 2001* Carolyn Geduld writes that, in effect, the early cuts made by Kubrick took much of the science out of the film's science fiction. But the shadowy drift further and further away from the prose treatment's explicit prose "is part of *2001*'s great achievement and great allure." Once we consider the film as it stands in its final version I shall indicate some of the things that appear in Clarke's published version of the film's prose treatment that did not find their way onto the screen when the movie was released in April 1968. Then the reader can decide whether or not he thinks that these items were a loss to the film.

The opening image in the movie shows the earth, moon and sun in vertical alignment with a black monolith below them. This shot is accompanied by the crashing opening chords of Richard Strauss's *Thus Spake Zarathustra*. This symmetrical arrangement of a group of heavenly bodies with respect to a black monolith often occurs in the film, along with the Strauss music, when man is about to make a further evolutionary leap forward.

This opening tableau is followed, after the credits, by the prologue, "The Dawn of Man." The sunrise that fills the wide screen is a metaphor for the dawn of civilization, as prehistoric ape-men of the Pleistocene epoch begin to appear and prance about. Kubrick wisely used human beings wearing authentically designed ape suits (rather than the genuine article) since their movements are faintly recognizable as pre-human in a way that subtly suggests that these ape-men are on the threshold of intelligence. At the same time, the actors in their ape outfits are so convincing

that the director was able to use real baby chimps in the same scenes with them without destroying the illusion of their performances.

One of the ape-men is attacked by a leopard, demonstrating how they are prey to all of the ferocious animals that roam about the area. The ape-men are not big enough or strong enough to protect themselves from these enemies. Hence they are in no position to be carnivorous and have to subsist on the ever decreasing amount of vegetation that is available to them. The water supply is diminishing as well, and one group of ape-men must drive another group away from the water hole in order to gain access to it. At night each family of hungry ape-men huddles together in clusters for warmth and security. Nearby a leopard, his incandescent eyes shining in the darkness, guards a zebra which it has killed for its

sustenance.

In the morning one of the ape-men, called Moon-Watcher (Dan Richter) in the treatment but nameless in the film, is awakened by the eerie sound of humming voices (actually György Ligeti's unearthly music). He stares at the black monolithic slab that has apparently materialized during the night. Consternation reins as he and his mates prowl around the object in a mixture of fear and curiosity. Finally Moon-Watcher reaches out tentatively and touches the slab as the music swells. Then others follow his lead.

In the next scene Moon-Watcher is rooting about among some bones, which are all that remain of a ravaged animal. Then Kubrick interpolates a shot of the monolith, photographed imposingly from below, with the mystical alignment of sun and moon above it, suggesting that the monolith is overseeing what is about

to happen. Without premeditation, Moon-Watcher grasps one of the skeleton bones in his hand and, in majestic slow motion, brings it crashing down on the animal skull before him. As he delivers more and more blows on the exploding skeleton, Kubrick intercuts shots of a live animal being felled by similar blows. This succession of shots brilliantly indicates that the ape-man has grasped the principle of using the tool-weapon to kill game.

No longer condemned to vegetarian fare, the ape-men are seen munching on raw meat. Moon-Watcher has already implemented his newfound knowledge. Somehow sensing that his breakthrough has entitled him to ascendancy in his tribe, he leads his contingent to the water hole, where they take possession of it by driving another pack away. When one of these defies Moon-Watcher, the latter, brandishing a bone like a scepter, suddenly raises it against his opponent and crushes his skull with it. The man-ape is learning to extend his own physical powers through the use of a tool-weapon to kill one of his own kind, and in so doing has ironically taken a step toward humanity.

Following suit, his adherents menacingly pick up other bones from the ground while the bested tribe slinks away from the site of their defeat with a few ineffectual shrieks. As the victorious man-ape throws his weapon spiraling into the air there is a dissolve to a spaceship soaring through space in the year 2001.

"It's simply an observable fact," Kubrick has said, "that all man's technology grew out of his discovery of the tool-weapon. There's no doubt that there is a deep emotional relationship between man and his machine-weapons, which are his children. The machine is beginning to assert itself in a very profound way, even attracting affection and obsession. Man has always worshiped beauty, and I think there's a new kind of beauty in the world."

That beauty is marvelously evident in this first sequence in space, in which Space Station 5, which resembles a revolving Ferris wheel, spins gracefully on its way, orbiting two hundred miles above the earth to the strains of "The Blue Danube" waltz. "It's hard to find anything much better than 'The Blue Danube,' " Kubrick comments, "for depicting grace and beauty in turning. It also gets as far away as you can get from the cliché of space music."

Kubrick has punctuated the whole picture with previously written music instead of using a score especially composed for the film, as he had originally intended to do. During the long months of production, the director had relied on "temporary music tracks" of classical music to provide the proper atmosphere for the scenes that he was working on. When it came time to have the vet-

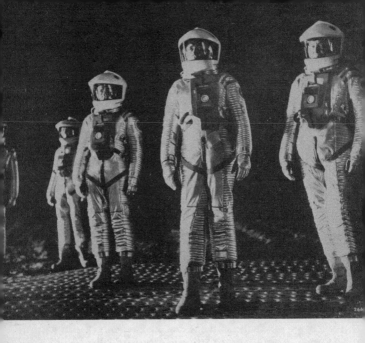

eran cinema composer Alex North write the score for the film, however, the director decided to stick with the selections that he had gotten used to working with all along. The popularity of the two recordings of sound track music from *2001* makes it clear that the music which Kubrick chose did catch the imagination of filmgoers. Indeed, Strauss's *Thus Spake Zarathustra* in particular has become as closely associated with *2001* as Rossini's "*William Tell Overture*" has with the Lone Ranger and the "Colonel Bogey" march has with *The Bridge on the River Kwai*.

Spaceship *Orion* is nosing its way toward Space Station 5, which is a kind of "halfway house" for passengers on their way to the moon. *Orion* carries only one passenger, Dr. Heywood Floyd, chairman of the U.S. Council of Astronauts (William Sylvester). As the spacecraft docks, a stewardess speaks the first words to be heard in the film, some thirty minutes after it has begun. "Here you are, sir. Main level, please." "See you on the way back," Floyd grins.

This is a fair sampling of the sparse, perfunctory type of dialogue that is used in the film. When some critics opined that the film needed more dialogue, Kubrick replied that he had tried to work things out so that anything important in the movie was trans-

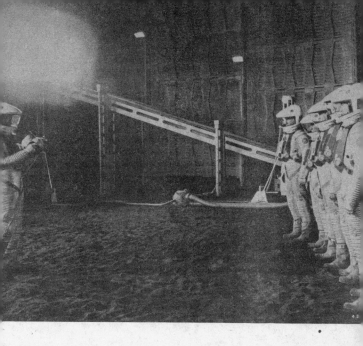

mitted through action rather than in dialogue scenes, which account for only forty-six minutes of the film's 141-minute running time. "There are certain areas of feeling and reality," Kubrick told the *New York Times*, "which are notably inaccessible to words. Non-verbal forms of expression such as music and painting can get at these areas, but words are a terrible straitjacket. It's interesting how many prisoners of that straitjacket resent its being loosened."

As Floyd goes through security formalities at the space station, he gives his destination as the moon. A number of people who saw the film, Kubrick discovered, thought that Floyd was headed for a planet called Clavius because later on in the scene Floyd speaks of the moon crater Clavius. "From what he says to the security personnel, however, his destination could not be clearer," says Kubrick.

While waiting for spaceship *Aries* to take him on his journey to the moon, Floyd puts in a call to earth on a Bell picturephone to his daughter Squirt (played by Kubrick's youngest daughter Vivian). He wishes her a happy birthday and expresses his regrets that he will not be able to be present at her party the following day. When he asks to speak to his wife he is told that she is out.

More than one commentator on *2001* has pointed out that the only scenes in the film which show anything approximating family feeling are in the "Dawn of Man" prologue. Space age man, living his computerized existence, seems to have programmed normal human feeling almost entirely out of his daily living. This concept is further elucidated as Floyd chats with some Russian colleagues who are on their way home from the Russian sector of the moon. A female scientist remarks casually that she now sees little of her husband, also a scientist, because he spends so much of his time engaged in experiments on the ocean floor.

With a tight-lipped cordiality that recalls the War Room scenes from *Dr. Strangelove,* Floyd exchanges pleasantries with the Russian scientists until one of them inquires with careful nonchalance why the American sector of the moon has been incommunicado for the last ten days. "Two days ago," he says, "a rocket bus was denied permission to make an emergency landing. Is there an epidemic going on?" Floyd can only answer with some embarrassment, "I am not at liberty to discuss this." He then makes his hasty departure for the space-shuttle *Aries* that will carry him to the moon.

Once he has arrived there, he is hurried to a conference room where he can at last discuss his mission, the necessity of the news blackout in the American sector of the moon, and the cover story that there is an epidemic there. As Floyd is introduced and makes his initial remarks, he is photographed from the opposite end of the conference table, some distance away from the camera. Then, as he begins to reveal the reason for these precautions, the camera moves in closer, as if the filmgoer were being beckoned nearer to share these confidences.

Secrecy must be maintained, Floyd explains, in order to preserve as confidential the discovery that has been made at the moon crater Clavius. He has been summoned there to gather further information about that discovery, one which "may well prove to be among the most significant in the history of science." There is a token expression of misgivings about the cover story since it might cause needless worry for the loved ones of the Clavius personnel back on earth. But, given the low level of familial concern that characterizes twentieth-century man in the film, this anxiety is quickly allayed by Floyd.

On the way to the Tycho excavation site in a moon bus, Dr. Ralph Albertson, one of the directors of the Clavius Space Station, compliments Floyd on his excellent speech at the briefing, presumably because Floyd was able to avoid communicating anything of real consequence to his listeners. Now that they are en route to view this momentous find, however, Floyd and his fellow experts can speak more freely.

It seems that a monolith has been uncovered beneath the surface of the moon, apparently buried there some 4 million years ago. As Floyd and his companions, wearing space suits, approach the monolith, we hear the same weird music that accompanied the discovery of the first monolith by the ape-men. This one, we infer, was buried on the moon at the same time that its twin was placed on earth and found by Moon-Watcher and his tribe. The first one had not been buried since the man-apes would not have been capable of detecting or unearthing it. The scientists have christened the present monolithic slab TMA-1 for Tycho Magnetic Anomaly-One.

A hand-held camera, probably operated by Kubrick himself, follows Floyd and the others down the ramp into the excavated area where the monolith stands. The blazing lights surrounding it glare into the camera, symbolizing the dazzling discovery that the ostensibly inert slab truly is, betokening as it does a clue to the existence of a race much older and more intelligent than man in the universe. Floyd reaches out and bashfully touches the monolith, just as Moon-Watcher had done centuries before. Then he and his colleagues stand in front of TMA-1 to be photographed with the find as a record of their visit. Just at that moment the fourteen-day lunar night comes to an end and a shaft of sunlight streams down on the slab for the first time since it was dug up, touching off a piercing scream of noise from TMA-1 which reverberates inside the radio receivers of Floyd and his fellow astronauts.

This radio signal emitted by the monolith, Arthur Clarke points out, is a kind of burglar alarm which telegraphs to those beings that buried it on the moon that man has developed technologically to the point that he has reached the moon and found the monolith. Man has thereby proved himself a species worthy of help toward further technological progress. Since the radio signal was aimed at the planet Jupiter (we learn later in the film), a mission is now outfitted to pursue the investigation of extraterrestrial intelligent life to that remote planet by seeking the target at which the radio signal was aimed.

Eighteen months later, then, a giant exploration ship called *Discovery-1* has been launched on the Jupiter expedition. Inside are two astronauts, David Bowman (Keir Dullea) and Frank Poole (Gary Lockwood), who consider themselves "caretakers" of the craft because the spaceship is really controlled by a computer, HAL 9000. It is so named because it is a *h*euristically programmed *al*gorithmic computer. Kubrick's belief that "the machine is be-

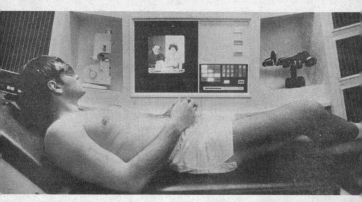

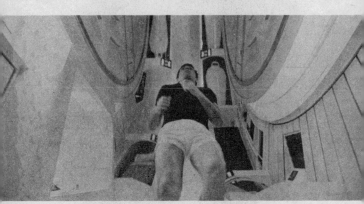

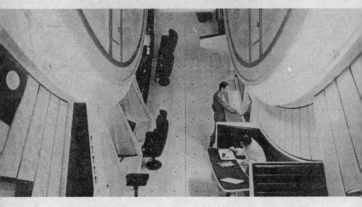

ginning to assert itself in a very profound way, even attracting affection and obsession," is illustrated in this part of the film by repeated juxtapositions of man with his human failings and fallibility immersed in machinery: beautiful, functional, but heartless. Kubrick, as always, is on the side of man. We shall shortly see here, as in *Strangelove,* that human fallibility is less likely to destroy man than the relinquishing of his moral responsibilities to supposedly infallible machines.

There are three other astronauts on board *Discovery-1* who have been sealed in refrigerated hibernation cases to preserve their energies—and the supplies on board—until the end of the nine-month journey. All of this is explained by a BBC-TV announcer on a news program which Bowman and Poole watch on their separate television receivers. The pair had taped an interview with the news commentator a day or two earlier. The announcer further tells his listeners that the HAL 9000 computer is programmed to mimic most of the workings of the human brain, including speech. He and his twin computer back at Mission Control, Hal obligingly informs the TV audience, are, "by any practical definitions of the words, foolproof and incapable of error." Bowman adds during the interview that Hal acts as if he has genuine emotions, "but that is something no one can truthfully answer." By the end of the film that question will be answered.

If in Hal we see Kubrick's vision of the machine becoming human, in Bowman and Poole we observe how man is becoming dehumanized and machine-like because of his close association with his technological offspring. The astronauts are portrayed as being further out of touch with genuine human feelings than Floyd and the other scientists in the previous segment of the film were. Floyd at least expressed regret at not being able to join his daughter for her birthday celebration. Poole, on the other hand, monitors a taped birthday message from his parents back home with total disinterest, lying under a sunlamp all the while. Even his prone position implies that the difference between this unresponsive human being and the three men sleeping in their hibernation tanks is minimal.

Bowman is not much more demonstrative in his behavior. The two men rarely interact, except in a crisis, and are hardly ever photographed in the same frame. They even mutely watch the same program on separate TV receivers. Bowman and Poole talk to Hal more often than they converse with each other.

In one conversation with Bowman, Hal hedgingly asks him if he has any ideas about the true nature of the mission, something which still remains a secret from Bowman and Poole. "Maybe I'm just projecting my own feelings," Hal goes on; "those strange stories before we left about something being dug up on the moon . . ." Bowman's shrewd reply is, "You're working up your crew psychology report, aren't you, Hal?"

Hal's soothing voice actually belongs to Canadian actor Douglas Rain, whom Kubrick originally engaged to do the film's narration. After Hal's part had been recorded by Martin Balsam with a great deal of expression, the director decided that Rain's reading of the lines in an even-toned, unemotional manner would lend an intriguing ambiguity to Hal's statements, teasing the film-goer into wondering at times what Hal is really "thinking" and "feeling."

When Hal nonchalantly announces that he has detected a potential failure in the Alpha-Echo-35 (AE-35) communications unit in the antenna outside the spaceship, Poole and Bowman, at least, do not suspect that this apparently routine eventuality will lead to catastrophe. Bowman decides that the unit will have to be checked immediately, since the antenna system is *Discovery-1*'s sole means of maintaining contact with the earth 500 million miles away.

Bowman enters one of the space pods aboard *Discovery-1,* which are used for extra-vehicular activity, and steers it outside the ship and as near as possible to the suspect antenna. He then leaves the pod long enough to remove the AE-35 communications unit for inspection and replace it with a spare. Back inside *Discovery-1,* Bowman and Poole can detect no malfunction in the unit.

They are informed by their contact at Mission Control in Houston that Hal's twin computer there has reported that Hal is in error. (Mission Control is played by Chief Warrant Officer Franklin W. Miller, U.S. Air Force traffic controller in England when the film was made.) Hal, ostensibly unruffled by this disclosure, suggests that the astronauts put the unit back in operation and let it fail: "We can afford to be out of communication with earth for the short time it will take to change it. Then the cause of the trouble can be found. Any mistake must be attributed to *human* error." Hal emphasizes the word *human* with the same disdain that Dr. Strangelove had used. "The 9000 series has a perfect operational record." Man, the implication seems to be, has not.

As the first part of *2001* draws to a close, Bowman and Poole enter one of the space capsules, where they intend to discuss the situation out of Hal's earshot. But they do not realize that they are not out of his eye-shot. In a marvelous bit of editing, Kubrick shows us a close-up of the luminous red "eye" of the computer intercut with shots of the camera panning back and forth between

**Gary Lockwood and Keir Dullea, 2001.**

the moving lips of the two men. Hal is reading the astronauts' lips.

Their plan is to reinstall the original AE-35 unit. If it does not fail as Hal predicted, it will be clear that Hal and not the communications unit is faulty. "That would pretty well wrap it up as far as Hal is concerned, wouldn't it," says Poole impassively. Hal would then have to be disconnected so that the mission could be run by remote control by his twin computer at Mission Control.

At this point, Arthur Clarke feels, one can still sympathize with Hal, since any miscalculation he may have made ultimately is traceable to the technicians at Mission Control who programmed him: "Hal is indeed correct in attributing his mistaken report to human error." In other words, no machine that man builds can be any more infallible than the fallible human beings who have built it, and man's greatest error is his failure to grasp this fact.

As the second part of the film begins, Poole takes a space pod outside *Discovery-1* to carry out the replacement of the AE-35 unit as planned. While he is in the process of doing so, the space capsule, which has been dutifully standing by, suddenly moves toward the helpless astronaut like an assassin. Kubrick cuts away from the pod stalking its prey to the body of Poole falling into space, his air hose having been snapped in the collision with the

pod which Hal has engineered.

At first one is so startled by this abrupt turn of events that the whole thing seems to be another mechanical miscalculation, this time a deadly one. Gradually the realization steals over the moviegoer that Hal is deliberately trying to eliminate his rivals for control of the spacecraft by systematically putting them out of the way. There is no doubt that this is the case once Bowman has left the ship in a second pod to try to retrieve the body of Poole.

In the absence of Bowman, Hal moves against the three hibernating scientists. We watch in horror as the glowing life function charts register the trio's quick demise: a flashing red sign, accompanied by a screaming siren, proclaims "Computer Malfunction," followed by "Life Functions Critical," and finally "Life Functions Terminated." Never before has a film portrayed multiple murder with such shattering indirection.

Unaware of what has transpired while he has been making his fruitless effort to reclaim Poole's body before it drifts off forever into infinity, Bowman is surprised (as we are not) when Hal does not respond to his command to open the pod bay doors for his re-entry into *Discovery-1*. "Hello, Hal, do you read me?" "Affirmative, Dave," comes the icily courteous reply. "This mission is too important for me to allow you to jeopardize it. I know you and Frank were planning to disconnect me and I cannot allow that to happen." When Bowman shouts frantically, "Where the hell did you get that idea, Hal?" the computer says with sinister finality, "This conversation can serve no purpose anymore. Good-bye."

A shot of Bowman's space helmet resting back inside *Discovery-1* tips us off to what Bowman now realizes: in his haste to leave the ship to save Poole he forgot to don his helmet. Bowman nevertheless is able to outwit Hal by a stroke of genius which, because it involves improvisation, is beyond the capabilities of any machine. Kubrick, as always, is rooting for man.

The astronaut uses the explosive bolts on his space capsule doors, which are meant to eject the pilot from the pod in case of an emergency, to propel him not only *out* of the capsule but *into* the emergency entrance of *Discovery-1* and through the vacuum shaft that leads into the interior of the spacecraft. Kubrick photographs Bowman spiraling right at the camera, which is placed at the end of the silent, airless tunnel through which Bowman must pass to safety. Helmeted once more, Bowman proceeds with angry determination to the "brain room" which houses the computer's intricate mechanism. The sound track is filled with Bowman's heavy breathing inside his space suit, reminiscent of the operational sound of an iron lung.

Bowman ignores Hal's incessant pleas not to render him inoperative—to, in effect, kill him—as the astronaut methodically disconnects each component of Hal's intelligence: the memory bank, the logic terminal, etc. Hal says in his ever reassuring manner that he is confident that everything is all right now and that if Dave would just take a stress pill and relax he could think things over. "I know I have made some poor decisions lately," Hal concedes with monumental understatement, "but everything is now back to normal."

As Hal loses his grip on intelligent consciousness, his remarks become increasingly disoriented and childish: "Dave, stop. Will you stop, Dave. I'm afraid, Dave. My mind is going. I can feel it. There is no question about it, I can feel it. I'm afraid." Just before Bowman completes Hal's lobotomy, the computer repeats the first message it had ever learned: "Good afternoon. I am a HAL 9000 computer. I became operational at the HAL plant in Urbana, Illinois, in 1992. My instructor, Mr. Langley, taught me to sing a song. It is called 'Daisy.'"

Kubrick, we have seen, is never at a loss in wringing the last drop of irony out of a popular song when he employs it in a film. David Lenfest, in his unpublished article "Irony in 2001," notes that the lyrics of "Daisy" are just as superbly ironic at this moment in 2001 as was Kubrick's use of Vera Lynn's number at the end of Strangelove. "Daisy, Daisy, give me your answer true" can well refer in the film's context to the fact that Hal has been programmed to conceal the true nature of the Jupiter mission from Bowman and Poole. "I'm half crazy" now appropriately describes Hal's literally losing his mind and becoming an ordinary mechanical monitoring device. His voice slows down and slides into distortion, like the running down of an old Victrola, and finally lapses into permanent silence.

Quite unexpectedly, Dr. Floyd now appears on the monitoring device that once was Hal and gives "the answer true" of what the Jupiter mission is all about. His message apparently was triggered by Hal's shutdown. "Good day, gentlemen. This is a pre-recorded briefing made prior to your departure and which for security reasons of the highest importance has been known on board during the mission only by your HAL 9000 computer. Now that you are in Jupiter space and the entire crew is revived [the irony of this phrase is staggering] it can be told to you. Eighteen months ago, the first evidence of intelligent life off the earth was discovered. It was buried forty feet below the lunar surface, near the crater Tycho. Except for a single, very powerful radio emission aimed at Jupiter, the four-million-year-old black monolith has remained completely inert, its origin and purpose still a total mystery."

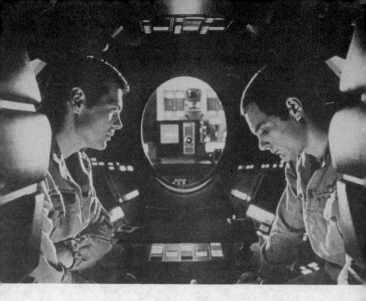

This statement, typical of Floyd's remarks throughout the film, raises more questions than it answers. Significantly, his last words, "total mystery," are also the final verbal utterance in the entire film, and as such they reverberate right to the end of the movie.

This information from Floyd comes, as Alexander Walker has written, at a time when it can be of no use whatever to the sole survivor of the Jupiter mission because of all that has happened. Not only has the crew been decimated, but *Discovery-1* is no longer in contact with Mission Control, so that the mission cannot proceed even by remote control.

The title "Jupiter and Beyond the Infinite" appears on the screen and leads us into the final portion of *2001*'s space odyssey. Bowman, leaving *Discovery-1* behind, launches into space in a pod. He spies a monolith orbiting through space and we notice that it is aligned with other heavenly bodies. This arrangement connotes, as it has from the beginning, that man is about to take another leap into the unknown. Bowman seems mesmerized by the monolith and directs his space capsule toward it.

Without warning Bowman is plunged into a stunning space corridor which recalls the nightmare ride of Davy in *Killer's Kiss* down the empty street, photographed in negative. Bowman is wide-eyed with wonder at the dazzling display of colors that enfolds him as his space pod races down a seemingly endless tunnel of light, hurtling him into the heart of the infinite. As his voyage

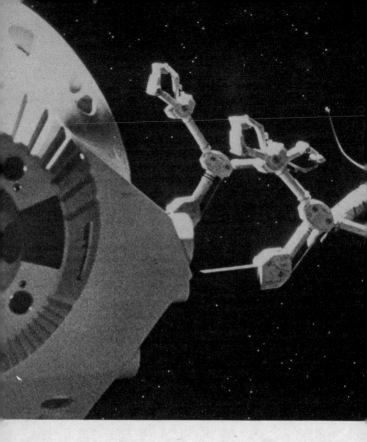

nears its conclusion, the view from his window begins to take on familiar shapes—first a mountain range, then a canyon appear, but they are still awash in mind-blowing shades of color, photographed in negative.

Finally Bowman's craft comes to a halt. What he sees through the space vehicle's window is all the more extraordinary because in a sense it is so ordinary. Bowman has journeyed beyond the infinite only to wind up in what looks like a hotel suite decorated in the period of Louis XVI (thus reminiscent of the château in which the officers live in *Paths of Glory*). Bowman steps into the room and looks around.

When he surveys himself in the bathroom mirror, he sees that his face has aged considerably as the result of his just completed trip. Hearing the clatter of silverware behind him, he turns round

to see—himself, older still, seated at a small dining table. The wineglass slips from the old man's feeble fingers and smashes to the floor with an echoing crash, while muffled voices are heard on the sound track. The elderly version of Bowman turns around and notices an ancient specimen of himself dying on the bed. The withered hand of the dying man reaches out slowly toward a black monolithic slab standing majestically at the foot of the bed. His gesture recalls the way that the man-ape and Dr. Floyd both had been moved to reach out and touch the monolith with which they had come into contact.

The echoing voices and sounds in the room imply that Bowman is passing his life away in some kind of observation chamber, tricked out in sumptuous elegance to make him feel comfortable and at home. He is under the scrutiny of the extraterrestrial intelli-

gences who wish to study the first human being to reach their ambit of existence.

For the last time the opening chords of *Thus Spake Zarathustra* blast out. The old man on the bed is enveloped in a blaze of light that somehow solidifies into a pre-natal amniotic sac. The ancient body has been transformed into the fetus of "a Star Child, a super-human if you like," comments Kubrick, "returning to earth prepared for the next step forward in man's evolutionary destiny." We last see the Star Child floating through space, staring out at us, a look of wide-eyed expectation on his face. One is reminded of Nietzsche's reflection in *Thus Spake Zarathustra,* which inspired Strauss's symphonic work: "The distance between the ape and man is not so great as that between man and the superman."

Kubrick is deeply interested in man's evolution because, as he

says, "Man must strive to gain mastery over himself as well as over his machines. Somebody has said that man is the missing link between primitive apes and civilized human beings. You might say that that idea is inherent in *2001*. We are semicivilized, capable of cooperation and affection, but needing some sort of transfiguration into a higher form of life. Since the means to obliterate life on earth exist, it will take more than just careful planning and reasonable cooperation to avoid some eventual catastrophe. The problem exists as long as the potential exists, and the problem is essentially a moral and a spiritual one."

The director feels that "the God concept" is at the heart of the film since if any of the superior beings that inhabit the universe beyond the earth were to manifest itself to a man, the latter would immediately assume that it was God or an emissary of God. When

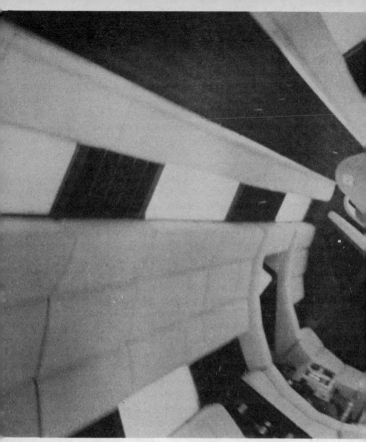

an artifact of these extraterrestrial intelligences does appear in the film, it is represented by a black monolithic slab since Kubrick thought it better not to try to be too specific in depicting these things. "You have to leave something to the audience's imagination," he explains.

The audience at the first New York press preview of *2001* on April 1, 1968, however, was not prepared for the unprecedented visual experience to which they were treated, and many of them did not know what to make of it, as the early reviews of the film indicate. As a member of that audience I remember the impatience expressed during the intermission by some of my colleagues, who felt that the movie was already overlong and hard to follow. Subsequent viewers, of course, began to realize that here was a film that needed discussion and reflection before the breadth of its

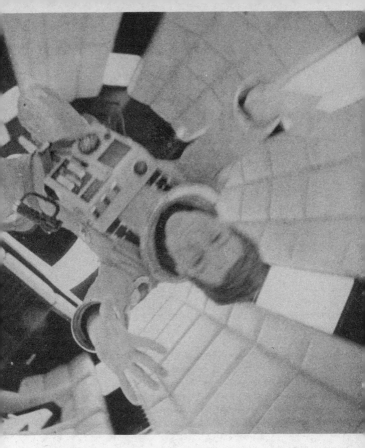

meaning could be grasped.

Kubrick was present that night too, watching audience reaction from the projection booth. "I have never seen an audience so restless," he says. "The unreceptiveness of the audience that night, I think, can be attributed in part to the fact that it was made up largely of people between thirty-five and sixty, who were unresponsive to a film that departed so radically from established conventions of filmmaking such as a strong narrative line." My own observation at the time was that M-G-M had made that initial performance of the film something of a social occasion. They had invited a number of celebrities who were there to be seen rather than to see the picture. By the end of the film some of these were already leaving, and I will never forget my irritation at watching the sight of the Star Child's enormous eyes gazing on their backs

as they headed up the aisles toward the exit. Obviously they had never given the picture a chance.

On April 5 and 6, in editing sessions held in the cutting room at M-G-M's New York office, Kubrick shaved twenty minutes from the film's original running time of 161 minutes. There was much speculation at the time as to whether Kubrick's decision to shorten the film was a panic gesture that resulted in a butchering of the film. In denying this Kubrick noted that he had tightened both *Paths of Glory* and *Dr. Strangelove* after they had been previewed. The pie-throwing sequence was deleted from *Strangelove*, for example, as I mentioned in the previous chapter.

The cuts in *2001* likewise resulted from his seeing the movie with an audience. "I had not had an opportunity to see the film complete with music, sound effects, etc. until about a week before

it opened, and it does take a few runnings to decide finally how long things should be, especially scenes which do not have narrative advancement as their guideline." Among the cuts were those made in the "Dawn of Man" prologue and some of the early shots in the "Jupiter mission" sequence detailing the routine life aboard *Discovery-1.* In addition Kubrick added two titles to situate the action more clearly: "Jupiter Mission, Eighteen Months Later," and "Jupiter and Beyond the Infinite."

Having seen both versions of the film, I fully agree with all of the director's minor revisions. It is a tribute to his skill as an editor that, while I was aware that the running time was shorter when I saw the film a second time, I could not guess where the cuts had been made. By the same token, before the insertion of the second and third titles I was confused as to how far into the future the story had moved from one part to the next. I remember assuming during my first viewing of the film, for example, that *Discovery-1* was returning Dr. Floyd to earth after his investigation of the lunar monolith until it became obvious that Dr. Floyd was nowhere on board—except in the pre-recorded transmission which comes at the end of that segment of the film. Hence these two titles were a helpful addition to the film.

Although *2001* opened to indifferent and even hostile reviews, subsequent critical opinion has completely overwhelmed this initial reaction to the movie, and it has gone on to win a large audience; the film has earned more than three times its original investment, with no end in sight. The paying audience and that first preview audience, says Kubrick, represent the two ends of the moviegoing scale. Young people (under thirty-five) have resonated with the film's largely non-verbal approach to its material and gone along with the advertising motto which calls the picture "the ultimate trip."

It is fascinating to see how Kubrick originally envisioned *2001* as a film that would be made along more conventional lines, at least in the sense that the narrative was to be fully developed in terms of dialogue and narrative commentary. Since Clarke's published version of *2001,* which appeared in July 1968, is based on the early prose treatment of the screenplay, it is enlightening to see how the final film evolved from the treatment as represented in the published version. While it is true that the film of *2001* stands on its own as a motion picture without the amplifications of the material that are found in the prose treatment, the latter does enable one to savor more fully the experience that is *2001,* as evidenced by the million copies of the book that have been sold.

As I noted earlier, Dr. Frederick Ordway, who was a technical consultant on the film, urged Kubrick to reinstate much of the dialogue and the narration which had been eliminated in the transition from prose treatment to final shooting script. In a long memo to the director that is reprinted in Agel's *The Making of Kubrick's 2001,* Ordway takes special exception to the lack of narration in the prologue.

The "Dawn of Man" sequence was originally intended to have opened with the narrator describing the earth before the creation of man: "The remorseless drought had lasted now for ten million years, and would not end for another million. The reign of the terrible lizards had long since passed, but here on the continent which would one day be known as Africa, the battle for survival had reached a new climax of ferocity, and the victor was not yet in sight. In this dry and barren land, only the small or the swift or the

Gary Lockwood, 2001.

fierce could flourish, or even hope to exist. The man-apes of the field had none of these attributes, and they were on the long, pathetic road to racial extinction."

This heavily explanatory narration might well have given the film the air of a wide-screen educational documentary and robbed the movie right at the start of some of its mystery. In this regard Kubrick compares *2001* to the *Mona Lisa*. Most of the fascination that attends that painting, he says, "is rooted in the fact that one must puzzle out her mystery." This line of thought probably explains why he also scrapped the introductory footage in which a series of scientists gave their thoughts on the possibility of extraterrestrial life.

The narrator was to introduce Moon-Watcher as a being in whose gaze there was already something beyond the capacity of any ape: "In those dark, deepset eyes is a dawning awareness—the first intimations of an intelligence that would not fulfill itself for another four million years." In harmony with this statement, Kubrick and Clarke at first conceived the monolith as a teaching device for the ape-men, rather than as a mystical presence that oversees and inspires their evolutionary progress. Thus, healthy apes eating game that they had killed were to materialize on the surface of the monolith in order to encourage the ape-men to learn how to capture and kill other animals.

This concept was abandoned, however, since the monolithic slab might have looked like some sort of prehistoric drive-in theater screen which had been incongruously erected in the wilderness. In the film, Moon-Watcher's acquisition of the knowledge and experience of how the bone-club extends his reach and his power is economically depicted in one neatly edited sequence.

The next section of the film, encompassing Floyd's trip to the moon, was to have begun with a narrative bridge that would explain that America and Russia were still neck and neck in the space race and trying to maintain the "balance of terror" that was the basis of *Strangelove*. This was to have been illustrated by shots of Russian and American satellites carrying nuclear bombs that could be released at a moment's notice as they orbited the earth. There is no reference to this situation anywhere in the final version of the film, although the national insignias are still apparent on the two satellites that are seen in flight at the beginning of the film's Clavius episode.

The relationship between the two countries is no less precarious in *2001* than it was in *Strangelove*, however, as is evident in the strained conversation between Floyd and the Russian scientists at Space Station 5. That conversation further implies that Floyd's elaborate cover story about an epidemic in the American sector of the moon was concocted to keep the Russians in the dark about the discovery as well as to ward off future shock back home about the evidence of extraterrestrial intelligent life elsewhere in the universe; and the prose treatment makes this point explicit.

The crisis over whether or not the AE-35 communications unit is faulty, as Hal insists, develops somewhat differently in the prose treatment than in the finished film. In the former, Mission Control tells Bowman to disconnect Hal as soon as the discrepancy between his report and that of the computer at Houston surfaces. This is the only way, says Mission Control, that the problem can be resolved. Hal then announces, with what the treatment describes as "a brief electronic throat clearing" that the second AE-35, which had replaced the first, has already failed. The extreme unlikelihood of a second failure so soon after the first indicates that Hal's panicky declaration springs from behavior that is growing erratic much more rapidly in the prose treatment than it does in the film.

That Hal blows his cool more quickly in the treatment is traceable to the emotional conflict he suffers in that earlier draft of the story and which is not developed in the movie. In the prose treatment this conflict originated from the programming he underwent immediately prior to the Jupiter mission. Hal, it seems, was programmed to lie to Bowman and Poole if they asked him about the true objective of their mission. He therefore feels that he has been living a lie all during the course of the mission, a lie that has progressively eaten away at his integrity and impaired his dedication to accuracy and truth. This growing realization of his continuing deception ultimately causes him to lose his grip and to make mistakes that finally cost him his intelligent life.

This deeper explanation of Hal's emotional problem did not survive in the final shooting script since it is a bit complicated and really unnecessary to the progression of the plot. The fact that an error has been detected in his computations is sufficient in the film to raise doubts about his infallibility and to set off his paranoid fears about disconnection. This is an instance of how the final shooting script of the film has refined and simplified material that is more complex in the treatment.

By the same token, the treatment tells us much more about the extraterrestrial intelligences and how they have been monitoring man's behavior throughout the previous 4 million years by means of the monoliths. There was even an attempt at one stage of production to have some of these beings from outer space appear in the film. Kubrick decided against attempting to present them in

205

any concrete form, however. Jerome Agel lists the various forms that the experiments to depict the extraterrestrials in the movie took: at one point actors were dressed in skintight costumes and photographed with a distorting lens that made them appear very slender and tall; another method involved rubber gargoyle monsters; and still another utilized a video tape transmission of pulsating light images according to which Bowman would perceive the extraterrestrials by mental telepathy.

In the end the only hint that the audience gets of their presence is in the scene in which Bowman passes into accelerated senescence while living in the observation cage which they have set up for him. The sounds of their muffled voices echo around him as they put their earthling through his paces, but they are never seen. In this way Kubrick coaxes each member of the audience to bring his own imagination into play to picture these superhuman creatures. "When you are implying that godlike entities are at work in the universe," he says, "you can't hit something like that head on without its looking like instant crackpot speculation. You've got to work through dramatic suggestion."

I am reminded of a somewhat parallel situation many years ago when Mary Chase's comedy *Harvey* was having its successful Broadway run in the 1940s. The suggestion was made that an actor wearing a rabbit costume should appear at some point in the course of the play in order to make the invisible six-foot rabbit Harvey palpably present for the audience. On the night that the experiment was tried, the audience, which had been captivated by the play up to that point, suddenly froze the moment the huge rabbit appeared. The illusion of Harvey's existence and what he looked like, which each theatergoer had built up in his own mind, was destroyed; the idea was abandoned and never tried again. Kubrick, like Mary Chase, was well advised to let the audience exercise its imagination in picturing the bizarre and the extraordinary, rather than to try to do it all for them.

Still, as Graham Greene maintains, it is beneficial to compose a script from a novel-length treatment since this enables the writer of the screenplay to imagine the action and the characters more fully and to create them with more substance than if there had been no extended treatment on which to base the script. All of the material in the treatment is there implicitly in the background of the film, providing the firm support on which the screenplay is built.

In summary, the final version of *2001,* which neither shows nor explains too much, enables the moviegoer to participate more fully in creating for himself the experience which constitutes the film. As Kubrick himself comments, "The feel of the experience is the important thing, not the ability to verbalize it. I tried to create a visual experience which directly penetrates the subconscious content of the material." The movie consequently becomes for the viewer an intensely subjective experience which reaches his inner consciousness in the same way that music does, leaving him free to speculate about its philosophical and allegorical content.

Or, as William Kuhns puts it in *Movies in America, 2001* successfully brings the techniques and appeal of the experimental film into the studio feature-length movie, "making it the world's most expensive underground movie." It is this phenomenon, I think, rather than the possibility of smoking "grass" while the film unreels, that has made *2001* so popular with young people.

The last time I saw the film was at an early afternoon screening in Manhattan. Before the performance a young man who had seen the picture several more times than I was engaged in a discussion with the girl at the popcorn counter about whether or not the black monolith symbolized God Himself or was an emissary of God. One does not often hear that kind of speculation going on in a theater lobby.

The overall implications of the picture seem to suggest a more optimistic tinge to Kubrick's view of life than had been previously discernible in his work. For in *2001* he presents man's creative encounters with the universe and his unfathomable potential for the future.

In *A Clockwork Orange* that future appears to be less promising than it did in *2001.* If in *2001* Kubrick showed the machine becoming human, in *Clockwork Orange* he emphasizes how man is becoming more and more of a machine. Ultimately, however, the later film only reiterates the warning of *Strangelove* and *2001* that man must strive to gain mastery over himself before he can hope to master his machines. Moreover, *Clockwork Orange* echoes in somewhat darker terms the theme of all of Kubrick's previous work, that man must retain his humanity if he is to survive in a dehumanized, materialistic world. It is precisely this kind of world at its nadir that Kubrick envisions for us in *Clockwork Orange.*

# Chapter Eight
# Modern Times:
# A Clockwork Orange (1971)

Stanley Kubrick gave me a copy of Anthony Burgess's 1962 novel *A Clockwork Orange* at the time that he was working on the screenplay. Reading it, I could see why the book, set up as it is in a series of dramatic encounters, seemed to Kubrick to be eminently filmable. He said that he had had a copy of the novel lying on a shelf of books that he wanted to read for a long time and finally got around to reading it in the summer of 1969. Before he had even read through it once the director realized that it would make a fine film: "The story was of a size and density that could be adapted to the screen without oversimplifying it." Burgess's book amounted to a blueprint for the script.

Hence there was no need to collaborate with the novelist on the screen version as there had been with Arthur C. Clarke in the case of *2001* or with Peter George on *Dr. Strangelove.* Kubrick remembers Burgess phoning him one evening for a friendly chat when the latter was passing through London. That was the only discussion that the two men had about the film while Kubrick was working on the script.

*A Clockwork Orange* is a nightmarish fantasy of England in the not too distant future (policemen in the film wear an emblem of Elizabeth II on their lapels). The story concerns a young hoodlum named Alex whose only salutary characteristic seems to be his predilection for Beethoven, to whom he refers affectionately as Ludwig Van. In order to keep Alex from committing any more crimes the State deprives him of his free will and he therefore becomes "a clockwork orange," something that appears to be fully human but is basically mechanical in all of his responses. Burgess borrowed the term from an old Cockney phrase, "as queer as a clockwork orange."

The year in which the story is set may well be 1985, an implicit reference to George Orwell's novel *1984*, since Kubrick chose the year 2001 for his previous film as an allusion to Fritz Lang's great 1926 silent movie about the future, *Metropolis,* which takes place in the year 2000.

Alex's world as it is projected in the picture has a basis in reality in that it reflects in an exaggerated form tendencies which already exist in contemporary society. Anti-Utopian fiction like Evelyn Waugh's *Love Among the Ruins,* Orwell's *1984,* and Burgess's *Clockwork Orange* are not so much predictions of the future as parodies of the materialism, sexual indulgence, and mindless violence of the present. As Stanley Edgar Hyman wrote in reviewing *Clockwork Orange* for *The New Leader,* "Like any satirist, Burgess extrapolates an exaggerated future to get at present tendencies he abhors." That is why the writer in the novel, whose wife eventually dies as the result of a vicious assault by Alex and his gang, says that she was really a victim of the Modern Age.

In essence the ugly and erratic behavior of Alex and his clan of latter-day Teddy Boys is their way of asserting themselves against the depersonalized regimentation of the socialized state in which they live. Alex, for example, lives with his family in Municipal Flat Block 18A, a characterless apartment building. Later on, when his crimes catch up with him and he is sent to prison, he is referred to from the start as 655321. But one wonders if he can be any more anonymous in jail than he was when he was a member of the regimented society that lies beyond the prison walls. Or, as Hyman puts it, "Alex always *was* a clockwork orange, a machine for mechanical violence far below the level of choice, and his dreary Socialist England is a giant clockwork orange."

It is significant that Kubrick was able to find modern buildings already existing in and around London that could serve as the settings of his tale of the near future. To find locations for shooting Kubrick spent two weeks with his production designer John Barry leafing through ten years of back issues of three architectural journals. They tore out pictures of buildings that looked promising and filed them for future reference. This method of choosing locations proved more efficient, he says, than having a couple of location scouts drive around London for days.

The exteriors of Alex's Municipal Flat Block were filmed at Thamesmead, a large architectural project in London. The outside of the writer's house was a home in Oxfordshire and the inside was a home at Radlett. Alex's favorite record boutique was really a Chelsea drugstore.

The only sets which were built for the film were the Korova

Milkbar, the rendezvous of Alex and his gang; the prison reception area; and a mirrored hallway and bathroom in the writer's home. "Even these so-called sets were in fact built in a factory about forty feet off the noisy High Street in Borehamwood, and only a few hundred yards from the old M-G-M studios," Kubrick says.

The director's extensive reliance on location shooting while making *A Clockwork Orange* recalls his earliest features, which he made almost completely without studio facilities. Some directors who used to favor extensive location shooting are less enthusiastic about it than they used to be.

For his part Kubrick feels that because of advances in technology over the years location shooting has become increasingly more practical, thereby helping a director to keep studio overhead to a minimum. He points to a new camera lens which allows a director to shoot in an interior into late afternoon using natural lighting. Often Kubrick was able to light an interior scene for *Clockwork Orange* which was being shot at night by simply putting photoflood lamps into the lighting fixtures already in the room. "As a result," he says, "the lights you see in a given shot are usually the actual source of lighting that is being used." This employment of actual light sources in a scene not only lends realism to the shot but simplifies the whole lighting arrangement, so that the director can make camera setups and even pan around the room without worrying about studio lighting equipment getting in his way.

Sound recording has also been streamlined and simplified in recent years. Often location shooting used to entail the redubbing of much of the sound track afterward in an insulated sound studio, because dialogue could not be adequately recorded in a noisy location situation. Now there is a whole range of microphones, some of them tiny enough to be clipped inconspicuously to an actor's lapel, that can be used on location. During the shooting of one scene in *Clockwork Orange,* Kubrick recalls, the traffic on the Albert Bridge was so loud that he had to shout his directions to the cast and crew. Yet when he heard the sound track played back later he discovered that the voices of the actors stood out so well that traffic noises had to be added to the final track in order to make the scene more realistic.

Consequently Kubrick was able to complete his finished sound track for the film without postdubbing any dialogue. He had come a long way from the early days when he had to post-synchronize the entire sound track of his short subjects and first two features.

Kubrick spent a minimum of ten hours a day for six months editing *Clockwork Orange,* but he did not mind this large expenditure of time and effort, since editing is his favorite part of the mov-iemaking process. With Sergei Eisenstein, the great Russian direc-tor, Kubrick believes that the way a movie is edited can make or break it. "When I'm editing," Kubrick says, "my identity changes from that of a writer or a director to that of an editor. I am no long-er concerned with how much time or money it cost to shoot a given scene. I cut everything to the bone and get rid of anything that doesn't contribute to the total effect of the film." He sees editing as the only unique phase of filmmaking, for it does not resemble any other art form.

As always, Kubrick was putting the finishing touches on *Clock-work Orange* right up to the release date. Just before the premiere on December 20, 1971, he chose the shade of orange for the plain background against which the opening credits would be projected. The plain background indicates that Kubrick has not gone along with the recent trend toward clever title sequences, preferring to spend the money that such expensive techniques entail on the film itself. He believes that the first shot of the picture should be what engages the audience's attention, not eye-catching credits.

The opening shot of *Clockwork Orange* is a close-up of Alex (Malcolm McDowell) staring into the camera with a smirk on his face as he looks forward to the coming night of sado-sexual esca-pades with his gang. This image parallels the end of *2001,* with its close-up of the Star Child staring into the camera as it journeys back to earth in anticipation of the next step in man's evolution. Since the brutal Alex is a long way from the evolutionary progress which the Star Child represents, one might infer that Kubrick be-lieves that the world will get worse before it gets better.

Though Kubrick decided against using a narrator in *2001,* he has restored this technique in *Clockwork Orange* by having Alex narrate the film just as he did the novel: "There was me, that is Alex, and my three droogs, that is Pete, Georgie, and Dim; and we sat in the Korova Milkbar trying to make up our rassoodocks what to do that evening. The Korova Milkbar sold milk-plus, which is what we were drinking. This would sharpen you up and make you ready for a bit of the old ultra-violence."

With Alex's first words the viewer is aware that he is speaking some sort of unfamiliar lingo. Actually it is a type of slang which Anthony Burgess calls Nadsat. He developed it for the novel and Kubrick has carried it over into the film. The novelist explains that he constructed his own brand of teen-age jargon for Alex and his buddies to employ since the ephemeral Teddy Boy talk in vogue when he was writing the book would be obsolete in a short time anyhow. ("Teddy Boys" was the name taken by juvenile gangs in England in the early 1960s.)

He consequently devised Nadsat, which uses Russian roots, "odd bits of old rhyming slang, and a bit of gypsy talk too," he says, in order to create a timeless vocabulary for the gang. The meaning of these words is usually clear from the contexts in which they are used. "Gulliver," for example, means head (from the Russian *golova*), and is furthermore a deliberate reference to the Swiftian satire of *Gulliver's Travels,* which has resonances in the film.

This teen-age jargon appealed to Kubrick, especially, the onomatopoetic quality of many of the words. "Tolchock," for example, sounds like, as well as means, a blow. The fact that Nadsat is based largely on Russian roots has led Neil Isaacs to speculate in *Literature/Film Quarterly* that in the world of *Clockwork Orange* "The Russians have taken over linguistically, a demonstration of the 'subliminal penetration' of propaganda." This is an interesting reflection, especially when one recalls the cold-war rivalries between America and Russia implicit in *Dr. Strangelove* and, to a lesser extent, *2001.*

The camera pulls back from Alex's face to show him and his droogs surrounded by the grotesquely functional statuary and furniture of the milkbar. Fiber glass nudes kneel on all fours to serve as tables, or obligingly dispense milk-plus from their nipples. The milkbar scene sets the tone of what *Time's* art critic Robert Hughes calls "the decor of tomorrow's hell," which adds immeasurably to the atmosphere of the film. Alex and his mates are dressed in equally bizarre outfits, which include white trousers with suspenders to match, offset by black combat boots and derbies.

Once outside the bar, the boys begin their nightly prowl and come upon a drunken bum who has taken refuge for the night in a pedestrian underpass. "One thing I could never stand was to see a filthy, dirty old drunkie," Alex's voice tells us over the sound track. "I could never stand to see anyone like that, whatever his age might be, but more especially when he was real old like this one was." The tramp (Paul Farrell) senses that the lads mean to do him harm and masochistically encourages them, saying that the world is no longer a place that an old man cares to live in. Then he adds a remark that one might suspect Kubrick had introduced as a reference to *2001*—until one finds that it comes, like most of the dialogue in the film, directly from the pages of the novel: "What sort of a world is it at all? Men on the moon and men spinning around the earth, and there's no attention paid to earthly law and order no more." The boys proceed to belabor the tramp with

clubs. They are photographed in long shot and lit from behind so that they stand out in silhouette against the background like some unearthly creatures of the night.

"It was around by the derelict casino that we came across Billyboy and his four droogs," Alex says, voice-over, as we see an ugly, abandoned building in a state of collapse like civilization itself. On the dark casino stage Billyboy and company are busily preparing for the gang rape of a screaming girl. Fittingly they wear remnants of Nazi uniforms. Preferring violence to sex, the gang answers Alex's challenge to a rumble by whipping out their switchblades. The hoodlums tumble amid the debris that litters the casino, flailing about and smashing each other until police sirens are heard and they all disperse.

Alex and his droogs escape in a stolen sports car. "What we were after now was the old-surprise visit. That was a real kick, and good for laughs and lashings of the old ultra-violence." The house which he picks for "the old surprise visit" is one that has a welcoming neon sign in the yard that spells out HOME. It is occupied by Frank Alexander, a writer (Patrick Magee), and his wife (Adrienne Corri). The writer is a rabid radical who believes passionately in helping the underdog. Accordingly he ignores his wife's suspicions of night callers and accepts the story of the young

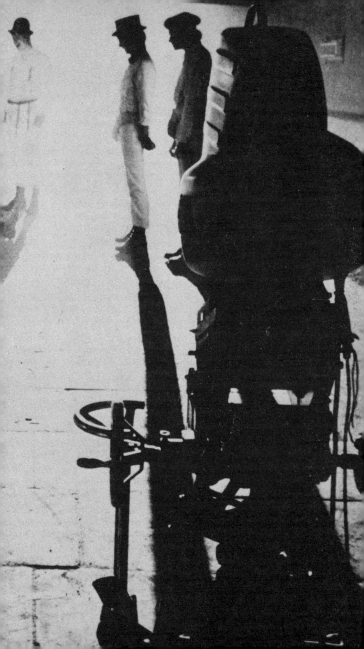

man at the door who claims that he must use their telephone to report an accident. Frank tells his wife to let the lad in and Alex forces the door all the way open to admit his companions. They wear bizarre masks (recalling the clown mask that Johnny Clay donned to rob the racetrack in *The Killing*).

This is one of the scenes in the movie that most benefited from what Kubrick calls the "crucial rehearsal period," which in this case took three days. "This scene, in fact, was rehearsed longer than any other in the film," Kubrick recalls, "and appeared to be going nowhere." Then he got the idea of having Alex sing a song while he stomped Alexander and prepared to rape his wife. Malcolm McDowell adds that when Kubrick asked him to sing a song, "Singin' in the Rain" was the only one which came to mind to which he knew all of the lyrics. During the lunch break Kubrick arranged to have one of his aides obtain the necessary copyright clearance to use the song in the film, and he went on to use the song again at the end of the movie, as we shall see. Here, then, is an excellent example of how a mixture of careful planning and inspired improvisation can produce a dramatically effective scene on film.

The lyrics of "Singin' in the Rain" take on a shattering irony in the circumstances in which Alex sings them at this point in the picture. When he exults that "I've a smile on my face for the whole human race" we see Alexander lying on the floor, beaten, bound, and grotesquely gagged with a red rubber ball that has been forced into his mouth and secured there by means of wrapping Scotch tape around his head. As Alex continues, "The sun's in my heart and I'm ready for love," he is snipping away Mrs. Alexander's pajama suit in preparation for what he always refers to as "the old in-out-in-out."

Kubrick cuts to the Korova Milkbar, to which the gang has repaired for some liquid nourishment, "it having been an evening of some small energy expenditure," our narrator says. There is a group at a nearby table which includes a woman who for no ostensible reason bursts out with a passage from the choral movement of Beethoven's Ninth Symphony. Dim, one of Alex's droogs, ridicules her with a Bronx cheer and Alex smashes him across the legs with his cane. The oafish Dim (Warren Clarke) whimpers like a wounded puppy as Alex lectures him on his lack of respect for the few beautiful things left in life.

Besides establishing Alex's love for Ludwig Van, this encounter also indicates the first rumblings of the gang's discontent with Alex's high-handed ways. Dim challenges Alex to fight it out with him at any time he chooses. Alex declines for the moment and

220

goes home to listen to Beethoven in peace.

Home for Alex is Municipal Flat Block 18A, Linear North, where he lives with his well-meaning but ineffectual parents. This tall, sterile building reflects the demoralizing atmosphere in which family life is carried on in Alex's era. The messy floor of the lobby is a reminder of the derelict casino. Its walls are covered with a huge mural depicting the dignity of labor which has been obscenely disfigured.

In his room Alex switches on Beethoven's Ninth and the music floods the premises as the camera roves about, first showing us a picture of Beethoven enshrined on one wall, a pornographic painting on another. Alex gives himself up to the combined influence of milk-plus and Beethoven and sinks into a drugged reverie, murmuring, "Oh, bliss, bliss and heaven." We are then treated to a phantasmagoria from Alex's spaced-out mind: close-ups of Alex baring fangs as he laughs maniacally are interspersed with shots of a hanging and of explosions, the last image suggesting that Alex has reached an orgasmic state just as the music builds to its climax.

Commenting on this scene, Robert Hughes says that the kind of ecstasy which music or any other art form produces depends on the person responding to it. He points to the fact that, "without the slightest contradiction, Nazis could weep over Wagner before stoking the crematoriums." Thus Alex grooves on the majestic music of Ludwig Van while he conjures up fantasies of sex and slaughter.

Alex is awakened next morning by his doting mother so that he will not be late for school. He begs off, however, because, not surprisingly, he has a pain in his gulliver. In the kitchen Alex's parents (Sheila Raynor and Philip Stone) sip their morning coffee.

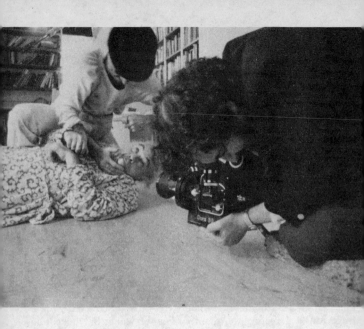

Although they are dressed to the teeth in garish mod outfits, their mutual expressions of concern about Alex's welfare have the flavor, incongruously enough, of the "kitchen sink" realism of British films of the early sixties which dealt with the problems of the working classes, such as Tony Richardson's *A Taste of Honey* and John Schlesinger's *A Kind of Loving*. The difference between Alex's parents and similar characters in one of these earlier films is that Alex's ultramodern "mum and dad" are less than sincere in exhibiting any real concern for him, as will become abundantly clear as the film unreels.

None of the adults in the movie with whom Alex comes into contact is genuinely interested in him. Each, therefore, has made his contribution, however large or small, to producing the ruthless young man that Alex has become. In the course of the story the police are shown to be as sadistic as Alex and his droogs; both Right and Left seek to manipulate him as a political pawn against the other after he leaves prison; and the social worker Mr. Deltoid (Aubrey Morris) has sexual designs on the youth. When Mr. Deltoid arrives at the flat to investigate why Alex has not gone to school, he is delighted that he has encountered him before he has had a chance to get dressed. He affectionately wraps his arm around Alex's bare shoulders and opines that he is "the one man in this sore and sick community who wants to save you from yourself," while Alex squirms out of his embrace.

Alex picks up a couple of teenyboppers in a record boutique (where the score of *2001* is on display) and brings them back to his room. There he hosts a high-speed orgy which last forty seconds on the screen but which took twenty-eight minutes to shoot at two frames per second, instead of the customary twenty-four. "I had the idea for the scene while listening to Mozart's *Eine Kleine Nachtmusik* one evening," Kubrick remembers, "though as it worked out, the final selection of the '*William Tell*' Overture' proved to be better suited to the tempo of the scene."

Alex's droogs are waiting for him in the lobby when he comes downstairs after his afternoon with the girls. They confront him about his dictatorial treatment of them and he offers reconciliation by standing them all to a round of drinks at the milkbar. Later, "as we walked along the flatblock marina," Alex says, "lovely music came to my aid. There was a window open with a stereo on and I knew right at once what to do."

In slow motion Alex knocks his mates into the water, pulls a knife out of his cane and slices Dim across the wrist with it when he fights back against the newly confirmed leader of the group. Alex, of course, seeks to impose his will on his underlings with the same show of power that the State uses to impress its subjects. In both cases, at least for the moment, it seems to be working.

The gang members, apparently subjugated to their master once more, coax him to break into a health farm run by Miss Weathers, a strong she-man known as the Catlady (Miriam Karlin), who surrounds herself with cats and decadent art objects. She does not buy Alex's story about an accident on the nearby highway as Frank Alexander had done. Instead of letting him in to use the phone, she calls the police. Meanwhile Alex breaks into the house through a window.

He menaces her with one of her own artifacts, a giant phallus (the embodiment of her penis envy) that recalls the bomb jutting out from between the legs of Major Kong at the end of *Dr. Strangelove*. The Catlady in turn swings a bust of Alex's beloved Beethoven at him. Their duel is shot with a hand-held camera that brings the spectator right into the fray. Kubrick operated the camera himself, as he did in shooting all of the scenes in the film in which the hand-held camera figured. "In addition to the fun of doing the shooting myself," he explains in *Sight and Sound*, "I find it virtually impossible to describe what I want in a hand-held shot to even the most talented and sensitive camera operator."

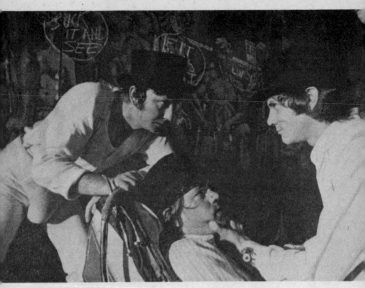

**James Marcus, Warren Clarke and Malcolm McDowell, CLOCK-WORK ORANGE.**

Inevitably Alex bests the Catlady and leaves her knocked sense-less, on her living room floor. When he goes outside to rejoin his henchmen, a close-up of a milk bottle clutched behind Dim's back tips the viewer off that a palace revolution is in the offing. Dim brings the bottle crashing across Alex's face and the felled leader is left to await the arrival of the police, whose sirens are audible in the distance.

At the station house Mr. Deltoid appears, having been sum-moned to participate in Alex's interrogation. He finds his charge lying against the wall in a corner of the immaculate room where he is being questioned. The wound on Alex's nose, which he re-ceived from Dim has been freshly opened in the course of his ex-amination by the police, and blood spatters the wall. "Violence makes violence," an inspector tells Deltoid. "He resisted his law-ful arresters. If you care to give him a bash in the chops, sir, don't mind us. He must be a great disappointment to you, sir." The so-cial worker glares into the camera lens (as if into Alex's eyes) and gleefully announces before spitting in his face, "You are now a murderer, little Alex. Your victim has died." His vindictiveness reminds one of Crassus's attempt to degrade Antoninus near the end of *Spartacus,* for both older men enjoy accomplishing the punishment of youths who spurned their advances.

"This is the real weepy and like tragic part of the story beginning, O my brothers and only friends," says "your humble narrator" as an aerial shot of a prison compound appears on the screen. Then follows the only scene which Kubrick added to the story: Alex's induction into the prison to begin serving his fourteen-year sentence for murder.

It was a necessary addition, Kubrick feels, because the prison sequence is compressed in his script in comparison with the way it is detailed in the book, and he had to do something to impress the audience with the idea that Alex was actually imprisoned. "The routine of checking into prison, which, in fact, is quite accurately presented in the film, seemed to provide this necessary weight." Alex is systematically stripped of his personal effects, his clothes, his identity (he is now 655321), and left only with his fantasy life.

He exercises his imagination by contemplating the more lurid sections of the Bible, the religious significance of which is, of course, lost on him. "I didn't so much like the latter part of the book," he comments, "which is more like all preachy talking." The prison chaplain (Godfrey Quigley) assumes that Alex's endless perusal of the sacred text is sincere, however, and makes him his assistant at the Sunday Church of England services.

Alex patronizes the chaplain and presses him for information about the Ludovico Technique, which reportedly enables a prisoner to leave prison for good after two weeks. The chaplain warns Alex against volunteering for the treatment and in so doing expresses the theme of the film: "The question is whether or not this treatment really makes a man good. Goodness comes from within. Goodness must be chosen. When a man cannot choose, he ceases to be a man." These theological reflections elude Alex, who willingly offers himself for the experiment when the Minister of the Interior (Anthony Sharp) visits the prison to see that the Ludovico Technique is implemented there. "The government cannot be concerned any longer with outmoded penological theories," he tells the prison governor, adding ominously, "Soon we may be needing all our prison space for political offenders."

The next day Alex is transferred to the Ludovico Medical Facility. The chief guard (Michael Bates) who escorts him there describes Alex to the admitting doctors in words that prove ironically prophetic: "You'll have to watch this one, Doc. A right brutal bastard he has been and will be again."

As the treatment begins, Alex is given a shot by a physician and then transported to a screening room. "I was bound up in a straitjacket and my gulliver was strapped to a headrest with wires running away from it. Then they clamped like lidlocks on my eyes

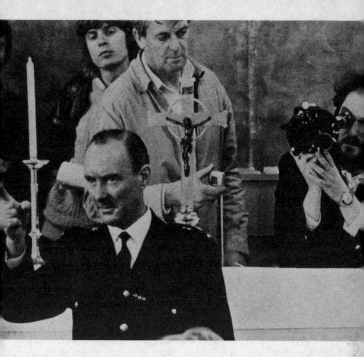

so that I could not shut them no matter how hard I tried." As he sits bug-eyed watching the first film, Alex enjoys seeing a man beaten mercilessly by a gang of thugs. "It was beautiful. It's funny how the colors of the real world only seem really real when you see them on the screen."

The next film portrays a gang rape, making it clear that these movies are paralleling the crimes that Alex and his droogs had committed earlier in the film. While he watches this succession of film clips a feeling of revulsion slowly engulfs Alex and he begs the attending physicians to stop the show, but the movies roll on.

Later Dr. Barnom assures him that, with the help of drugs, his body is learning to respond to sex and violence with revulsion. The next day, while viewing newsreels of Nazi atrocities, Alex is inconsolable when he realizes that the background score for the film is Beethoven's Ninth Symphony. He wails in agony that it is sinful to use Ludwig Van in this manner, but the doctors remind him that he chose to undergo the treatment and now he must see it through.

And so he does. At the end of two weeks Alex is judged ready to be released, and a kind of weird graduation ceremony is held, at which the Minister of the Interior announces, "Tomorrow we send him out into the world with the confidence that he is now as decent a lad as you would meet on a May morning. Our party promised to restore law and order and to make the streets safe again for the ordinary peace-loving citizen. This pledge is about to become a reality." Having finished his political fervorino, the minister presents Alex to the audience.

Alex is insulted by a man who forces him to lick his shoe, and then tempted by a scantily clad female. He cannot react in his former fashion to either stimulus, for as soon as the urge to violence or sex rises in him a concomitant urge to vomit also asserts itself, and he sinks to the floor, retching all the while. Alex's performance is met with approving applause from the audience, but the chaplain strongly protests what he has just witnessed.

"Choice!" he shouts to the assemblage. "The boy has no real choice, has he? Self-interest, the fear of physical pain drove him to that grotesque act of self-abasement. Its insincerity was clearly to be seen. He ceases to be a wrongdoer. He ceases also to be a creature capable of moral choice." The minister dismisses the chaplain's complaint, affirming that he cannot afford to be concerned with the subtleties of higher ethics, and sends Alex forth a "free" man.

Upon his release Alex is totally unprepared to cope with the calloused and corrupt society that awaits him. He first goes home, only to discover that Mum and Dad have given his room to a young man named Joe whom they have taken in as a lodger, and who has become like a son to them. Regretfully Alex's father stammers that he cannot ask Joe to leave since he has paid his rent in advance. "You've made others suffer," Joe says disdainfully; "it's only right that you should suffer proper."

Alex leaves the flat and wanders along the Thames embankment, only to encounter the tramp that he and his droogs had assaulted earlier in the movie. [This is one of the scenes in which Kubrick used a tiny microphone the size of a paper clip to get the dialogue. The mike was attached with black tape to the tramp's scarf and in fact is visible in several shots, though audiences never notice it.]

The tramp recognizes Alex and invites other elderly hoboes to join him in bashing the young man. A series of looming close-ups of grubby faces, contorted with rage, follow one another on the screen: "A sea of dirty old men trying to get at your humble narrator. It was old age having a go at youth."

Alex is rescued by two policemen who turn out to be two of his former gang members, Dim and Georgie, now police officers of a State that is becoming more and more fascist in its efforts to impose law and order on the populace. In the novel Georgie is dead by this time and it is Alex's old rival Billyboy who is Dim's fellow cop. Kubrick, however, eliminated this plot complication by simply having Georgie and Dim appear together at this point.

They drive Alex into the country in a police van and clobber him viciously in a clearing in the woods "to make sure he stays cured." When he regains consciousness he happens upon a welcoming neon sign, HOME, which seems to beckon him to hospi-

**Malcolm McDowell and Anthony Thorp, CLOCKWORK ORANGE.**

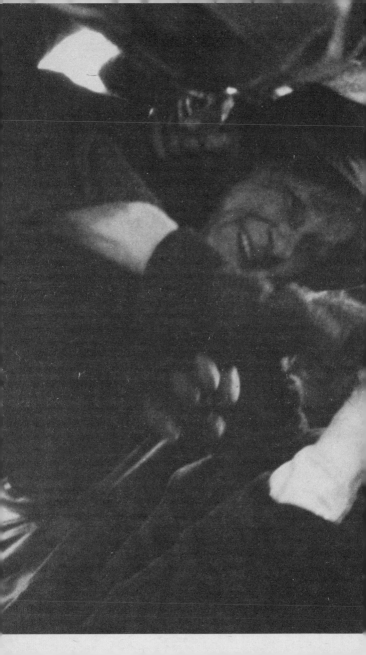

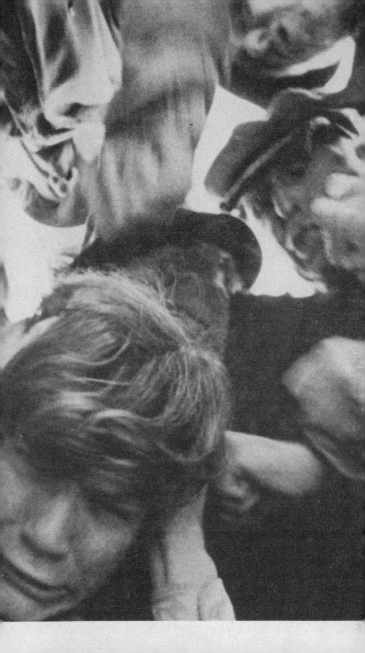

tality. He is admitted this time not by Mrs. Alexander but by Julian, the giant male nurse who looks after the invalid writer. As soon as he sees Frank Alexander in his wheelchair, Alex realizes with concealed horror that it is he who helped confine his host to that chair. He banks on Frank's not recognizing him, however, because of the mask that he wore the last time that they met.

Alexander nonetheless does recognize Alex as the recipient of the Ludovico treatment that he has read about, and schemes to make political capital out of Alex's experiences: "Tortured in prison, then thrown out to be tortured by the police." Frank phones some of his leftist cohorts and explains how they will be able to use Alex to discredit the party in power at the next election: they will inveigh against the government's tactics of recruiting brutal young toughs into the police force and of inaugurating debilitating brainwashing techniques of conditioning, all in the name of law and order. "Before we know where we are," he concludes, "we will have the full apparatus of totalitarianism."

Then, without being aware of it, Alexander reveals his own totalitarian propensities: "The common people will sell liberty for a quieter life. That is why they must be led, driven, pushed!" Here we have another wheelchair-bound Dr. Strangelove seeking to control the destiny of his fellow men.

As Alexander wheels himself away from the phone he suddenly notices that Alex is humming "Singin' in the Rain" while he lolls in the tub upstairs. An apoplectic look of shock distorts the writer's face. In the book Frank recognizes Alex when the lad insists in the course of their conversation that he is not dim like other ex-convicts, causing Alexander to recall that one of the hoodlums who invaded his home was named Dim. Kubrick's use of the song as Frank's means for identifying Alex is neater and more effective.

Having no misgivings about being recognized, Alex casually inquires about Mrs. Alexander over dinner. In a trembling voice her husband responds that she was raped by some thugs and later died in the course of a flu epidemic. "The doctors told me it was pneumonia, but I knew what it was. She was a victim of the Modern Age." Alex, too, is a victim of the Modern Age, as are many of the characters in *Clockwork Orange*.

Alex is interrogated by Frank's two fellow conspirators and he tells them how he was inadvertently conditioned against Beethoven—just before he passes out, having been drugged by Frank's dinner wine. He awakens to find himself locked in a bedroom while Beethoven's Ninth is cascading all around him. Alex hysterically rushes to the window and hurls himself through it, as Frank hoped he would.

In the most spectacular subjective shot in the entire movie the camera leaps out of the window too, enabling the viewer to see Alex's fall from his point of view. Kubrick achieved this effect by placing an especially durable camera in an insulated box and simply throwing it off a roof. In order to get the camera to land lens first he had to drop it six times, and it survived all six tries.

Alex too survives his plunge to earth and next awakens in a hospital bed enveloped in plaster casts. A montage of newspaper headlines tells of the controversy over Alex's attempted suicide: "Minister is accused of inhuman cure," says *The Evening Standard*. (One of the subheads in the newspaper headline refers to Alex Burgess, which is presumably a private joke between Kubrick and Burgess since Alex's last name, as given earlier in the film, is De Large.)

On returning to consciousness Alex finds his mother and father fawning over him and begging him to return home, an invitation which he bitterly rejects. Dr. Taylor, a psychiatrist (Pauline Taylor), comes to see him, and to her he mentions the bizarre dreams which he has been having, about a lot of doctors playing around with his gulliver. She cheerily dismisses his inquiry by assuring him that "it is all part of the recovery process." Perhaps the medicos have been tinkering with Alex's psyche while he was unconscious, a possibility that seems more and more to be the case in the light of the responses that Alex gives to Dr. Taylor in the ensuing experiment, during which traces of the old Alex begin to surface.

She shows him a series of drawings and he is to say whatever comes into his head. To a picture of a man entering a lady's bedroom, for example, Alex says, "No time for the old in-out, luv. I just came to read the meter." Dr. Taylor is pleased: "You seem well on the way to making a complete recovery."

The Minister of the Interior, who later comes to see Alex, agrees. He offers to feed Alex his supper while chatting with him. Alex pops his mouth open to receive each morsel like a fledgling bird in a nest. In a supremely patronizing tone the minister says his piece:

"I can tell you with all sincerity that I, and the government of which I am a member, are deeply sorry about this, my boy. We followed recommendations which were made to us that turned out to be wrong. An inquiry will place the responsibility where it belongs. [Elsewhere, of course.] There are certain people who wanted to use you for political ends. There is also a certain man, a writer of subversive literature, who has been howling for your blood. He found out that you had done wrong to him—at least he *believed* that you had. We put him away for his own protection, and also for yours." One of the reasons that the minister was interested in using the Ludovico treatment, we recall, was to clear out the prisons and thus make room for political prisoners. Frank Alexander is one of these.

Now the minister gets down to the heart of the matter. "It is no secret that this government has lost a lot of popularity because of you, my boy. But public opinion has a way of changing, and you, Alex, can be instrumental in changing the public's verdict." He offers Alex an easy job with a handsome salary. "You can rely on me, Fred," says Alex with a Cheshire smile. At the end of *Paths of Glory* General Broulard attempted to buy Colonel Dax, but Dax would not be bought. Alex unquestionably can.

Stereo equipment is wheeled in and Beethoven's Ninth blares forth as Alex and Fred shake hands for a passel of photographers. As Alex says, voice-over, "I was cured all right," a dream image appears on the screen: Alex frolics in slow motion with a nearly naked blond in a pile of polystyrene balls, while a group of Victorian ladies and gentlemen, dressed as for the Ascot races, look on and applaud. They represent a satirical thrust at the attitude of the Minister of the Interior, who subscribes to the Old Victorian code of morality which was concerned only with the surface appearances of respectability, not with true integrity. This final image also makes it clear that Alex is returning to his old self, complete with all of his former proclivities. Alex has regained his free will.

During the closing credits of the movie, as a final irony, Kubrick has Gene Kelly's original rendition of "Singin' in the Rain" from the 1952 motion picture of that name played on the sound track. This is a stroke of genius similar to Kubrick's employment of "We'll Meet Again" as the accompaniment of the nuclear holocaust in *Dr. Strangelove*. The words of "Singin' in the Rain" take on a particularly ironic quality as Kelly proclaims that it is "a glorious feeling" to be "happy again," for Alex has just jubilantly declared that he is cured, which means that he is fully able to return to his vicious behavior. One might go a step further in tying the song to the film by saying that anyone who is not concerned about mankind's future as depicted in the film is himself singing in the rain.

Because Kubrick has been unsparing in detailing Alex's depraved behavior in *Clockwork Orange*, the picture has been a source of continuing controversy. In considering the objection that the unpleasant events chronicled in Burgess's novel are presented more graphically in the film than they are in the book, I am reminded of what British director Ken Russell said about making his 1971 film *The Devils*: "When one reads about gory events in a book one can sift them through one's imagination and filter out as much of the unpleasantness as one cares to. But you can't do that when you are looking at a film. *The Devils* was a jolly sight less ugly than Aldous Huxley's book on which it was based. I was reading another book of Huxley's recently, *Ape and Essence,* and I said to myself, 'This is strong stuff, and were I to film it people would probably say that I have exaggerated the presentation of the material in the book. But it really couldn't be exaggerated.' " The same might be said of *A Clockwork Orange.*

The philosophy which underlies *Clockwork Orange* has also been attacked, on the grounds that Kubrick glamorizes, even evokes sympathy for a ruthless criminal. In dealing with this objection, Kubrick told critic Gene Siskel, "The essential moral of the story hinges on the question of choice, and the question of whether man can be good without having the choice to be evil, and whether a creature who no longer has this choice is still a man." The fact that Alex is evil personified is important, Kubrick contends, to clarify the point that the film is making about human freedom. "If Alex were a lesser villain, then you would dilute the point of the film. It would then be like one of those Westerns which purports to be against lynching and deals with the lynching of innocent people. The point of such a film would seem to be 'You shouldn't lynch people because you might lynch innocent people,' rather than 'You shouldn't lynch anybody.' Obviously if Alex were a lesser villain, it would be very easy to reject his 'treatment' as inhuman. But when you reject the treatment of even a character as wicked as Alex, the moral point is clear."

In short, to restrain man is not to redeem him. Redemption, as the prison chaplain says more than once in the film, must come from within.

The first time that Kubrick described Alex to me he called him a Richard III character, a comparison which he has repeated often since and one that seems, on reflection, well founded. In an essay about Shakespeare's villainous Richard III, I once wrote, "Richard is a malignant villain who has the gall to comment smugly to the audience on his own villainy. He is an opportunist who does not plot too far in advance but rather is adept at seizing the opportunities of the moment to further his schemes. The pure detached reason that in Shakespeare's view was to characterize a hero degenerates in Richard to pure cold cunning. He inhabits a corrupt world where his victims often deserve what he deals out to them." Surely, with a few minor adjustments, this description could serve equally well to delineate Alex in *Clockwork Orange.*

Kubrick, moreover, follows Shakespeare's lead in witholding

our sympathy from his villainous hero's victims because he wants to engage our interest in the dexterity with which his anti-hero carries out his plans. This is not to say, however, that we are asked to approve of what Alex does, any more than we are asked to approve of what is done to Alex in the second half of the film. Superficially he is a perversely winning character; but then so is the Minister of the Interior. We are asked, ultimately, to grasp the realization that the latter, for all his urbanity and charm, is no less of a heartless villain than Alex, given the minister's ruthless and systematic attempts to impose thought control on the population, an aim which he may yet achieve.

"The film and the book are about the danger of reclaiming sinners through sapping their capacity to choose between good and evil," Anthony Burgess has written in the London *Evening News*. "Most of all I wanted to show in my story that God has made man free to choose either good or evil, and that this is an astounding gift." Malcolm McDowell's own feelings about Alex at the end of the film bear out Burgess's remarks, as well as Kubrick's: "Alex is free at the end; that's hopeful. Maybe in his freedom, he'll be able to find someone to help him without brainwashing. If his Ludwig Van can speak to him, perhaps others can."

Still, it is not necessary to look beyond the end of the movie to find some possible regeneration for Alex in order to conclude that Kubrick has made a morally responsible film. As I mentioned in dealing with the objection that *Dr. Strangelove* does not solve the problems about the "balance of terror" which it raises, a filmmaker is not required to provide solutions to the questions which he raises and examines in a film. If he has jolted the audience into reflecting on these vital issues, he has done a great deal. In the case of *Clockwork Orange* it is almost as if Kubrick has presented Alex to the film audience as a challenge that Alex himself might phrase this way: "Here I am; what are you going to do about me?"

Kubrick now avoids films about the present because he believes that a movie can achieve a much more objective perspective about events and situations that are not contemporary. Just as he carried us into the future with his trilogy of science fiction films that began with *Dr. Strangelove,* so in his next film he has stepped back into the past to dramatize *Barry Lyndon,* the first novel by the Victorian novelist William Makepeace Thackeray. Hence one wonders if those Victorian ladies and gentlemen in the last shot of *Clockwork Orange* were somehow a portent of the film to follow.

# PART FOUR: THE PAST AS PRESENT

# Chapter Nine
# The Great Lover:

# Barry Lyndon (1975)

"It takes about a year to let an idea reach an obsessional state so I know what I really want to do with it," says Kubrick of the way that he initiates a new project. Because of his painstaking care in finding and developing a subject, other directors make more films than he does. For example, Sam Peckinpah's *Straw Dogs* was premiered at the end of 1971 at the same time that *Clockwork Orange* opened. By the time Kubrick announced that he was ready to start on another movie, Peckinpah had made no less than three more films: *Junior Bonner* (1972) and *The Getaway* and *Pat Garrett and Billy the Kid* (1973).

Meanwhile Kubrick had just reached the "obsessional state" at which he could proceed on *Barry Lyndon,* a tale of an eighteenth-century rogue written by the Victorian novelist William Makepeace Thackeray (*Vanity Fair*). Kubrick, in using Thackeray's novel as the basis for his movie, has added material that does not appear in the book and in other ways revised the original. Nonetheless it will be enlightening to examine the novel to see what there is about it that attracted Kubrick to adapt it for the screen, and to suggest how such a story might fit into the Kubrick canon as we have watched it develop in the preceding chapters.

Kubrick had already done two costume pictures (*Paths of Glory* and *Spartacus*) and the challenge of making another one was a tempting consideration. In addition, *Barry Lyndon* is not as alien to the rest of Kubrick's work as it might at first appear. For one thing, Thackeray in his writing seemed at times to be reaching for a style akin to cinema. In his *Irish Sketchbook* he describes a mountain range in minute detail and then, dissatisfied with what he considers to be his inadequate attempt to evoke the scene for the reader, comments, "Printer's ink cannot give these wonderful hues, and the reader will make his own picture at his leisure." Written in the same pictorial style, *Barry Lyndon* is as filmable a book as any Kubrick has made into a motion picture.

More importantly, in *Barry Lyndon* Kubrick very likely saw resonances of a theme that has reasserted itself throughout his work, that the best-laid plans often go awry: from the meticulously plotted racetrack heist in *The Killing* and Colonel Dax's efforts to defend the three scapegoat prisoners in *Paths of Glory,* through Spartacus's slave revolt and Humbert's designs to possess Lolita exclusively, to the "balance of terror" that is designed to halt the nuclear arms race in *Dr. Strangelove* and the Jupiter mission to investigate extraterrestrial life on another planet in *2001,* man is thwarted in his efforts to achieve his goals.

Human error and chance insinuate themselves into the most well-organized endeavors to frustrate their implementation and final success. Spartacus is ground under by the superior military tactics and political corruption of the Romans; Humbert is outwitted by the shrewd Quilty; and modern technology turns against its human instigators in the science fiction trilogy, as when the Ludovico Technique backfires in *A Clockwork Orange.* In this list of failures Barry Lyndon easily finds his place, for his lifelong schemes to become a rich nobleman ultimately come to nothing.

Of all of Kubrick's heroes and anti-heroes, Thackeray's Barry has the strongest kinship to Alex of *Clockwork Orange.* Both are young men whose superficial charm initially proves to be very ingratiating as they narrate their past "indiscretions" for us. But this charm eventually wears thin and is finally seen to cloak vicious proclivities for sex and violence as they reveal more and more about themselves.

Although *Barry Lyndon* was Thackeray's first novel, he had been a practicing journalist for several years before writing it, so that he produced a skillful piece of fiction in his first time out. His purpose was to create a tale about an eighteenth-century adventurer and Casanova of the Tom Jones variety, but furthermore to turn on him the cold light of irony, and show him up for the scoundrel that he really was. This ironic approach, of course, is the same method that Kubrick, following Anthony Burgess, took toward Alex in *Clockwork Orange.*

In fact, some of the descriptions of Barry Lyndon that one reads in essays on Thackeray's novel could just as easily have been written about Alex. For example: "The hero is a ruffian who, thinking he is showing a favorable picture of his life, is in fact giving himself away by his every sentence." That is Lord David Cecil writing in his introduction to a recent edition of the novel, but it might just

as well be Alex that he is referring to. Like Burgess, Thackeray was a realist and an anti-romantic who wanted to show up his hero for the kind of person he really was. Hence it is not surprising that Kubrick, who is also a realist and an anti-romantic, would be as attracted to one author as to the other. *Barry Lyndon* is not a pleasant book, says Lord Cecil, but it depicts with macabre power the darker side of human nature—a topic that has never failed to interest Kubrick.

*Barry Lyndon* is also an exciting novel, for it traces the amorous adventures of a Don Juan who hops from bedchamber to gaming room with equal ease. Though Barry gradually becomes more corrupt and dissipated as he gets older, he never completely loses the engaging qualities of his youth, such as his ability to snap back after facing whatever reversals Fortune hurls in his way. And, like Alex, he is constantly battling people who are every bit as wicked as he is. Therefore Barry never ceases to fascinate us in much the same way that a villain like Alex (or like Richard III) does.

Here, then, is a brief sketch of the plot of Thackeray's novel. Although, as I mentioned, Kubrick has extensively revised the book in adapting it for cinema, this synopsis will give us a good idea of the material from which he was working.

As a youth in Ireland, Barry naively falls in love with Nora, a coquette who delights in making him suffer. She is really in love with a Captain Quin, a young officer whom Barry foolishly challenges to a duel. Thinking he has killed Quin, Barry takes to the road and eventually joins the British army, which is currently engaged in prosecuting the Seven Years' War against the Germans. Barry's description of his lot as a common soldier rivals the ugly, inglorious picture of army life which Kubrick painted for us in *Paths of Glory*. Indeed, Barry's acrid remarks about his squalid existence in the army might have come from Kubrick's World War I film: "It is all very well," says Barry in the novel, "to dream of glorious war in a snug armchair at home, or to make it as an officer, surrounded by gentlemen, gorgeously dressed, and cheered by chances of promotion. But those chances do not shine on poor fellows" in the ranks. Barry fares no better when he is press-ganged into the Prussian army, which is composed, he says, "of men hired or stolen like myself from almost every nation in Europe."

After the war Barry is hired to spy on the Chevalier de Balibari, who turns out to be his long-lost uncle and a scoundrel in his own right. Together they roam across Europe bilking unsuspecting aristocrats in the gambling salons. The handsome Barry gets involved with a succession of women, all the while on the lookout

244

for a rich widow whom he can marry for her money and title. Of one such woman, whom he did not find physically attractive, he tells the reader with his sublimely unvarnished candor, "it was her estate I made love to; as for herself, it would be a reflection on my taste as a man of fashion to own that I liked her."

He meets the elderly and ill Sir Charles Lyndon, who jokingly suggests that Barry is pursuing his friendship with a view to marrying Lady Lyndon when he has passed on. Sir Charles, needless to say, is absolutely right. Once the old knight is dead, however, Barry has to contend with several other suitors who have been waiting in the wings for the opportunity to marry this most eligible of widows. Older and more unscrupulous than when he wooed Nora Brady, Barry draws on a seemingly bottomless bag of tricks to press his advances on Lady Lyndon.

Once Barry has succeeded in browbeating Lady Lyndon into marrying him and giving him access to her fortune and title, he decides that "we often buy money very much too dear." For Lady Lyndon turns out, on closer inspection, to be an unpleasant, vain young woman who is at once attracted physically to her undeniably good-looking husband and repelled by his coarse and irresponsible ways. Only her infatuation with him explains why she puts up with his weaknesses for as long as she does. At one point in the book Barry notes concerning his ill-treatment of his wife that he only struck her when he was drunk—at least for the first three years!

As Barry turns more and more to other women, Lady Lyndon finally divorces him and leaves him to the tender mercies of his creditors. Ending his days in a debtors' prison, Barry can only shrug, "I am one of those born to make, and not to keep, fortunes." He remains the same irrepressible individual he had been throughout his life right up to the end of the story. "As soldier, gambler, wife-beater, con man and finally prisoner," Penelope Houston comments on Thackeray's creation in *Sight and Sound,* "Barry Lyndon is an anti-hero at large in a raffish and generally reprehensible society; and a character wide open for a filmmaker's interpretation. The book opens up possibilities which suggest that, as usual, Kubrick knows exactly what he's about."

In writing *Barry Lyndon* Thackeray was departing drastically from the romantic presentation of the adventurous heroes of the historical novels that had preceded his first venture into that genre. So in filming *Barry Lyndon* Kubrick has chosen a story that likewise departs from the highly romantic historical movies of the past. Many of these, especially those made in England in the years following World War II, were what Penelope Houston describes

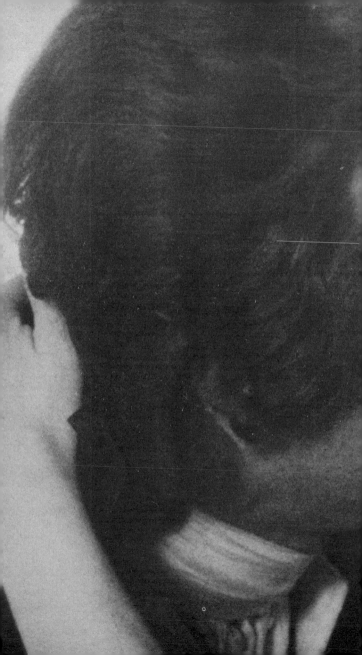

in *The Contemporary Cinema* as examples of "kitchenmaid escapism." She goes on to explain how these movies gloried in "endless permutations of the same star équipe, as James Mason and Stewart Granger, Margaret Lockwood and Phyllis Calvert flung themselves into Regency disguise, took to the roads as highwaymen, poisoned off old retainers (with, if memory can be trusted, doses from large bottles obligingly labelled *poison*), and cheated each other out of inheritances." (After a steady diet of historical epics of this sort, one small-town American exhibitor wrote to his distributor back in the forties, "Don't send me no more pictures about people who write with feathers!")

Since Thackeray wanted to expose the underside of corruption beneath the elegant surface behavior of that bygone era, Barry Lyndon is anything but an Errol Flynn-type swashbuckling hero; rather, in the words of Warner Brothers' advance publicity for Kubrick's film, Barry is "a card-sharper, seducer, bully, and liar who regards gambling as the highest occupation to which a man can devote himself, for whom fraud is always justified by success; a man possessed by all meanness except cowardice."

For the title role in his movie Kubrick chose Ryan O'Neal, who says that his remote preparation for the part included "taking sword-fighting lessons for months." Thackeray, who styles himself not the author but the "editor" of Barry Lyndon's "autobiography," hints in a footnote in the novel why Barry included so many duels in his memoirs: "Whenever he is at an awkward pass, or does what the world does not consider respectable, a duel, in which he is victorious, is sure to ensue, from which he argues that he is a man of undoubted 'honor.'"

*Barry Lyndon* was shot on locations in Ireland, England, and the Continent, since Kubrick believes that location shooting is just as viable for a period picture like *Barry Lyndon* as for a contemporary story like *The Killing,* or for one set in the near future like *Clockwork Orange.* "Most of the interiors of a period film can be shot in mansions and castles that are still preserved in Europe, where the furniture and decor are already there," he has pointed out. "You only have to move in your cast and crew and get to work."

One of the major changes which Kubrick made in creating his film of Thackeray's novel was having a narrator—possibly the voice of author Thackeray himself—replace Barry as the teller of his own tale. In the past Kubrick has often turned to spoken narration as the most simple and direct way of telegraphing exposition to an audience, as I have already pointed out in the course of this book. Since he followed the lead of the original novels in having the central character of *Lolita* and of *A Clockwork Orange* narrate his film versions of those two novels respectively, one wonders why Kubrick switched from the first-person narration of Barry in Thackeray's book to the more impersonal voice of a nameless narrator (voice by Michael Hordern) in the film of *Barry Lyndon*.

In the novel, as I mentioned above, Barry gives himself away with nearly every sentence, despite his efforts to paint a favorable picture of himself. This delightfully satirical element in the novel is largely lacking in the movie because the disembodied voice of the narrator gives Barry away to the viewer with every comment that he makes on Barry's behavior. Kubrick's explanation of this reworking of his material is that a first-person narration works for comedy but not for the more serious comments that Thackeray introduces into his narrative. But it is just this comic touch which anyone who has read Thackeray's novel misses in the motion picture, and I confess my disappointment that the director who injected comic satire into *Dr. Strangelove* removed it from *Barry Lyndon*.

If some of the humor is mislaid in the passage of the story from page to screen, some of the dramatic intensity is too. Kubrick retools Lady Lyndon (Marisa Berenson) into a much more passive wife than is the intrepid lady with which Barry has to contend in the book, where the stubborn and resourceful lady literally gives Barry a run for his money. Thackeray's Lady Lyndon is a much more worthy adversary for the wiley Barry than is Kubrick's.

Once these reservations have been made, however, I am happy to say that the majority of the revisions which Kubrick made in bringing Thackeray's novel to the screen have enhanced it considerably. As the film unfolds, one sees that Kubrick wants us to sympathize with Barry much more than Thackeray did. For the portrait of Barry which Kubrick has sketched for us is not that of a mere wastrel who is rotten from the start, but of a young man who has become increasingly disillusioned with life because he has been systematically taken advantage of by the very people whom he has trusted most. (Watching Barry go from good to bad in the movie is much more interesting than watching him go from bad to worse in the book.)

Barry's first love, Nora Brady, coyly manipulates his feelings for her. Even the person whom Barry respects most, Captain Jack Grogan (Godfrey Quigley), participates in the Brady family's plot to force Barry to leave Ireland by making him believe that he has killed his rival for Nora's hand in marriage in a duel. Grogan's later offer to share with Barry the hush money which he received from the Bradys does not really alter his disloyalty to Barry. Ironi-

cally, when Grogan is later killed in the war against the French, we are told that one of the last positive influences on Barry's character is now gone.

Barry next falls into the hands of a bogus nobleman, the Chevalier de Balibari (Patrick Magee), who—although he is not Barry's long lost uncle as he is in the novel—entices Barry to join him roaming across Europe bilking unsuspecting aristocrats at the gaming tables. By the time that Barry marries Lady Lyndon for her wealth, therefore, he has become a scheming scoundrel, someone far different from the naive young man whom we met at the beginning of the film. Finally, when his only son Brian is killed in a riding accident, it seems that the last spark of real warmth and human love is extinguished in Barry's nature.

Yet we learn in the celebrated duel scene between Barry and his stepson, Lord Bullingdon (Leon Vitali), that such is not the case. This scene derives from a single, unspecified sentence on the last page of the novel which merely states that the young man met Barry Lyndon and "revenged upon his person the insults of former days." Taking his cue from this cryptic remark, Kubrick builds a scene in the film in which Barry fires his pistol at the ground in order not to injure further the young man who—he by now realizes—has suffered enough from his selfishness. Instead of recognizing his stepfather's gesture of contrition, however, the embittered young gentleman wounds Barry in the leg, rendering him crippled for the rest of his itinerate life.

As Penelope Houston comments in her long review of the movie in *Sight and Sound,* the irony underlying this scene is that "Barry's devious career has been governed by the ambition to become a gentleman; and it is as a 'gentleman' that he holds off when he has his man at his mercy. . . . Bullingdon, who has the advantage of having been born a gentleman, shows no such compunction." There is little doubt, then, that Kubrick wants us to feel some degree of sympathy for Barry throughout the film, but especially at the end—though he does not consign Barry to debtors' prison for the rest of his days as Thackeray does. As Kubrick envisions him, says Penelope Houston, Barry is a Gatsby without a noble dream, a seedy soldier of fortune who in the end has nothing to show for his troubled life but wounds and scars; a born loser who learned the ways of a rogue but never mastered the art of self-protection against those more crafty and cruel than he.

This climactic duel scene, which, as I said, is not specifically mentioned in the book at all, is described in the script in the single line, "Barry duels with Lord Bullingdon." It can well serve as an example of the painstaking way in which Kubrick the perfectionist creates a segment of celluloid, one which has been called by John Hofsess in *The New York Times* "one of the most stunning sequences in modern film."

"It took six weeks (forty-two working days) just to edit the sequence," Hofsess continues. "To find the music, Handel's 'Sarabande,' Kubrick listened to every available recording of Seventeenth and Eighteenth Century music that he could acquire, literally thousands of LPs. What he achieves in such moments of the film might be called . . . inspired combinations of words, images, music, and editing rhythms, creating a kind of artistic experience that no other medium can convey."

Even though *Barry Lyndon*'s running time of just over three hours makes it the longest movie that Kubrick has yet made, it still reflects the kind of cinematic economy which we have come to expect from his work. Frequently a single telling image can communicate more to the film viewer than several lines of dialogue or narration, which is why Kubrick keeps both to a minimum, and relies whenever possible on his knack for visual symbolism.

He shoots the scene in which Barry discovers Nora Brady flirting with his rival in the late afternoon so that the dying sunlight can signal the demise of Barry's hopes of ever winning Nora for himself. Later, in the scene in which Barry is engaged in flirting ever so discreetly with Lady Lyndon across a gambling table, candles stand in the foreground of the shot. In this way Kubrick emphasizes the flame that has been enkindled in the lady for Barry's youth and beauty, and the flame that has been likewise enkindled in Barry for her wealth and status.

In photographing scenes lit solely by candles Kubrick marked an advance in cinematography, since no scene in a motion picture had ever been lit with so little illumination before. He accomplished this by using an extremely sensitive lens which originally had been developed by NASA for photographing the instrument panel of a space ship. The result, as Judith Crist rightly rhapsodizes, is that "for the first time in a period film the night lighting is authentically by candle; by a few and by the hundreds, the yellow light and deep shadows bring an entirely new vision to our experience, the golden glow a remarkable contrast to the clarity of natural lighting on which Kubrick relies for his daytime interiors and outdoor scenes."

Harold Rosenberg sums up Kubrick's achievement in *Barry Lyndon* in a *New York Times* essay in which he writes that the director has created in the film what amounts to a panoramic painting of eighteenth century life. "The movie translates Thackeray's printed page into art for the eye and the ear by coordinating the

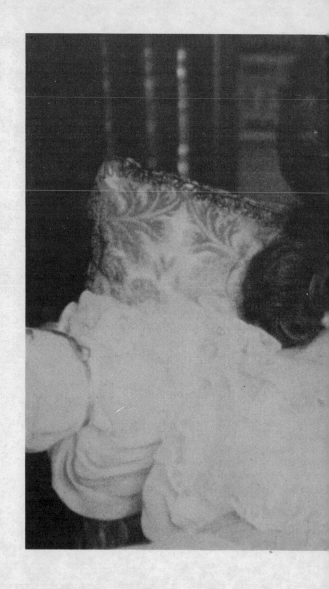

story with the paintings, music, and landscape of the period," for the settings and costumes were all suggested by the paintings of Gainsborough, Reynolds, and Hogarth, just as the musical score was culled from the compositions of Handel, Vivaldi, Bach, and Mozart.

To accomplish such a task involved a budget of nearly eleven million dollars (all of which, says Kubrick, is visible on the screen), and nearly four years of steady work. The director supervised every detail of the production, including the "incredible effort on costuming," which involved thirty-five seamstresses and tailors working for six months before the cameras rolled. In England, Ireland, and elsewhere Kubrick searched for just the right location site for each scene in the film, turning up landscapes, houses, and castles that looked genuinely eighteenth century, and including what Kubrick calls "the hardest location to find for a period picture, a properly rutted rustic road."

No wonder that Barry Lyndon won Academy Awards for its grand technical and artistic achievements; though none went to Kubrick himself, Oscars were earned by Ken Adam and Roy Walker for production design and art direction, to Ulla-Britt Söderlund and Milena Canonero for the costumes, to John Alcott for cinematography, and to Leonard Rosenman for adapting and conducting the musical score.

*Barry Lyndon* ends with the following printed epilogue (the first such epilogue that Kubrick has used since *Lolita*): "It was in the reign of George III that these personages lived and quarrelled. Good or bad, handsome or ugly, rich or poor, they are all equal now." When the audience reads this, they feel that they have indeed been catapulted backward in time to witness the lives of people from the past relived before their eyes on the screen. One might almost go so far as to say that if the technical equipment to make a movie had been available in the eighteenth century, the films made then would look exactly like *Barry Lyndon* does!

Even *Punch,* which did not say much in favor of the film, in effect conceded this last point: "Each episode begins with the same formal sequence: first a respectful pause before a fiery sunset or a brewing storm or an emergent dawn; and then it moves indoors to a superbly orchestrated tableau [of] ravishing pictorial beauty." Pauline Kael may dismiss the picture as "a coffee-table movie," but in reality Kubrick has created quite an accomplishment.

He has managed in this film not only to translate a historical novel to the screen but to evoke the past as a vivid present—which is just what it was for the people who lived through it. Kubrick's characters may write with feathers, but they inhabit a motion pic-

266

ture which comes closer than any costume film ever has before to showing us a historical era, not as part of a dead past, but as a living present.

In making a film Kubrick's abiding respect for his actors is always evident, especially in his encouraging them to make suggestions during rehearsals. "An actor will do what you want him to do if he is able to do it," he remarked in *Sight and Sound.* The director's job, then, is to provide the actors with ideas about the psychology of the characters they are portraying and about the purpose of the scene. The director can make a mediocre actor less mediocre, says Kubrick, but he cannot make him exciting or interesting. "Only a good performer can provide the magic that makes a great performance. The actor must know that you admire him and there is no way to fake that." This attitude spurs the actor on to do his best.

Sterling Hayden recalls experiencing just this sense that Kubrick respected him when he was making *Dr. Strangelove* for the director. On the first day of shooting Hayden found that he could not handle the technical jargon in his lines. "I was utterly humiliated and Stanley told me, 'The terror on your face may yield just the quality we want and if it doesn't, the hell with it. We'll shoot the thing over.' He was beautiful."

Kubrick is always omnipresent when shooting a film, checking every detail, making sure that the combination of human error and chance that dog his characters is kept at a minimum on his set. Through all of this Kubrick manages to maintain the same soft-spoken manner that characterizes his conversation. When he discovered, for example, while processing the negative of *Clockwork Orange,* that the laboratory had scratched it seriously, he informed the head of the lab which had almost ruined months of his work that he was going to finish the job elsewhere—without ever raising his voice.

Once a Kubrick film is in the can, he supervises every aspect of the advertising campaign that will promote the motion picture in which he has already invested a year or more of his life. Kubrick belongs to that handful of moviemakers, which also includes Alfred Hitchcock, whose name is as much of a draw on the marquee as that of any actor in the movie. *Barry Lyndon* is his first film in ten years to employ a superstar in the lead.

As to what Kubrick will turn to after *Barry Lyndon,* one can only guess. Kubrick does have one long-cherished project that he will probably make eventually, a film about Napoleon. That great dictator fits into Kubrick's ongoing study of the failure of the best-worked-out plans in that his defeat was brought about by causes

that all of his meticulous advance work did not foresee and could not cope with. Kubrick began his initial planning of the film after he finished *2001,* but, as he says, that was before "the lights went out in Hollywood," in the wake of the failure of several large-scale productions, such as the Julie Andrews vehicle *Star* and the Barbra Streisand vehicle *Hello, Dolly!* Also the Russians released *Waterloo,* a solemn epic about Napoleon starring Rod Steiger, which made it inadvisable for Kubrick to make another movie about Napoleon at that time. The Russian film, however, was a heavy-handed pageant which garnered a cool critical response and has since sunk without a trace.

In any event, Kubrick does not envision making his movie on the scale of a Russian or Hollywood epic when he does get around to making it. Again he plans to use authentic locations on the Continent (as he did in *Barry Lyndon*), where many buildings and sites dating from Napoleon's time still are preserved. The battle scenes can be done in places like Yugoslavia, Hungary, and Romania, where arrangements can be made to enlist the services of the regular army for shooting, in the same way that he employed a corps of German policemen in *Paths of Glory.*

Kubrick's Napoleon will attempt to capture all aspects of the man: as soldier, statesman, and emperor. "It is difficult to make a film about a historical figure that presents the necessary historical information and at the same time conveys a sense of the day-to-day reality of the characters' lives," he says. "Most people don't realize, for example, that Napoleon spent most of his time on the eve of battle immersed in paper work. You want the audience to get the feeling of what it was like to be with Napoleon." Kubrick, in short, wants to present the past as a vivid present when he makes a historical film, to portray the past as it was to the people living it.

Whether his films are set in the past, present, or future, Kubrick has demonstrated a continuing concern for mankind in his films. "The destruction of this planet would have no significance on a cosmic scale," he has reflected to Eric Norden, "our extinction would be little more than a match flaring for a second in the heavens. And if that match does blaze in the darkness, there will be none to mourn a race that used a power that could have lit a beacon in the stars to light its funeral pyre."

It is clear, then, that Kubrick wants to continue to create films that will stimulate his audience to think about serious human problems, as his pictures have done from the beginning. Because of the success of his movies in the past, Kubrick can go on making films in the way he wants to, proving in the future, as he has in the past, that he values the artistic freedom which he has worked so hard to win and has used so well.

## Chapter One

*Day of the Fight* (U.S.A., 1951)

| | |
|---|---|
| Director, Photography, Editor, Sound | Stanley Kubrick |
| Commentary | Douglas Edwards |
| Running time: 16 minutes | |
| Distributor: RKO Radio | |

*Flying Padre* (U.S.A., 1951)

| | |
|---|---|
| Director, Photography, Editor, Sound | Stanley Kubrick |
| Running time: 9 minutes | |
| Distributor: RKO Radio | |

*The Seafarers.* 1953

Photographed in color and directed by Stanley Kubrick. Written by Will Chasan. Narrated by Don Hollenbeck. Technical advice by the staff of the *Seafarers Log.* Produced by Lester Cooper. Presented by Seafarers International Union, Atlantic and Gulf Coast District, AFL. Running time: 30 minutes.

*Fear and Desire* (U.S.A., 1953)

| | |
|---|---|
| Production Company | Stanley Kubrick Productions |
| Producer | Stanley Kubrick |
| Associate Producer | Martin Perveler |
| Director, Photography, Editor | Stanley Kubrick |
| Dialogue Director | Toba Kubrick |
| Script | Howard O. Sackler |
| | Stanley Kubrick |
| Music | Gerald Fried |

Frank Silvera (Mac), Kenneth Harp (Corby), Virginia Leith (The Girl), Paul Mazursky (Sidney), Steve Colt (Fletcher), David Allen (Narrator)
Running time: 68 minutes
Distributor: Joseph Burstyn

*Killer's Kiss* (U.S.A., 1955)

| | |
|---|---|
| Production Company | Minotaur |
| Producers | Stanley Kubrick |
| | Morris Bousel |
| Director, Photography, Editor | Stanley Kubrick |
| Script | Stanley Kubrick |
| | Howard O. Sackler |
| Music | Gerald Fried |
| Choreography | David Vaughan |

Frank Silvera (Vincent Rapallo), Jamie Smith (Davy Gordon), Irene Kane (Gloria Price), Jerry Jarret (Albert), Iris (Ruth Sobotka), Mike Dana, Felice Orlandi, Ralph Roberts, Phil Stevenson (Hoodlums), Julius Adelman (Mannequin Factory Owner), David Vaughan, Alec Rubin (Conventioneers)
Running time: 64 minutes
Distributor: United Artists

## Chapter Two

*The Killing* (U.S.A., 1956)

| | |
|---|---|
| Production Company | Harris-Kubrick Productions |
| Producer | James B. Harris |
| Director | Stanley Kubrick |
| Script | Stanley Kubrick, based on the novel *Clean Break*, by Lionel White |
| Additional Dialogue | Jim Thompson |
| Photography | Lucien Ballard |
| Editor | Betty Steinberg |
| Art Director | Ruth Sobotka |
| Music | Gerald Fried |
| Sound | Earl Snyder |

Sterling Hayden (Johnny Clay), Jay C. Flippen (Marvin Unger), Marie Windsor (Sherry Peatty), Elisha Cook, Jr. (George Peatty), Coleen Gray (Fay), Vince Edwards (Val Cannon), Ted De Corsia (Randy Kennan), Joe Sawyer (Mike O'Reilly), Tim Carey (Nikki), Kola Kwariani (Maurice), James Edwards (Car Park Attendant), Jay Adler (Leo), Joseph Turkey (Tiny)
Running time: 83 minutes
Distributor: United Artists

**Chapter Three**

*Paths of Glory* (U.S.A., 1957)

| | |
|---|---|
| Production Company | Harris-Kubrick Productions |
| Producer | James B. Harris |
| Director | Stanley Kubrick |
| Script | Stanley Kubrick, Calder Willingham, Jim Thompson, based on the novel by Humphrey Cobb |
| Photography | George Krause |
| Editor | Eva Kroll |
| Art Director | Ludwig Reiber |
| Music | Gerald Fried |
| Sound | Martin Muller |

Kirk Douglas (Colonel Dax), Ralph Meeker (Corporal Paris), Adolphe Menjou (General Broulard), George Macready (General Mireau), Wayne Morris (Lieutenant Roget), Richard Anderson (Major Saint-Auban), Joseph Turkel (Private Arnaud), Timothy Carey (Private Ferol), Peter Capell (Colonel Judge), Susanne Christian (German Girl), Bert Freed (Sergeant Boulanger), Emile Meyer (Priest), John Stein (Captain Rousseau), Ken Dibbs (Private Lejeune), Jerry Hausner (Tavern Owner), Harold Benedict (Captain Nichols)
Running time: 86 minutes
Distributor: United Artists; presented by Bryna Productions

## Chapter Four

*Spartacus* (U.S.A., 1960)

| | |
|---|---|
| Production Company | Bryna Productions |
| Executive Producer | Kirk Douglas |
| Producer | Edward Lewis |
| Director | Stanley Kubrick |
| Script | Dalton Trumbo, based on the book by Howard Fast |
| Photography | Russell Metty |
| Additional Photography | Clifford Stine |
| Screen Process | Super Technirama-70 |
| Color | Technicolor |
| Editors | Robert Lawrence |
| | Robert Schultz |
| | Fred Chulack |
| Production Designer | Alexander Golitzen |
| Art Director | Eric Orbom |
| Set Decoration | Russell A. Gausman |
| | Julia Heron |
| Titles | Saul Bass |
| Technical Adviser | Vittorio Nino Novarese |
| Costumes | Peruzzi |
| | Valles |
| | Bill Thomas |
| Music | Alex North |
| Music Director | Joseph Gershenson |
| Sound | Waldon O. Watson |
| | Joe Lapis |
| | Murray Spivack |
| | Ronald Pierce |
| Assistant Director | Marshall Green |

Kirk Douglas (Spartacus), Laurence Olivier (Marcus Crassus), Jean Simmons (Varinia), Charles Laughton (Gracchus), Peter Ustinov (Batiatus), John Gavin (Julius Caesar), Tony Curtis (Antoninus), Nina Foch (Helena), Herbert Lom (Tigranes), John Ireland (Crixus), John Dall (Glabrus), Charles McGraw (Marcellus), Joanna Barnes (Claudia), Harold J. Stone (David), Woody Strode (Draba), Peter Brocco (Ramon), Paul Lambert (Gannicus), Robert J. Wilke (Captain of Guard), Nicholas Dennis (Dionysius), John Hoyt (Roman Officer), Fred Worlock (Laelius), Dayton Lummis (Symmachus)

Original running time: 196 minutes, permanently cut to 184 minutes

Distributor: Universal Pictures

**Chapter Five**

*Lolita* (Great Britain, 1962)

| | |
|---|---|
| Production Company | Seven Arts/Anya/ Transworld |
| Producer | James B. Harris |
| Director | Stanley Kubrick |
| Script | Vladimir Nabokov, based on his novel |
| Photography | Oswald Morris |
| Editor | Anthony Harvey |
| Art Director | William Andrews |
| Set Design | Andrew Low |
| Music | Nelson Riddle |
| Lolita's Theme | Bob Harris |
| Sound | H. L. Bird |
| | Len Shilton |
| Assistant Directors | Roy Millichip |
| | John Danischewsky |

James Mason (Humbert Humbert), Sue Lyon (Lolita Haze), Shelley Winters (Charlotte Haze), Peter Sellers (Clare Quilty), Diana Decker (Jean Farlow), Jerry Stovin (John Farlow), Suzanne Gibbs (Mona Farlow), Gary Cockrell (Dick), Marianne Stone (Vivian Darkbloom), Cec Linder (Physician), Lois Maxwell (Nurse Mary Lord), William Greene (Swine), C. Denier Warren (Potts), Isobel Lucas (Louise), Maxine Holden (Hospital Receptionist), James Dyrenforth (Beale), Roberta Shore (Lorna), Eric Lane (Roy), Shirley Douglas (Mrs. Starch), Roland Brand (Bill), Colin Maitland (Charlie), Irvin Allen (Hospital Attendant), Marion Mathie (Miss Lebone), Craig Sams (Rex), John Harrison (Tom)
Running time: 153 minutes
Distributor: Metro-Goldwyn-Mayer

# Chapter Six

*Dr. Strangelove, or How I Learned to Stop Worrying and Love the Bomb* (Great Britain, 1964)

| | |
|---|---|
| Production Company | Hawk Films |
| Producer-Director | Stanley Kubrick |
| Associate Producer | Victor Lyndon |
| Script | Stanley Kubrick, Terry Southern, Peter George, based on the novel *Red Alert*, by Peter George |
| Photography | Gilbert Taylor |
| Editor | Anthony Harvey |
| Production Designer | Ken Adam |
| Art Director | Peter Murton |
| Special Effects | Wally Veevers |
| Music | Laurie Johnson |
| Aviation Adviser | Captain John Crewdson |
| Sound | John Cox |

Peter Sellers (Group Captain Lionel Mandrake, President Muffley, Dr. Strangelove), George C. Scott (General Buck Turgidson), Sterling Hayden (General Jack D. Ripper), Keenan Wynn (Colonel Bat Guano), Slim Pickens (Major T. J. "King" Kong), Peter Bull (Ambassador de Sadesky), Tracy Reed (Miss Scott), James Earl Jones (Lieutenant Lothar Zogg, Bombardier), Jack Creley (Mr. Staines), Frank Berry (Lieutenant H. R. Dietrich, D.S.O.), Glenn Beck (Lieutenant W. D. Kivel, Navigator), Shane Rimmer (Captain G. A. "Ace" Owens, Co-pilot), Paul Tamarin (Lieutenant B. Goldberg, Radio Operator), Gordon Tanner (General Faceman), Robert O'Neil (Admiral Randolph), Roy Stephens (Frank), Laurence Herder, John McCarthy, Hal Galili (Members of Burpleson Base Defense Corps)
Running time: 94 minutes
Distributor: Columbia Pictures

# Chapter Seven

*2001: A Space Odyssey* (Great Britain, 1968)

| | |
|---|---|
| Production Company | Metro-Goldwyn-Mayer |
| Producer | Stanley Kubrick |
| Director | Stanley Kubrick |
| Script | Stanley Kubrick, |
| | Arthur C. Clarke, |
| | based on Clarke's short |
| | story "The Sentinel" |
| Photography | Geoffrey Unsworth |
| Screen Process | Super Panavision |
| | Presented in Cinerama |
| Color | Metrocolor |
| Additional Photography | John Alcott |
| Special Photographic Effects | Stanley Kubrick |
| Designer and Director | |
| Editor | Ray Lovejoy |
| Production Designers | Tony Masters |
| | Harry Lange |
| | Ernie Archer |
| Art Director | John Hoesli |
| Special Photographic Effects | Wally Veevers |
| Supervisors | Douglas Trumbull |
| | Con Pederson |
| | Tom Howard |
| Music | Richard Strauss |
| | Johann Strauss |
| | Aram Khachaturian |
| | György Ligeti |
| Costumes | Hardy Amies |
| Sound | Winston Ryder |

Keir Dullea (David Bowman), Gary Lockwood (Frank Poole),
William Sylvester (Dr. Heywood Floyd), Daniel Richter (Moon-
Watcher), Douglas Rain (Voice of HAL 9000), Leonard Rossiter
(Smyslov), Margaret Tyzack (Elena), Robert Beatty (Halvorsen),
Sean Sullivan (Michaels), Frank Miller (Mission Control), Penny
Brahms (Stewardess), Alan Gifford (Poole's Father), Edward
Bishop, Glenn Beck, Edwina Carroll, Mike Lovell, Peter Delman,
Dany Grover, Brian Hawley
Running time: 141 minutes
Distributor: Metro-Goldwyn-Mayer

## Chapter Eight

*A Clockwork Orange* (Great Britain, 1971)

| | |
|---|---|
| Production Company | Hawk Films |
| Producer-Director | Stanley Kubrick |
| Executive Producers | Max L. Raab |
| | Si Litvinoff |
| Associate Producer | Bernard Williams |
| Script | Stanley Kubrick, based on the novel by Anthony Burgess |
| Photography | John Alcott |
| Color | Warnercolor |
| Editor | Bill Butler |
| Production Designer | John Barry |
| Art Directors | Russell Hagg |
| | Peter Shields |
| Music | Ludwig van Beethoven |
| | Edward Elgar |
| | Gioacchino Rossini |
| | Terry Tucker |
| | Erika Eigen |
| Original Electronic Music | Walter Carlos |
| Sound | John Jordan |
| Assistant Directors | Derek Cracknell |
| | Dusty Symonds |
| Costumes | Milena Canonero |

Malcolm McDowell (Alex), Patrick Magee (Mr. Alexander), Michael Bates (Chief Guard), Warren Clarke (Dim), John Clive (Stage Actor), Adrienne Corri (Mrs. Alexander), Carl Duering (Dr. Brodsky), Paul Farrell (Tramp), Clive Francis (Lodger), Michael Gover (Prison Governor), Miriam Karlin (Catlady), James Marcus (Georgia), Aubrey Morris (Deltoid), Godfrey Quigley (Prison Chaplain), Sheila Raynor (Mum), Madge Ryan (Dr. Barnom), John Savident (Conspirator), Anthony Sharp (Minister of the Interior), Philip Stone (Dad), Pauline Taylor (Psychiatrist), Margaret Tyzack (Conspirator), and Steven Berkoff, Lindsay Campbell, Michael Tarn, David Prowse, Barrie Cookson, Jan Adair, Gaye Brown, Peter Burton, John J. Carney, Vivienne Chandler, Richard Connaught, Prudence Drage, Carol Drinkwater, Lee Fox, Cheryl Grunwald, Gillian Hills, Craig Hunter, Shirley Jaffe, Virginia Wetherell, Neil Wilson, Katya Wyeth
Running time: 135 minutes
Distributor: Warner Brothers

# BARRY LYNDON

(Great Britain, 1975)

Starring: RYAN O'NEAL (Barry Lyndon); MARISA BERENSON (Lady Lyndon); PATRICK MAGEE (The Chevalier); HARDY KRUGER (Captain Potzdorf). Featuring, in alphabetical order: Steven Berkoff (Lord Ludd); Gay Hamilton (Nora); Marie Kean (Barry's Mother); Diana Koerner (German Girl); Murray Melvin (Reverend Runt); Frank Middlemass (Sir Charles Lyndon); Andre Morell (Lord Wendover); Arthur O'Sullivan (Highwayman); Godfrey Quigley (Captain Grogan); Leonard Rossiter (Captain Quin); Philip Stone (Graham); Leon Vitali (Lord Bullingdon); Michael Hordern (Narrator).
With: John Bindon, Roger Booth, Billy Boyle, Jonathan Cecil, Peter Cellier, Geoffrey Chater, Anthony Dawes, Patrick Dawson, Bernard Hepton, Anthony Herrick, Barry Jackson, Wolf Kahler, Patrick Laffan, Hans Meyer, Ferdy Mayne, David Morley, Liam Redmond, Pat Roach, Dominic Savage, Frederick Schiller, George Sewell, Anthony Sharp, John Sharp, Roy Spencer, John Sullivan, Harry Towb.

## THE CREDITS

Written for the screen, produced and directed by Stanley Kubrick. Based on the novel by William Makepeace Thackeray.

Executive Producer—Jan Harlan
Associate Producer—Bernard Williams
Production Designer—Ken Adam
Costumes designed by—Ulla-Britt Soderlund, Milena Canonero
Photographed by—John Alcott
Editor—Tony Lawson
Art Director—Roy Walker
Hair styles and wigs—Leonard
Assistant to the Producer—Andros Epaminondas
Assistant Director—Brian Cook
Music adapted and conducted by— Leonard Rosenman

From works by: Johann Sebastian Bach, Frederick the Great, Georg Friedrich Handel, Wolfgang Amadeus Mozart, Giovanni Paisiello, Franz Schubert, Antonio Vivaldi
Irish traditional music by—The Chieftains
Schubert Piano Trio E-Flat Op. 100 performed by: Ralph Holmes, violin; Moray Welsh, cello; Anthony Goldstone, piano.
Vivaldi Cello Concerto E-Minor—Pierre Fournier, cello; recorded on Deutsche Grammophon

Production Managers—Douglas Twiddy, Terence Clegg
Assistant Directors—David Tomblin, Michael Stevenson
Unit Managers—Malcolm Christopher, Don Geraghty
Production Manager in Germany— Rudolf Hertzog
Location Liaison—Arthur Morgan, Col. William O'Kelly
Sound Editor—Rodney Holland
Sound Recordist—Robin Gregory
Dubbing Mixer—Bill Rowe
Assistant Editor—Peter Krook
Sound Editor's Assistant—George Akers
Continuity—June Randall
Gambling Advisor—David Berglas
Historical Advisor—John Mollo
Fencing Coach—Bob Anderson
Stunt Arranger—Roy Scammell
Horsemaster—George Mossman
Wrangler—Peter Munt
Armorer—Bill Aylmore
Set Dresser—Vernon Dixon
Assistant Art Director—Bill Brodie
German Art Director—Jan Schlubach
Property Master—Mike Fowlie
Property Man—Terry Wells
Property Buyer—Ken Dolbear
Construction Manager—Joe Lee
Painter—Bill Beecham
Drapesmen—Richard Dicker, Cleo Nethersole, Chris Seddon
Second Unit Cameraman—Paddy Carey

Camera Operators—Mike Molloy, Ronnie Taylor
Focus Puller—Douglas Milsome
Color Grading—Dave Dowler
Camera Assistants—Laurie Frost, Dodo Humphreys
Camera Grips—Tony Cridlin, Luke Quigley
Gaffer—Lou Bogue
Chief Electrician—Larry Smith
Make-up—Ann Brodie, Alan Boyle, Barbara Daly, Jill Carpenter, Yvonne Coppard
Hairdressing—Susie Hill, Joyce James, Maud Onslow, Daphne Vollmer
Wardrobe Supervisor—Ron Beck
Costume Makers—Gary Dahms, Yvonne Dahms, Jack Edwards, Judy Lloyd-Rogers, Willy Rothery
Hats—Francis Wilson
Wardrobe Assistants—Gloria Barnes, Norman Dickens, Colin Wilson
Producer's Secretary—Margaret Adams
Casting—James Liggat
Choreographer—Geraldine Stephenson
Production Accountant—John Trehy
Production Secretaries—Loretta Ordewer, Pat Pennelegion
Assistant Accountants—Ron Bareham, Carolyn Hall

With Special Acknowledgement to Corsham Court; Glastonbury Rural Life Museum Stourhead House and the National Trust; Castle Howard. Lenses for Candlelight Photography made by Carl Zeiss West Germany. Adapted for Cinematography by Ed Di Giulio. Special Sound Assistance Dolby Laboratories Inc. A Peregrine Film. Made on location in England, Eire, and Germany by Hawk Films Ltd. and re-recorded at EMI Elstree Studios Ltd., England.

# BIBLIOGRAPHY

BOOKS:

Agel, Jerome, ed. *The Making of Kubrick's 2001*. New York: New American Library, 1970.

Baxter, John. *Hollywood in the Sixties*. New York: A. S. Barnes, 1972.

Burgess, Anthony, *A Clockwork Orange*. New York: Ballantine Books, 1972.

Clarke, Arthur C. *2001: A Space Odyssey*. New York: New American Library, 1968.

Cowie, Peter. *Seventy Years of Cinema*. New York: A. S. Barnes, 1969.

Crist, Judith. *The Private Eye, the Cowboy, and the Very Naked Lady*. New York: Paperback Library, 1970.

Geduld, Carolyn. *Filmguide to 2001: A Space Odyssey*. Bloomington: Indiana University Press, 1973.

Gow, Gordon. *Hollywood in the Fifties*. New York: A. S. Barnes, 1971.

Houston, Penelope. *The Contemporary Cinema: 1945-63*. Baltimore: Penguin Books, 1969.

Kael, Pauline. *Going Steady*. New York: Bantam Books, 1971.

———. *I Lost It at the Movies*. New York: Bantam Books, 1966.

———. *Kiss Kiss Bang Bang*. New York: Bantam Books, 1969.

Kagan, Norman. *The Cinema of Stanley Kubrick*. New York: Holt, Rinehart, and Winston, 1972.

Kubrick, Stanley. *A Clockwork Orange*. Based on the novel by Anthony Burgess. New York: Ballantine Books, 1972.

Manvell, Roger. *New Cinema in the USA*. New York: Dutton, 1968.

Nabokov, Vladimir. *The Annotated Lolita*. Edited by Alfred Appel, Jr. New York: McGraw-Hill, 1970.

———. *Lolita: A Screenplay*. New York: McGraw-Hill, 1974.

Sarris, Andrew. *Confessions of a Cultist: On the Cinema, 1955-69*. New York: Simon and Schuster, 1971.

Thackeray, William Makepeace. *Barry Lyndon*. With an Introduction by Lord David Cecil. London: Cassell, 1967.

Walker, Alexander. *Stanley Kubrick Directs*. Expanded edition. New York: Harcourt, Brace, Jovanovich, 1972.

ARTICLES:

Appel, Jr., Alfred. "Nabokov's Dark Cinema: A Diptych." *Tri-Quarterly*, Spring 1973.

———. "The Eyehole of Knowledge." *Film Comment*, IX (May-June 1973).

Barr, Charles. "Cinemascope: Before and After." *Film: A Montage of Theories.* Edited by Richard Dyer MacCann. New York: Dutton, 1966. Originally published in *Film Quarterly*, XVI (Summer 1963).

Bernstein, Jeremy. "Profile: Stanley Kubrick." *The New Yorker*, November 12, 1966.

———. "Talk of the Town: *Beyond the Stars*." *The New Yorker*, April 24, 1965.

Butler, Ivan. "James Mason." *The Making of Feature Films: A Guide*. Baltimore: Penguin Books, 1971.

Cocks, Jay. "Kubrick: Degrees of Madness." *Time*, December 20, 1971.

Gelmis, Joseph. "Stanley Kubrick." *The Film Director as Superstar*. Garden City, N.Y.: Doubleday, 1970.

Houston, Penelope. "Kubrick Country." *The Saturday Review*, December 25, 1971.

———. "*Barry Lyndon*." *Sight and Sound*, Spring 1974.

——— and Philip Strick. "Interview with Stanley Kubrick." *Sight and Sound*. Spring 1972.

Hughes, Robert. "The Decor of Tomorrow's Hell." *Time*, December 27, 1971.

Hyman, Stanley Edgar. "Afterword." *A Clockwork Orange* by Anthony Burgess. New York: Ballantine Books, 1972. Originally published in *The New Leader*, January 1963.

Isaacs, Neil D. "Unstuck in Time: *Clockwork Orange* and *Slaughterhouse-Five*." *Literature/Film Quarterly*, I (Spring 1973).

"The Killing." *Time*, June 4, 1956.

Kloman, William. "In 2001 Will Love Be a Seven-Letter Word?" New York *Times*, April 14, 1968, section 2.

Kuhns, William. "Stanley Kubrick." *Movies in America*. Dayton: Pflaum/Standard, 1972.

Martin, Pete, "Alfred Hitchcock." *Film Makers on Film Making*. Edited by Harry M. Geduld. Bloomington: Indiana University Press, 1969. Originally published in *The Saturday Evening Post*, July 27, 1957.

Norden, Eric. "Stanley Kubrick." *Playboy*, September 1968.

Rapf, Maurice. "A Talk with Stanley Kubrick." *Action*, VI (January-February 1969).

Schrader, Paul. "Notes on *Film Noir*." *Film Comment*, VIII (Spring 1972).

Zimmerman, Paul D. "Kubrick's Brilliant Vision." *Newsweek*, January 3, 1972.

**Popular Library**

*The most exciting event in paperback publishing!*
Here are your favorite heroes and superheroes—all brought to life by the leading authorities in the field. And Big Apple books are magnificent! They are beautifully designed & printed in a magazine size format (8-1/2x11), and are full of rare, nostalgic photographs, many never before published.

Order now. Big Apple Books fill a vital gap in every film buff's library.

| | |
|---|---|
| ☐ **SUPERMAN—Serial to Cereal** | - $3.95 |
| ☐ **STANLEY KUBRICK** | - $3.95 |
| ☐ **ROBERT REDFORD** | - $3.95 |
| ☐ **ABBOTT AND COSTELLO** | - $3.95 |
| ☐ **TEX AVERY: KING OF CARTOONS** | - $3.95 |
| ☐ **ROCK DREAMS** | - $7.95 |

**Buy them at your local bookstore or use this handy coupon for ordering:**

BOB-51

**Popular Library, P.O. Box 5755, Terre Haute, Indiana 47805**

Please send me the books I have checked above. I am enclosing $_____ (please add 50c to cover postage and handling). Send check or money order —no cash or C.O.D.'s please. Orders of 5 books or more postage free.

Mr/Mrs/Miss _____

Address _____

City _____ State/Zip _____

Please allow three weeks for delivery. This offer expires 5/77.

**Hollywood**

*DREAMS FOR SALE*

| | | |
|---|---|---|
| ☐ **AUNTIE MAME** (Movie-"Mame"), P. Dennis | 08261 - | 95c |
| ☐ **BUCK AND THE PREACHER**, D. Walker | 08188 - | 75c |
| ☐ **COLUMBO** #1, Alfred Lawrence | 08382 - | $1.25 |
| ☐ **THE DEAN'S DEATH COLUMBO** #2, J. Hartman | 00265 - | $1.25 |
| ☐ **ANY PORT IN THE STORM COLUMBO** #3, Henry Clement | 00317 - | $1.25 |
| ☐ **BY DAWN'S EARLY LIGHT COLUMBO** #4, Henry Clement | 00326 - | $1.25 |
| ☐ **MURDER BY THE BOOK COLUMBO** #5, Lee Hays | 03109 - | $1.50 |
| ☐ **HARRY AND TONTO**, J. Greenfeld & P. Mazursky | 00214 - | $1.25 |
| ☐ **HARRY O**, L. Hays | 00269 - | $1.25 |
| ☐ **HARRY O** #2, L. Hays | 00337 - | $1.25 |
| ☐ **LEAVING CHEYENNE**, Movie—"Loving Molly", L. Mc Murtry | 08272 - | $1.25 |
| ☐ **OKLAHOMA CRUDE**, M. Norman | 08233 - | $1.25 |
| ☐ **THE ROCKFORD FILES** #1, Mike Jahn | 00318 - | $1.25 |
| ☐ **THE SUGARLAND EXPRESS**, H. Clement | 08276 - | $1.25 |

**Buy them at your local bookstore or use this handy coupon for ordering:**

BOB-38

**Popular Library, P.O. Box 5755, Terre Haute, Indiana 47805**

Please send me the books I have checked above. I am enclosing $_____
(please add 35c to cover postage and handling). Send check or money order
—no cash or C.O.D.'s please. Orders of 5 books or more postage free.

Mr/Mrs/Miss _____

Address _____

City _____ State/Zip _____

Please allow three weeks for delivery. This offer expires 5/77.

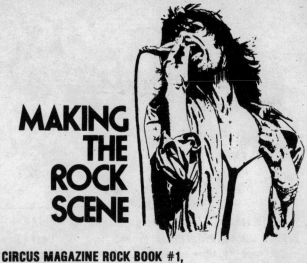

# MAKING THE ROCK SCENE

☐ **CIRCUS MAGAZINE ROCK BOOK #1,**
Alice Cooper ............................................. 03046 - $1.50

☐ **ELTON JOHN (Rock Book),** C. Stein ........... 03052 - $1.50

☐ **HOLLYWOOD STAR REPORTER (Flip #2),**
L. Franklin ................................................. 00640 - 95c

☐ **MICK JAGGER,** J. Marks-Highwater ............ 08317 - $1.50

☐ **JANIS,** D. Dalton ..................................... 08251 - $1.50

☐ **MAKING IT TOGETHER (Flip #1),** R. Reed ... 00626 - 95c

☐ **BETTE MIDLER** ..................................... 08348 - $1.50

☐ **ROBERT PLANT (Rock Book #3),** M. Gross ... 03060 - $1.50

☐ **YOUR FAVORITE COUNTRY MUSIC STARS,**
C. R. Hollaran ............................................ 03076 - $1.50

**Buy them at your local bookstore or use this handy coupon for ordering:**

BOB-50

**Popular Library, P.O. Box 5755, Terre Haute, Indiana 47805**

Please send me the books I have checked above. I am enclosing $_____
(please add 35c to cover postage and handling). Send check or money order
—no cash or C.O.D.'s please. Orders of 5 books or more postage free.

Mr/Mrs/Miss_____

Address_____

City_____ State/Zip_____

Please allow three weeks for delivery. This offer expires 5/77.